MANAGING INFORMATION AS A CORPORATE RESOURCE

PAUL L. TOM
Acadia University

The Scott, Foresman Series in
Computers and Information Systems
Thomas H. Athey, Consulting Editor

SCOTT, FORESMAN AND COMPANY
Glenview, Illinois   London, England

Acknowledgments: Figures 2–2 (p. 31), 10–1 (p. 255), 10–2 (p. 259), 10–5 (p. 267), and 10–6 (p. 274) from Forbes Advertising Supplement PERSONAL COMPUTING: THE CHALLENGE TO MANAGEMENT dated May 21, 1984. Copyright © 1984 Forbes, Inc. Reprinted by permission of *Forbes Magazine*. Figure 3–A (p. 45) from "Citicorp's Growth Under Walter Wriston" from *The New York Times,* April 21, 1985. Copyright © 1985 by The New York Times Company. Reprinted by permission. Figure 3–1 (p. 51) from "The Plunging Price of Memory Chips," *Business Week*. Reprinted from the May 30, 1985 issue of *Business Week* by special permission. Copyright © 1985 by McGraw-Hill, Inc. Figure 3–2 (p. 52) from "Thanks to the Plummeting Cost of Random Access Memories . . . Demand for Ram Chips is Exploding," *Business Week*. Reprinted from the April 2, 1984 issue of *Business Week* by special permission. Copyright © 1984 by McGraw-Hill, Inc. Figures 5–2 (p. 118), 5–3 (p. 119), 5–4 (pp. 120–1), 5–5 (p. 122), 5–6 (p. 124), 5–7 (p. 126), and 5–8 (pp. 128–9) from INFORMATION SYSTEMS PLANNING CHARTS by Arthur Andersen and Company. Copyright © Arthur Andersen and Company. Reprinted by permission. Professional Application, Chapter 12, pages 298–301, from "The Unfinished Revolution" by Dennis Kneale from TECHNOLOGY IN THE WORKPLACE from *The Wall Street Journal,* September 16, 1985. Reprinted by permission of *The Wall Street Journal*. Copyright © Dow Jones & Company, 1985. All Rights Reserved.

Library of Congress Cataloging-in-Publication Data

Tom, Paul L.
    Managing information as a corporate resource.

    (The Scott, Foresman series in computers and
information systems)
    Bibliography: p. 309–10
    Includes index.
    1. Industrial management—Information services—
Case studies. I. Title II. Series.
HD30.35.T65   1987   658.4'038   86-22084
ISBN 0-673-18309-2

123456 KPF 919089888786

MANAGING INFORMATION AS A CORPORATE RESOURCE

PREFACE

Computer-using organizations are entering a rapidly changing, high-risk period that will require careful planning and close supervision. The changes include integrating microcomputers with mainframes, installing automated office systems, and developing integrated telecommunications. Perhaps not since the big conversion days of the 1960s has there been such a need for well-considered plans showing what the information systems should look like five to eight years hence and how organizations will use them. The availabilty of information and low-cost hardware and software to process that information has made it critical for management to control this vital corporate resource and manage its use. The ability to access more and more data has given rise to the recognition that information is a corporate resource and must be managed, just as the financial, manufacturing, and personnel resources of a company are managed.

The objective of this text is to provide, through vignettes and professional applications, a discussion of how to manage information as a corporate resource. It is not a technically oriented book; it will not discuss "how to" build systems, develop data bases, or decide between hierarchical and relational data bases. There are many texts on the market today that will provide that type of information. What this text will do is to provide the reader with problems in managing information drawn from actual consulting experiences. Each chapter starts with a professional application or vignette drawn from the author's consulting experience. These cases present a live environment for the discussion that follows. It allows the student to study the text with a management problem in mind. It also permits the instructor to critique the actual solution and develop alternative approaches based on emerging technologies. The professional applications and their solutions are presented to describe both the problem and one approach to solving those problems. Concepts and theories underlying the problem areas are presented as background information. It is hoped by presenting a professional application, and then the concepts and principles that apply to it, that the book can be used to stimulate discussion on both the theory and the solution.

This text is directed at: (1) business students in an MBA program or at the upper-division undergraduate level; (2) information systems managers who must implement the corporate information plan; (3) executives who are responsible for managing the corporate information resource.

Today's literature in the information-processing field emphasizes computer literacy, programming, system analysis and design, and management information systems. There are very few books on the management of information as a corporate resource, and those few available devote half their pages to describing the resource being managed: what is a computer, what is a system, what is data and what is information. All these books are technically oriented or describe information from the technician's point of view. Perhaps most important, many textbooks in use today are based on the research activities of academics rather than the experience of people who have devoted their lives to the field of information processing at the technician and executive levels. Hopefully, this text will provide students and practitioners with a discussion of managing information resources based on practical experience in the business world. It presupposes that the reader has a background in information processing, either having worked in the field or having taken the basic computer and management information courses at the university level.

Many texts use the case approach. Usually this means that cases are presented at the end of each chapter to serve as homework assignments or to be used as class discussion vehicles. Rarely are the solutions given in the text. This book starts each chapter with a professional application or vignette taken from the author's consulting experience. The situations described in the applications are used to illustrate problems and management techniques are used to solve the problems. The reader is presented with how the application was actually handled and solved. The names of some of the applications have been altered at the request of the companies since nothing has been omitted from their description. Some of the facts presented do not portray the company in the best light, so they have asked that their real names not be used and their identity disguised.

Professors are urged to draw on their experience in leading the class discussions using this approach. The chapters accompanying each professional application will present some concepts and techniques, but to generate lively discussions, alternative approaches and solutions should be presented to the students for debate and discussion. It is not the intent of the author to present the ''correct'' solution to the applications. The solutions implemented by the companies were the result of many factors, such as time and budget constraints, political considerations, the ability of the organization to absorb change, the competence of technical personnel, and the support of the user groups within the organization. Today's technology may present new solutions and alternatives not available at the time the application took place. It is hoped that class instructors will be able to use the applications, as a vehicle for generating thoughts on how this application might be handled today.

Managing information as a corporate resource involves teamwork from everyone in the organization. The systems expert and the computer technician, despite their technical skills, are often insensitive to the human and organizational implications of their activities and to the problems caused by change. Thus, the study of how to manage information as a resource is necessary for both the manager, who uses the information, and the technician, who supplies the information. Both must understand the process of initiating and controlling change in an increasingly complex world. The major objective of this book is to contribute to that process.

Paul L. Tom

TABLE OF CONTENTS

MANAGING INFORMATION AS A CORPORATE RESOURCE

1

THE INFORMATION AGE

ISSUES

- Top management's discomfort with computers

- The early focus on data and transaction processing

- Recognizing information as a business resource and competitive weapon

- Levels in the information hierarchy:

  discovery, surprise, disillusionment, motivation, knowledge

- Why can management not "manage" their data-processing organization?

- Systems development—art or science?

- Is automation today labor intensive?

- How up-to-date are today's computer applications?

- The communication gap between executive management and information-

  processing management

- The new breed of information executives—what is their role?

The computer age is over; the information age has begun. In the 1960s when the computer age started, business people bought computers because it was the thing to do. It held high hopes for making their businesses more efficient, more profitable. Answers to problems could be obtained at the push of a button. Unfortunately, few of the expectations came true, and if they did, it was with great effort and cost. Today, business people do not buy computers because it is the thing to do. No one buys a power drill because he wants a drill; he buys it because he wants a hole. The same is now true of computers. Management does not want computers, it wants results in the form of reduced costs, increased revenues, improved customer service, or better information—and everyone knows that the computer is the fastest, surest, most predictable way of getting what you want or at least that is how it should be.

Any current survey of senior management will find that most executives will not agree that the computer is the fastest, surest, and most predictable way of getting what you want. They will not claim to understand information processing, and many even distrust those associated with it. Most senior executives today are 50 years old or older. If they went to college, they graduated prior to 1955. There were no computer science programs in the universities prior to 1960. Academics in the 1960's were predicting that the number of computers would not exceed 100 in the world and that they would be used for complex scientific and mathematical calculations in advanced research laboratories. Even Thomas Watson, founder of the present IBM Corporation, did not have much optimism over the demand for computers. Since the present senior executives were not taught computers in school nor exposed to them in their early business careers, few understood them or felt comfortable talking to people who did. Those executives who made an effort to learn about computers by talking to their data-processing staff found an immediate communications barrier. Computer people had a tendency to use technical jargon and computer buzz words. Most were technicians with little knowledge of how businesses were run and the information management needed for decision making. They were problem oriented, enjoyed developing the logic towards solving a predefined problem rather than understanding the problem itself and the impact the solution might have on the business as a whole. Executives, on the other hand, put blind faith in the computer's ability to solve business problems, gave up trying to understand computers, and hoped that the people they hired to run the computer department knew what they were doing.

In terms of technological innovation, the computer has been a success, unparalleled by any other modern development except the telephone. Even the space program, an astounding feat of science and engineering, depended on the computer for its success. In terms of the computer's contribution to cost savings and improved operations, most would agree that there has been some. In terms of its contribution to the business information needs of the senior executive, most would believe that it has failed to meet its potential.

For the past 30 years businesses have been fascinated with hardware. This fascination for machinery has given way to heightened interest in the uses to which it is put. The popular press has used the term the "Computer Age" to refer to the love affair with hardware, and the term "Information Age" to refer to the trend toward treating information as a corporate resource.

Actually, the age we are living in is well named as far as business is concerned. In the early days of computers, the focus in electronic **data** processing (EDP) was on replacing manual tasks with the computer, making procedures more routine and efficient, and above all, on **data.** There was very little emphasis on turning that data into information for management decision making. The early efforts to develop true "management information systems" floundered due to the lack of software, lack of understanding by management of what a computer could and could not do, and the inability of computer technicians to communicate with executives. On the other hand, executives wanted, "at the press of a button", information that was not available and that often could not even be collected. Their work was not predictable, involved more exceptions than rules, and resisted systematization. The result of all of these factors reinforced the tendency to use the computer for processing data rather than in helping executives make better business decisions.

What has changed? If the "Computer Age" was characterized by the processing of data, what has caused the beginning of the "Information Age" when the computer will supply executives with the necessary information for more effective decision making?

THE END OF THE COMPUTER AGE

The passing of the computer age was brought about by several developments:

- The development of time-sharing in the late 1960s started the trend towards interactive computing and provided users with a decentralized resource.
- The development of mini- and microcomputers provided users with computer power at relatively little cost.
- Advances in telecommunications allowed users to link their terminals or small computers to a host computer where their data was stored.
- Software advances in application packages, data management systems, and high-level end user languages provided the end users with tools to build their own systems if the computer department could not, or would not, help them meet their processing needs.
- Wide acceptance by executives of the personal computer as a decision support tool accelerated the need for access to information stored in the central computer files to support the management decision-making process.

These hardware and software advances have caused a major shift in how the computer is used in many organizations. System designers who spent most of their time in the past decade designing transaction systems now find that users not only want information systems, but want the information presented at their desks, on their personal computers, and in a format which allows them to manipulate it with software developed for the personal computer.

How did these executives become computer smart all of a sudden? If they did not understand the computer in the 1970s, how did they acquire the knowledge to write programs for their own personal computers in the 1980s? Most of them did not attempt to write their own programs. Advances in software permitted them to buy application packages that were very user friendly. Following directions given by prompts, they could manipulate data and do computations rather easily. Once the executive mastered the use of an electronic spreadsheet, he was "hooked" on the computer and began to learn more about using it. Decision makers who do not want to spend time learning how to use their computers (having your own personal computer is now the latest corporate status symbol) can hire college students to build whatever models or programs they want at very little cost. Once this is done, they can train their secretaries or administrative assistants to use the program and get them the information they want.

The information age begins with a shift away from the traditional data-processing environment to one where managers have access to information stored in the corporate data base and can access this information directly from their desks. The implications of this are enormous. Does this mean that job security for computer analysts and programmers, so carefully nurtured for the past 30 years, is over? Will they all be replaced by executives armed with their own desktop computer? How will executives with their newly found computer tool manage this resource so that they do not again suffer the disillusionment of the 1960s and 1970s? That is what this book is about. Managing information resources: hardware, software, systems, personnel, organizations. To guide us, we will look at the mistakes of the past, profit from those mistakes and avoid repeating them in the future. To do this, a series of cases will be used to describe actual management problems in managing information resources. These cases are actual cases that the author worked on as a consultant to the companies involved. Because many of the mistakes and problems are still an embarrassment to company management, the names of the companies and their management team have been changed. The basic facts remain as the author found them on his assignments.

Before looking at how to manage information resources better in the future, let us look at where we are heading and set the stage for further discussions.

PROGRESSION TO THE INFORMATION AGE

Increasingly, information will be recognized as an important business resource, perhaps even vital to the effective management of a business enterprise in the 1990s. The "haves" and the "have nots" of the business world will divide on the basis of who has the best information. Information will become a competitive weapon. We will grow increasingly dependent on computers in our business and personal lives. We cannot escape the fact that those who learn to wring the fullest potential from their computers will hold a critical edge over those who do not. The computer will become a primary source of information—first about the business itself, then about the environment in which the business exists: the market, the competition, the economy. As management begins to appreciate the computer's potential as an agent of change, this role will take precedence over its role as a processor of data. Then the computer will begin a slow, deliberate move from the clerical floor to the executive suite.

Today, business executives are faced with a dilemma: is there a choice on whether or not to computerize? Most of them would say that the computer has not lived up to their expectations. Many of them have extensive experience in weighing the promise of the computer against what seems like astronomical costs and major disruptions in their business, and the inevitable unpleasant surprises. If the computer and the people who developed the systems on the computer have disappointed them in the past, how will there ever be a new role for the computer in the 1990s and how will computer information ever be a corporate force? To answer these questions, let us look at how we got to where we are today.

Business literature is replete with accounts of how we got here. Many authors have described their view of the stages a company moves through in its use of computers, some looking at the business applications being addressed, some at computer technology. As early as 1974, Gibson and Nolan[1] categorized EDP growth into four stages: initiation, expansion, formalization, and maturity. They contended that all EDP facilities go through these four stages and they described the management problems in each stage. If we look at management's reaction to the problems in automating its activities, we can discern five periods that closely parallel the Nolan stages of growth. These are the periods of discovery, surprise, disillusionment, motivation, and knowledge or dependency. These periods may also be viewed as levels in an information hierarchy that we must experience before arriving at the stage which Nolan refers to as maturity (see Figure 1-1).

Discovery

During the period of discovery, the computer is introduced with excitement, enthusiasm and anticipation. Its early applications are relatively simple, they are designed to reduce clerical activity and costs. The information is used primarily by the accountants but management is interested and supportive. The computer is primarily a data processor and the focus is on processing, not information. Most of the reports that are generated are prepared on a fixed schedule and much of the data is historical for the purpose of comparing one period to another. Management's reaction is one of enthusiasm and high hopes.

1. Gibson, Cyrus and Nolan, Richard, "Managing the Four Stages of EDP Growth," *Harvard Business Review,* Jan.-Feb., 1974.

FIGURE 1-1   INFORMATION HIERARCHY

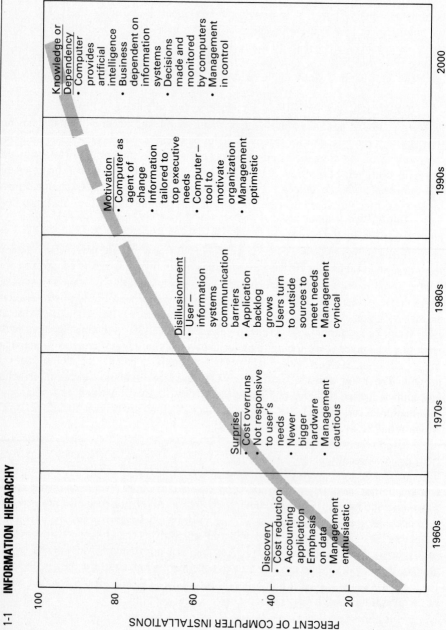

1960s

Discovery
- Cost reduction
- Accounting application
- Emphasis on data
- Management enthusiastic

1970s

Surprise
- Cost overruns
- Not responsive to user's needs
- Newer bigger hardware
- Management cautious

1980s

Disillusionment
- User—information systems communication barriers
- Application backlog grows
- Users turn to outside sources to meet needs
- Management cynical

1990s

Motivation
- Computer as agent of change
- Information tailored to top executive needs
- Computer—tool to motivate organization
- Management optimistic

2000

Knowledge or Dependency
- Computer provides artificial intelligence
- Business dependent on information systems
- Decisions made and monitored by computers
- Management in control

PERCENT OF COMPUTER INSTALLATIONS

100   80   60   40   20

Surprise

The second level of the hierarchy is the period of surprise. Management sees the potential for expanding the tool of accounting to provide information to help control operations, resources, production, and purchasing, but a problem is beginning to emerge. Management is continually surprised by cost overruns, delays in implementing systems, systems that are not responsive to users' needs, and the need for newer and bigger hardware. If you listen to computer managers during this period, they think that the users cannot make up their minds, demand continual change, and do not understand the real potential of computers. Senior management, on the other hand, think computer managers have only two goals:

1. to get the newest computers and software, and
2. to convince management that cost overruns and delays are normal and should be expected.

During this period, new information is developed for many new users in the enterprise, but their expectations for each new system are never quite realized and management's enthusiasm turns to caution. By the time the company has reached level three, the period of disillusionment, management's caution has turned to cynicism.

Disillusionment

A typical situation during this period is as follows: Management is considering a major decision, perhaps a marketing matter, and wants to evaluate revenue projections as they relate to manufacturing capacity and the distribution network. With high hopes for what the information-processing department might be able to provide, management asks for a forecast only to be told that it cannot be done, or that it will take so long that it will no longer be a forecast.

Even where the computer staff is superb and eager to be responsive, it is usually not strategically placed in the organization at a level that allows it to understand fully corporate strategy and priorities. It is also a prisoner of the past. Its financial, manufacturing, and inventory programs may not be compatible and to answer the question may take at least a year, a much bigger computer and many more systems analysts and programmers. Management stalks off wondering what good all those computers are doing. For their part, the data-processing people cannot understand why management could not have anticipated this need months ago and given the department the resources necessary to solve the problem.

At this point, disillusionment is complete. Management and data processing begin to build a wall between themselves. The wall usually becomes so impenetrable that management and data processing figuratively throw their requests for information and the resulting answers over the wall at each other. Neither side makes an effort to ensure that requests are realistic and feasible or that the information provided serves a useful function. No-one accepts responsibility.

Some companies adopt the philosophy that the information-processing department is a "service organization," there to provide computer and software resources to any user willing to pay for them. It is a classic dichotomy with one team saying, "Be responsive to my needs," and the other saying, "Do whatever you wish and I'll send you a bill."

As this period progresses, the backlog of demand for new systems grows, the users turn to purchased software to meet their needs, to outside consultants or software houses, to service bureaus, or to their own mini- or microcomputers. The data-processing department becomes consumed with the maintenance of aging systems. Some would estimate that today, about 80 percent of all companies that have been using computers for 10 years or more are stuck somewhere in the period of disillusionment.

It is enough to make one want to discard the whole thing and go back to nonautomated systems. But that is looking at the wrong culprit. The culprit is not the computer, it is management. Management have learned to manage many complex processes, but with computers, their sense of management somehow has been misplaced. Because they did not understand how computers worked, they abrogated their management responsibilities. There really is no option to turn back because the amount of information to be classified is already staggering and will continue to grow at a fantastic pace. By the time our young children graduate from college, the amount of information in the world will be four times greater than now. By the time that same child is 50 years old, it will be 32 times greater. At that time, 97 percent of everything known in the world will have been learned since the time the child was born. We are going to need computers.

Most businesses stuck in the period of disillusionment cannot turn back. They can stay where they are or they can move ahead into the next level, the period of motivation. However, the conviction and effort required to move through the period of disillusionment is considerable. Management generally views information processing as a high-technology function; it is not. Although the hardware that processes data is a product of advanced technology, the way businesses use that hardware is preindustrial in both technique and results. What are some of the characteristics of the information-processing field that have frustrated management?

- Work is done by individual artisans independent of one another.
- Trial and error experimentation is common.
- There is little useful interchange.
- There is more art than science involved.
- The standards of measurement are poorly defined.
- The results are unpredictable and hard to duplicate.

If these characteristics sound familiar, it is because they are encyclopedia references to the chief characteristics of the cottage industry of 200 years ago. Historically, the term "cottage industry" refers to the method of production in use before the mid-eighteenth century, the time when the Industrial Revolution began. Systems automation is still a cottage industry. A tremendous amount of unique, innovative, trial-and-error effort is applied to the design and programming of most of today's computer systems. The automation of information is somewhat like taking an order for a car, then starting to build a bumper, then a fender, and then something else. The principles of mass production, so familiar to all of us and embodied in most areas of a business enterprise, have not been applied to the systems automation process.

One of the reasons this has happened is the common misconception that it has to be this way—systems development is an art. It has become a self-fulfilling prophecy. A second reason is the misconception that data-processing costs have been falling because of the decline in the cost of hardware. We hear, for example, that the cost of labor has tripled since 1955 although people work at the same pace. In the same period of time, computers now work 1000 times faster and today it costs only one cent for what used to cost $1.26 in 1955. If automobiles had developed at the same pace as computers over the last 30 years, the automobile today would be capable of getting 1000 m.p.g., would cost $10, require no maintenance, and be two inches long.

If hardware were the major factor, data-processing costs would be small enough so that management should not be concerned. The problem is that the automation process has become labor intensive. Furthermore, two thirds of all data-processing costs are related to the maintenance of existing programs and systems. A computer program ages with change, not with time. As changes are added, documentation becomes even less reliable, changes take longer and longer, the individual artisan who developed the program becomes more and more indispensable, and the process becomes even more labor intensive and fragile.

There are those who contend that the automation of information is an art form and any attempt by management to impose control and structure will stifle creativity. Most experienced managers would disagree. That same philosophy was common, and costly, among manufacturers before it was destroyed by the era of standardized, interchangeable parts, and assembly line and automated production processes.

The reason most companies experience the problems of the period of disillusionment is that they are tolerating a preindustrial cottage industry approach to information systems. The company that wishes to progress to the fourth level in the information hierarchy and to participate in the promise of the 1990s has to abandon cottage industry techniques and manage its information resources as it manages the other components of its business.

Motivation

When we abandon the cottage industry approach to information systems, we can progress to the next level in the information hierarchy, the period of motivation. The term motivation refers to the prediction that, as senior management becomes the major user of automated information, the enterprise will begin to recognize the potential of the computer as an agent of change, a source of motivation.

Most computer applications today support clerical functions. They keep records, do vast amounts of simple arithmetic, and generally make simple calculations appear complex and sophisticated. Many of these applications were defined and developed by the computer staff without adequate participation from the management of the department using the application. Some are holdovers from the days of punched card accounting machines, reprogrammed several times during conversion to more up-to-date equipment. Basically, the logic in use during the 1950s is still in use today.

These routine operations produce byproduct information that filters up to management and becomes one element of input used by management to make decisions about the company's operations, but a minor element in most companies. When a company moves into the period of motivation, instead of this buttom-up development of information, it will adopt a top-down process in which management becomes the major user of information tailored to the needs of senior executives; information about the unique requirements of the specific enterprise operating in its environment. Management could define the strategic issues that are unique to its business. The computer could analyze these strategic issues and suggest alternative ways of viewing the organization's business. When senior management has chosen the direction in which it wishes to take the enterprise, management's job will be to push this information down the organizational ladder.

The information systems can then be designed to serve as guideposts for middle management and others to follow in implementing the strategies adopted by executive management. When that is working, senior management is no longer dependent upon byproduct information. It is receiving the information it needs and is using that information as an agent of change, as a tool to motivate the organization to move in the strategic direction defined by senior management.

Knowledge or Dependency

There is another period emerging from the period of motivation. It is viewed dimly through a haze at this point by the futurists. Optimists label it the period of knowledge, where computers handle so much of the daily corporate operations that senior executives are finally freed from their preoccupation with events inside the organization and can concentrate on focusing on the external environment in which their business operates. This is the age of artificial intelligence, the "fifth generation" of computers that can think.

Pessimists might call it the period of dependency. It has a dark side too. Businesses may be wagering their very existence on computers. The computer will make decisions based on a set of predefined rules. It will be a barometer to compare activities to plans or principles, then adjust the activities automatically. An extreme case of the bad side was illustrated in a movie entitled *War Games,* released in 1984. In this film, computers were programmed to take over the defense of the Western world because human beings could be too emotional to execute an order to fire missiles that would destroy civilization. Unfortunately, a teenage computer genius managed to access this computer and initiated a war game that could end the world. Pure science fiction, but thought-provoking in what could happen if the next period turns out to be the period of dependency instead of the period of knowledge.

Our immediate concern is not what will happen in the future, but how to progress from the period of disillusionment to the period of motivation. The challenge to any business enterprise that wishes to participate in the migration to the period of motivation is to develop techniques to manage its information as a corporate resource, just as it manages its human resources, manufacturing resources, and financial resources. The information-processing function requires the same level of executive management direction as do the business functions of marketing, operations, and finance. Management and the information-processing department have to tear down the wall they have erected between themselves during the period of disillusionment. Both must understand each other's perspective and work out a solution that both can live with. From the executive or user management perspective, the information systems area is viewed as follows:

- Information-processing costs are rising while its contributions to business goals are often difficult to measure.
- Development projects take too long and cost too much.
- Surprise requests for computer hardware result in last minute decisions and become unplanned capital expenditures.
- System plans are not fully integrated with business objectives.
- User complaints are frequent and difficult to put in perspective.
- Turnover of information-processing personnel results in communication and systems support problems.
- Proliferation of personal computers throughout the organization requires rethinking on how computer resources are to be managed within the company.

From the information-processing management perspective:

- Management and user commitment to major systems projects is difficult to obtain and sustain.
- Users and management require continuing education in information-processing concepts, the development process, and the degree of commitment required.
- User complaints may be unjust and the positive contribution of information processing is difficult to communicate.
- Users must understand that present systems are not structured to allow easy access to data from personal computers or remote terminals. To restructure data files to permit easy access will require resystemization that is time-consuming and costly.

These issues, if not effectively addressed, result in a communication gap between executive/user management and information-processing management. As a consequence, executive management becomes frustrated and disillusioned by efforts to bridge this gap and becomes increasingly concerned about information-processing activities.

A NEW APPROACH TO INFORMATION MANAGEMENT

Today's information systems managers have much broader jobs than their predecessors, data-processing managers. In the past, when top management focused on goals and strategies, they seldom thought of information as a corporate resource and a competitive tool. The data-processing manager used to focus on how to translate management's goals and strategies into information requirements and provide the systems (hardware and software) to supply this information. In the environment of the 1980s and 1990s, the information systems manager must become part of the top management team and participate in developing the goals and strategies of the corporation. The information systems manager must cope with a growing computer literacy among users and their desire to have immediate access to corporate data files. The need to integrate microprocessors with mainframes, user-developed applications with application packages and custom coded systems, local area communications with long distance networks, word processing with data processing, and on-line inquiry with periodic printed reports, all under a security system that guards against unauthorized access, requires that we take a new approach to managing this vital resource.

The information environment is continually changing. As hardware prices fall and processing power increases, the trend towards distributed and decentralized processing will continue. Users will want computer power in their hands. The days of a centralized facility supplying all computer services to users is rapidly drawing to an end. Yet, today over 80 percent of all computer users are provided with centralized processing services. Even with information resources distributed to end users, the central processing facility will still exist. It will house the corporate data base, handle the high-volume transaction based systems, serve as a message-switching center, the hub of a communications network. Most likely, the present single location site will be converted to a multilocation center to provide better security and backup.

The new information environment will include host computers in many locations, data base systems sending information to distributed computers, stand-alone minis providing computer resources for unintegrated applications, personal computers in offices linked to receive data from corporate data files and other personal computers. The communication network will be unlike any we have today. Each office will have its own local area network to link the equipment in an automated office environment. Communication lines will link each office together into a nation-wide network. Satellite communication will link host computers in different countries. The corporate information manager will have instant access to information on a worldwide basis for decision making. This environment is considerably different from that of the 1960s and 1970s. To manage information resources in this new environment requires both technical skills and knowledge of the functional areas of a business. The new breed of information executives must be:

1. **Planners**—They should be ready to participate in developing corporate strategies and planning for supplying the necessary information for use as a competitive tool in executing these strategies. In the past, information-system planning centered around hardware/software strategies, migration from one generation of equipment to another, and replacement planning. While these will still be important, the information manager in the 1980s must take a broader horizon; planning must integrate information strategies into corporate strategies and use information as a corporate resource and competitive tool.

2. **Catalysts for change**—Since most businesses today are still struggling to emerge from the period of disillusionment, it will be up to the new breed of information managers to act as catalysts for change and bring their company into the period of motivation. Change may be upsetting to the corporate manager because it implies the unknown and upsets the status quo. Change in an unfamiliar technical area is doubly upsetting. It will be the role of the new information manager to develop programs for initiating change that will not be threatening to the corporate line operations executives. The benefits of new technology must be patiently explained to them to involve them in the process of change so that they accept rather than resist new technology. By being an active participant in the business-planning process, by showing line management how information can gain them a competitive edge, the information system manager can overcome the fear of change and work with management to develop new techniques that will give the company the best that technology can offer and keep it ahead of its competitors.

3. **Information consultants**—One way of breaking down the walls built up between the old data-processing department and the functional areas of the business is to reestablish communications between the two groups. The new breed of information managers must be information consultants. They must develop the trust of line personnel so that the information function is viewed as a helpful tool for their work rather than a threat to them. The concept of the information center has been very helpful in building this trust. As an example, when personal computers were proliferating in 1980–82, General Foods' headquarters in White Plains, New York established an information center that provided many of the more popular brands of microcomputers for use by General Foods' managers. They were able to go to the information center and get information on how to use these computers, the application software packages available, and actually sit down and play with each computer. Managers found this extremely helpful in evaluating whether or not to acquire one for their personal use. Moreover, a feeling of helpfulness and trust developed between the information center and user personnel so that, when the corporation set standards on personal computers for use in its offices, the resistance was minimal due to the good feeling developed between the two groups. This effort

dramatized for management what can be done when the information manager becomes a true consultant to the users and can communicate with them in ways they can understand and appreciate.

4. **Seasoned business executives**—In addition to being technical experts and information consultants, information executives must also be seasoned business executives. They must manage people, equipment resources, financial resources, development projects, capital expenditures, user relations, management interfaces, and technology. Since all aspects of a business today are affected by systems, information managers are continually involved in all parts of the company's business. In many cases, because of the very detailed work that goes into the design and construction of a business information system, the information manager will know more about how a particular area of a business operates than the operating manager in charge of that area. The information manager must be seen as an effective manager in designing and developing systems, but also as capable of performing as a general manager, one able to manage the operations of the business as a whole. To reach this stage, the information manager must apply commonly used management techniques to managing information resources.

The key to effective management of information resources is the application of formal management techniques to this function. The types of management techniques commonly applied to business functions such as marketing, operations and finance are largely applicable to information processing. For example, most companies develop and execute a marketing plan, report performance and evaluate results for the next planning effort. This closed-loop concept, however, has not been widely adopted as the foundation for managing information processing. Too often the management cycle is not closed due to inadequate management reporting and inadequate evaluation of information-processing activities. Failure to close this loop can frustrate all levels of management: executive, user, and information processing.

FIGURE 1-2   **CLOSED-LOOP MANAGEMENT CYCLE**

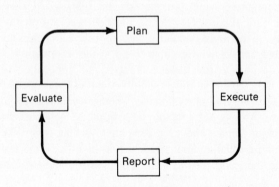

We will use the major phases of the closed-loop management cycle (see Figure 1-2) to organize our discussion on managing information resources. Planning is the starting point for managing information as a corporate resource. Chapters 2, 3, and 4 will cover Information Strategic Planning, Technology Planning, and Systems Planning. Executing, or putting plans into effect, will be discussed in six chapters covering: Systems Development, Production System Support, Computer Operations Management, Information and Systems Security, Human Resource Development, and the linking of Micros and Mainframes. To complete the closed-loop management cycle, we will look at Management Control Information Processing. Professional applications are used in each chapter to illustrate the topics covered.

CHAPTER 1   **DISCUSSION QUESTIONS**

1. Up to now, most will agree that the computer has not lived up to its potential in contributing to the information needs of senior executives. Why? What do you think will happen in the next 10 to 15 years?

2. In the 1960s, a lot of talk and publicity was given to "MIS—management information systems." Why? Will there be future attempts to build management information systems? Will these attempts be successful?

3. What characterized the "Computer Age" and what events marked the transition from the computer age to the information age?

4. Is systems development an art? Does it not require creativity, imagination, and craftsmanship, the same attributes required of an artist?

5. Why has management not devoted as much attention to managing information systems as it has to managing finance, marketing, production, and the other functional areas of a business?

6. How long do you think it will take for management of today to start managing information as a corporate resource, and how will they get from here to there?

2

INFORMATION STRATEGIC PLANNING

ISSUES

- What is strategic planning? How do information systems fit in?

- How is performance measured in strategic planning?

- Concept of a chief information officer

- Applying strategic information techniques

- Role and composition of a project-steering committee

UNITED FOOD AND BEVERAGES, LTD.

Paul Williamson was looking out his window high atop the Place Ville Marie overlooking Montreal and the St. Lawrence River. Corporate headquarters of United Food and Beverages (UFB) in New York City had appointed Paul the new chief executive officer of its Canadian subsidiary. Not bad for someone not quite 40, Paul thought. Moving to Canada, especially to French-speaking Montreal, had been a concern to both Paul and his family, but he had been offered French language lessons for the whole family as well as a fluently bilingual administrative assistant.

As he gazed down at the city sparkling in the summer sun, he was not as worried about adjusting to a bicultural environment as he was about how to handle a festering problem in the Canadian subsidiary. He had called his accounting firm and asked that they send over someone who knew the company and the problems in the data-processing department. Paul had been told that a new computer based distribution control system (DCS) under development for over four years would have to be scrapped. Although over one million dollars had been spent on the development, it was nowhere near completion, and another $500,000 or more would be needed to complete the system. In the most recent annual audit, the accounting firm had recommended that the project be scrapped and its costs written off. Much to his amazement, Paul found that the other executives, mainly the vice-president of marketing and the vice-president of distribution agreed with the recommendation. His director of data processing had tendered his letter of resignation. Paul also found that the data-processing department was held in extremely low regard throughout the Canadian head office. Most executives referred to it as a joke and had little or no contact with their people. "I see those guys once a month for four hours at the steering committee meeting," said one of the executives. "They give me a headache." Paul was preparing for the meeting with his auditors and mentally drawing up a list of questions to ask them.

United Food and Beverages Ltd., Canada, was a wholly owned subsidiary of United Foods Inc., one of the largest food-processing companies in the world with worldwide sales of over 2.85 billion dollars. UFB Canada contributed $850 million in sales in 1986. The company was projecting sales of over one billion dollars by

1990. Its products ranged from a complete line of consumer packaged foods (cereals, breads, cookies, candy, snacks) to beverages (coffee, tea, soft drinks) and wines and spirits. They also manufactured and distributed cooking and baking ingredients. The Canadian operations were the largest outside the U.S. and consisted of 30 manufacturing plants and 12 regional distribution centers. It had a total work force of over 5000 employees. While the company had operated in Canada for over 100 years, its most rapid growth had been in the past 10 years through an aggressive program of mergers and acquisitions. Every time the U.S. company bought a company, its Canadian operations would be merged into UFB Canada as an operating division. The officers of the acquired company would become division officers in UFB Canada. Ten division presidents reported to Paul as well as the five corporate vice-presidents: manufacturing, marketing, finance, distribution, and administration. Most of the ten division presidents were in their late 50s and early 60s. Two would be retiring within the year. UFB permitted voluntary retirement at age 62, with mandatory retirement at age 65. At 39, Paul was the youngest CEO in the company. He was vice-president of marketing at corporate headquarters before being appointed to this job one month ago.

At two o'clock, his secretary admitted Mr. Michel Lozeau, partner-in-charge of the management advisory services practice at his accounting firm. Michel had reviewed the systems area of UFB Canada during the annual audit and made the recommendation that the one million dollar write-off be taken and the project scrapped. Paul had met Michel during the get-acquainted meetings held before his move to Montreal. Also, Paul had attended meetings in New York where Michel made presentations on computer systems.

"Bonjour, Michel, comment allez-vous?"

"Tres bien, merci, et vous?" replied Michel.

"Well, you got me, after one lesson, I shouldn't be trying my fractured French on you, Michel."

"On the contrary," Michel replied in English, "You should use every opportunity to practice your French. You'll be amazed how quickly you will speak it well with constant practice."

Paul then indicated to Michel the reason for this meeting: "As you know, I am new here. Imagine my surprise to find that my first big problem was your recommended write-off of the DCS project. I am not questioning your recommendation, your report made it very clear why you thought the project would not work, and that to continue it would be pouring money into an open hole. I will have some detailed questions about the project for you later, perhaps. Now, I want to ask you to tell me about the history of the data-processing organization. The people here are so negative about the department that I would like to hear your viewpoint. How long have you been assigned to our account?"

"I've worked on the UFB account since I was a senior consultant, over 10 years ago," replied Michel. "I think I can give you a brief history of data processing here. UFB installed an EAM system in the late 50s."

Paul interrupted: "What's an EAM system?"

"Sorry, EAM stands for electrical accounting machine, it's a punched card system. The applications were payroll, general accounting, and financial statements. The company was smaller then, and automating these accounting functions saved many man-hours of work. When IBM came out with the 1401 system,[1] UFB converted to it in 1962. That conversion was easy since the input was still punched cards. All they had to do was write the 1401 programs in autocode, and IBM helped them do most of that. As the company grew, they needed more memory and storage capacity than that afforded by the 1401, so in 1967 IBM convinced them to replace the 1401 with an IBM 360 Model 30. Unfortunately, none of the 1401 programs worked on the 360, so all of them had to be rewritten in a programming language called COBOL. We recommended at the time that they redesign some of the applications to take advantage of new technology such as disks and data management software. The data-processing manager thought that redesign would be too expensive and too time-consuming so he just hired some part-time programmers to recode the existing programs from 1401 autocoder to 360 COBOL. By then, many changes had been made to the 1401 programs and the documentation wasn't exactly up to date. The conversion effort took much longer than anticipated, and many of the new programs didn't work. Management wasn't too pleased with the whole effort.

"By 1972, they needed more computer power and IBM suggested converting to a 370/135. The controller thought that too much money was being spent on new computers and vetoed the idea to upgrade to a 370. Instead, he arranged to take over the lease of a 360 Model 40 from a third party and returned the Model 30 to IBM." Paul interrupted to ask if the 360/30 was on rental from IBM for over 5 years. Michel replied: "UFB always rented from IBM. The controller didn't want to tie up capital in equipment, especially in computers which he said changed every other year. As the company started its expansion program in the mid 1970s, the Model 40 couldn't handle the added volume. IBM suggested that they should go to an on-line data base system with a 3301 system. That's when the situation exploded. Your predecessor, Paul, literally blew up when he got the recommendation from IBM. He said that for over 15 years, all the company did was change computers and recode programs. The cost of data processing was skyrocketing. The staff was growing by over 20 percent each year, hardware costs were going out of sight, and not a single new application has been implemented since the days of the punched card machines. As far as he was concerned, we could throw out all of the computers and return to the manual systems."

"Did they?" Paul asked.

"Yes and no, they threw out the computers and went to a service bureau. That was in 1978. Just about everyone in the department quit. The only ones who stayed were the original crew from punched cards days. They were close to retirement and couldn't find a job elsewhere if they tried."

Paul indicated that he would ask Michel for his opinions on the quality of the data-processing staff later, for now he wanted to hear the rest of the story.

Michel continued: "All the computer hardware was removed and the data cen-

---

1. See Appendix A for a description of the IBM family of computers.

ter torn down. An RJE (remote job entry) terminal was placed in each user department. Printers were placed in the accounting department. After a job was processed at the service bureau, the output was printed in the accounting department and distributed to the user departments. It was a way of saving money, not having to give each user department a printer. Most of the processing was for the accounting department anyway. The applications were payroll, billing, receivables, payables, general ledger, and financial statements. Systems under development were: order entry and cash management. Since the vice-president of distribution did not want to do her processing at a service bureau, she somehow managed to find the money to buy a minicomputer and five terminals. She hired systems analysts and programmers (moonlighters) to develop an order entry system strictly to meet her requirements. The cash management program was killed by the controller who decided to do it by hand.''

"Two questions," Paul said. "If we went to a service bureau, and I assume that we are still there."

"That's correct," Michel replied.

"Then why are there so many data-processing people on the payroll, and why do I see computer equipment listed as assets in the financials?''

"Ah, you see, only corporate data processing got rid of its computers and went to the service bureau. When the company started acquiring companies, the Canadian branches of those companies all had their own computer systems which they brought along with them after being merged into UFB. There was no way those applications could be merged in the UFB system; they didn't have the resources or the know-how to do it. Moreover, the added transaction volume would make the service bureau alternative extremely costly. As an aside here, Paul, you are at the point now where your volume suggests that it would be more economical to consider doing your own processing in-house again, especially considering the recent drop in hardware costs. As for people, you have an enormous staff maintaining existing programs. The staff from the acquired companies are included in the data-processing personnel numbers. They are primarily doing maintenance work on their systems. What was your second question?''

"Oh yes, how did the DCS project get started?''

Michel replied: "Actually distribution control system is a misnomer. It started at the request of the marketing people. You know how competitive the food industry is. Profit margins are razor thin and the marketing group here never had the information to assess the success or failure of its promotional programs, nor did they know what was selling or what wasn't as a result of the programs. The information was being collected through the order entry and sales systems, but by the time it came out the other end of the system, it was too late to be of any use. Marketing wanted a rapid response system so that they could analyze market and sales information and answer 'what if' type questions at a terminal. They knew that the competition had this type of system, so why couldn't they?''

Good question, Paul thought. This type of marketing information system was available in the U.S. Of course the computers in the U.S. were much more powerful than those here, nevertheless, Paul thought, why not . . .

Michel continued: "Of course you could have that here, but we would have to redesign the order entry system to make it on-line, design it as a data base system, and permit user queries. Furthermore, the existing order entry system is extremely limited since it is designed for one user on a minicomputer. By redesigning the system, we can generalize it and make it useable for all divisions in the company. Then we can throw out all of the obsolete systems in place and replace them with a single system that will provide marketing with all the information for all divisions within the company. But first, we will have to redo the distribution system."

Paul noticed how Michel was beginning to refer to UFB as "we". Michel continued: "The data-processing people, with the help of marketing, convinced the vice-president of distribution that this should be done. She agreed to the project only if the costs were to be split 25–75 percent. She would fund 25 percent and marketing would fund 75 percent. Her arguments were that (1) she didn't need the system, her present one suited her purpose very well, and (2) most of the benefits would be better information for marketing. Therefore, they should bear the brunt of the costs. Marketing was so desperate for information by then, they agreed, and the project was under way.

"A steering committee composed of representatives from every division and the corporate staff was created to monitor and control progress. A project team was established that would first survey all the divisions to determine requirements, then design the most advanced system using relational data bases and on-line inquiry. Most of the steering committee did not understand any of the technical jargon, but it all sounded good and the two sponsors were enthusiastic, so the project got started.

"Almost immediately the team ran into trouble. The analysts did not know the business. As they interviewed users in the divisions, there was no communication. Moreover, it appeared that each division did order entry differently, and each had different unique requirements. The division requirements did not seem to match what the corporate programs were doing. Months were going by and very little was being accomplished. After three months of study, the team still could not define the scope of the project. These problems were brought up at the steering committee meetings and the answers from the division representatives were: tell us what you want to know and we will help you. The data-processing people did not know how to tell the division presidents that they did not understand the food-processing and distribution business, consequently, they could not understand what the requirements were, even when told by the division people. Needless to say, things weren't helped any by the technical jargon used by the analysts.

"As time pressures mounted, they turned to the existing system. If they could upgrade the existing system, make it on-line and data base oriented, at least marketing could get corporate information from the system. Divisional information could be added later. Unfortunately, the existing system was written in FORTRAN for the minicomputer, was poorly documented, and the documentation was not current. Programmers were sent to school to learn FORTRAN and to do the translation from it to COBOL. There were practically no logic changes, there wasn't time. The final result was that the existing system was recoded into COBOL and tested on the large IBM systems at the service bureau. It didn't work and no one could figure out how to make it work. They could not find the original programmers who worked on the system as moonlighters. The documentation they had left was worthless. Changes had been made to the programs and they were not documented. The users were told that the existing system would be converted as is, then enhanced by adding bells and whistles. It all sounded very logical to the steering committee.

"Turnover on the project team was high because people did not like recoding programs. They were hired to do original, creative work. This work was not only not state of the art as advertised, but tedious and boring. Everytime someone left the project, more experience was lost. By now, project personnel turnover was almost 100 percent. Finally, when we looked at the project last year, they were completely lost. People were writing individual programs, there was no overall system schematic to show interrelations between programs, the scope was still fluid, and specifications changed every time the analyst talked to another user. There was very little hope that the system would ever be useable. Even the project manager admitted that the chance of success would be quite low. That's when we decided to recommend scrapping the project before more money was wasted."

Paul whistled, "I just can't understand how things could go on for so long without someone pulling the plug. What about the steering committee? Who was on it and why didn't they do something?"

Michel replied: "The steering committee was formed according to the book. It was chaired by the vice-president of marketing, since he would have been the major user of the system. Each division was represented by its president. In addition, all your vice-presidents were members. All told, there were 15 members plus the director of data processing. At the initial meeting, your predecessor told everyone present that this was a momentous project, it would move the company into the 'cutting edge of technology' and provide management with much needed information to fight the competition. Everyone was to give it their complete support. He then left the meeting and never attended another one. Initially, the meetings were rather short with data processing giving progress reports. Soon, the presidents stopped attending and sent representatives, usually the chief financial officer in each division. They all asked questions and got satisfactory answers. Whenever there was a problem, a logical solution was also presented by data processing. The schedule kept on slipping but data processing assured them that they could make up the time. Originally, the project was scheduled to be completed in 30 months. About midway through, it was stretched to 36 months. To make that date, they had to give up some features, like the data base and on-line access. At the meetings I attended, there were always arguments on what all these terms meant. Soon it became apparent that finishing the project was more important than what it provided for the user. When the vice-president of marketing realized that he would not get what he wanted after three years of development effort, he called us and asked us to take a close look at the project to see if it would provide him with the information before too long. You have my report." Michel concluded his briefing with a big sigh.

"Thank you for a very honest and comprehensive briefing. Let me ask you some brief questions," Paul continued. "What do the top management team here think of data processing?"

"I've never heard them say much about it." Michel answered. "They don't see any computer generated reports, the data-processing budget is less than one percent of sales, so they probably think that they are getting good processing for what it costs them. They hear from others in the organization that data processing is a joke, but most of their counterparts in other business organizations feel the same way about their departments. Data processing reports to the vice-president of finance, and he is happy with the service provided. It has reduced the number of accounting clerks significantly, especially in the order-processing areas. Actually, outside of accounting, data processing isn't much used."

"What about marketing?" Paul asked. "Surely they use the computer for market analysis, pricing, and promotional analysis."

"Not really," Michel replied. "Jerry, the vice-president of marketing, would love to, but he hasn't had much success getting anything done promptly from the data-processing department. That's why he was so enthusiastic about this project. There are some analysts in marketing using their own personal computers (Apple II and the IBM PC) to do their own data manipulation."

"Where do they get the information?" Paul asked.

"From the order entry system. They asked the data entry clerks to give them a transaction listing of all their inputs each night and they enter it on their personal computers in the morning. Actually, they have hired some college kids to do it, Jerry's son, who is a business student at McGill does most of the analysis and programming, he and his buddies. You don't mind that, do you?" Michel asked.

"Not if he is any good," Paul replied. "Let me ask you something else, why is the computer only used for accounting? Isn't there an information plan? What's on the back burner for development?"

"That's a good question." Michel answered. "Nothing is on the back burner for development. You'll find out, if you haven't already, that planning is not a popular word around here. Most of the top management team grew up as 'doers', not planners. They have a gut feel for the market and the competition. They like to cut deals, give trade discounts. There is a standard price for each of your products, but it is rarely used. Each customer can cut a deal based on volume or trade promotion and get a unique price for the product. There is no time for planning, you have to react to competition. Things change rapidly in this industry, any plan today would be obsolete by tomorrow. Moreover, I hope you don't mind my saying this, Paul, most of your executives feel that they don't have to plan on what to do. They will be told what to do by head office in New York. That's why there is no corporate strategic plan and no information plan."

Paul reacted: "Wow, I appreciate your telling me this, Michel. You don't believe it, do you?"

"Believe what?" Michel replied. "That the nature of the business precludes planning? Of course not, but Paul, you must remember that most of your management team is close to retirement. They have never had to develop a strategic plan. UFB has been part of the U.S. operations for over 100 years. All the planning has been done in New York and sent to Montreal to be implemented. Even when they disagree with the plan here, they have always had the attitude, why fight city hall?

If you plan on developing a strategic plan for UFB Canada, you have a lot of training to do.''

"Do I have the people to do it?'' Paul asked.

"Boy, do you. Every one of your operating divisions has a young second-in-command. When these companies were merged into UFB, your head office put bright young people into the second slots to help the president make the transition over to the UFB way of doing things. Many of them had been frustrated, but few have left because they see themselves as a replacement for the president. After all, as one of them said to me, they can't all live forever. Of course, you know that your own corporate staff is superb, all very young and very frustrated over the lack of information to help in their decision making. They learned a long time ago not to take this to your predecessor; doing that only meant a long-winded lecture on how to run a business without the 'new fangled computers'.''

Paul laughed: "Sounds like you have had that lecture before.''

"Many times,'' Michel replied. "The only area you have problems with, Paul, is data processing. You just lost your director. He was the third in the past 10 years. All of them had rather be the 'genius' system analyst that younger people could come to with problems, than be an effective data-processing manager. Why, the last two directors also did coding. Said that it helped keep them technologically current.''

Paul: "How much did we pay them?''

"About $35,000. Fred, your controller, did not feel that they should make more than the chief accountant. After all, they do the same thing, basically.''

Paul looked at his watch and saw that it was past 6:00 P.M. He rose from the desk and apologized for keeping Michel so late. He knew he would be working late tonight, thinking about what to do to turn this company around. They were doing well financially by reacting to actions taken in the U.S., but think of how much more they could be doing by developing their own market in Canada. However, that would take planning, new attitudes, better information . . .

The experience presented in the United Food and Beverages application is becoming frustratingly common. Senior management identifies an opportunity to use information systems for strategic advantage, a chance to analyze and target specific markets, lock in customer relationships, achieve a significant reduction in operating expenses, or deliver new products and services. A project team is formed, expectations are high, and valuable executives commit a lot of time to the system development task. Several years later, deep disenchantment has set in. The complexity of the effort, both in business and technical terms has risen markedly, as has its costs. No one is certain when results will be achieved, although a stripped-down version of the system is being pursued on a crash basis. Meanwhile, marketing management wonders what happened to the original, seemingly simple idea and worries that the opportunity has been lost.

Paul Williamson CEO of UFB, Canada, has several alternatives to consider. He can take the approach that the problem lies in the way the project was managed, therefore, a more structured approach is needed. Or, he can say that traditional system development is too slow, and what is needed is more productivity aids, more end user involvement in development. He might also say that the technical risks are too high, and better risk measurement tools are needed. All of these will be discussed in Chapter 5, Systems Development. While all these approaches to the problem are helpful, they do not deal with the fundamental issue: the business value of the proposed system and how the system fits into the company's strategic plans.

In most cases, once a system has been approved for development and the design effort started, the original focus on business value is lost. Each division has new and changing requirements and corporate management wants an integrated system. There are discussions about the integration of data with the technical architecture. New technologies are explored, the latest in software is evaluated. But the basic questions remain unasked: What is this really worth to the business, and how does it all fit into our strategy?

Before looking at how Paul Williamson attacked his problem, let us look at the need for information strategic planning, and at the need for evaluating systems based on their place in the company's strategic plan and their worth to the business.

STRATEGIC INFORMATION

More than 95 percent of the Fortune 500 companies claim to be doing some type of strategic planning. While many executives hold this methodology in high regard, their experience with strategy execution, mobilizing an organization to change, has left them somewhat dissatisfied. The reputation of strategic planning is beginning to be blemished and will not survive the 1980s unless more businesses develop an effective program for strategy execution. What is needed is a ''change agent'' that can motivate an organization to move in whatever strategic direction the CEO chooses. Information can be that agent for change.

Most CEOs consider strategic planning their single largest concern and their greatest personal responsibility. That planning responsibility is divided into strategy development and strategy execution. While development has been successfully accomplished in many organizations, execution has not. Effective strategy development and execution require two kinds of strategic information. The first monitors external change and is used in strategy development. This information is readily available and used effectively today. The second monitors internal change and is used in strategy execution. It is the second kind of information that has not been used effectively.

To solve the problems of strategy execution, the CEO must use strategic information in a new role, a role that will help overcome the basic orientation differences between business executives and computer professionals, and move the computer from the clerical floor to the executive suite. Before this move can occur, organizations will have to understand fully the value of strategic information.

The right kind of strategic information can serve as the instrument of change the CEO needs to move his organization in the direction he has chosen. It can be used to describe the expectations of corporate leadership and their concept of ideal performance, and also measure progress toward specific goals. In this role, information becomes the means to encourage change in highly motivated people. If people know that a certain measure will be used to judge their performance, they will strive to do well according to that measure. Most successful members of corporate management are strongly motivated to excel when prompted by the expectations of corporate leadership. They will change to meet those expectations, if the expectations are clear. Effective leadership, therefore, demands that the CEO's goals are clearly understood by everyone in the organization.

To implement a successful strategic plan, management must define the target as well as the organization's concept of ideal performance in meeting that target. Part of the strategic-planning process should be to define this concept in terms of strategic success factors.

STRATEGIC SUCCESS FACTORS

Strategic success factors are not new to business. Arthur Andersen & Co. developed responsibility reporting in the 1960s as a forerunner to this approach. Hundreds of companies used responsibility reporting to focus on containable costs in each responsibility level. Containable costs was identified as the strategic success factor in each level in the management structure and was then carefully monitored. In the late 1960s, D. Ronald Daniel, now managing director of McKinsey & Co. expanded the concept of success factors. Instead of relating them to responsibility reporting, he tied them to executive compensation. John Rockart of the MIT Sloan School Center for Information Systems Research documented a methodology for defining critical success factors in the article, "Chief Executives Define Their Own Data Needs".[2] He focused on data that were not always collected but that contributed to the success of the particular management level involved. His technique for defining critical success factors consisted of the following steps:

- Interviewing top management and discussing goals
- Analyzing goals and determining critical success factors
- Defining the prime measures of the critical success factors
- For hard information, defining report formats and/or subsystems
- For soft information, recording the appropriate data manually.

Rockart suggests that critical success factors be arrayed hierarchically and used for communication, either as an informal planning aid or as part of the formal planning process. These factors can be an excellent approach for executives to clarify priorities both for business planning and management information requirements.

Today, most companies, if they use strategic success factors at all, define a small number, 10 to 12, that will dramatically affect an organization's success. Since these factors can measure successful performance, they constitute the strategic information on which to base strategy execution. To execute strategy successfully, management must continually pay close attention to these factors and also carefully define them for their employees. Terms like growth and profitability are too broad and poor definitions of strategic success factors. If misrepresented, or misinterpreted, these factors can lead employees down a path that diverges from management's original purposes.

For example, one bank adopted fees generated by each division as a strategic success factor. Shortly thereafter it found offices aimed for high-volume customers rather than good credit risks. As a result, the net fees declined considerably. A company that focuses on sales as a strategic success factor may find that their personnel are poaching on each other's territory or are asking customers to sign orders with the understanding that the merchandise will never be delivered. These examples illustrate that the wrong strategic success factors can be counterproductive.

How does one select the right strategic success factor? Several criteria come to mind. First, the factor should be measurable, since performance will be evaluated based on how successful management is in meeting the goal for that factor. Second, the factor should have some business value. If the factor is the key to success in meeting a certain goal, what is the business value of that goal. Finally, the factor should be easily understood by those who will have to work with it as a performance indicator. For example, some firms use return on investment (ROI) as a strategic success factor. However, ROI often becomes a numbers game between those sub-

2. Rockart, John, "Chief Executives Define Their Own Data Needs," *Harvard Business Review,* Mar.-Apr., 1979.

mitting projects for approval, and approving management. Whether the target is met depends on who is doing the measuring and the criteria for return on investment. It is not an easily understood factor.

Let us assume that the mission of United Food and Beverages is to be the dominant food-processing company in Canada, supplying its products to the most profitable market segment in Canada. One segment of their strategic plan might look like Figure 2-1.

These strategic success factors are measurable, have business value, and are understandable. Moreover, each factor can be used to develop key performance indicators to measure individual performance. For example, the last strategic success factor in Figure 2-1 is "Low material costs." Key performance indicators that can be developed for that factor are:

- Actual material costs vs. longterm target
- UFB percent material costs vs. industry average
- Material price as percent of standard price
- Change in material price as percent of Consumer Price Index.

FIGURE 2-1   **STRATEGIC PLAN FOR UFB**

Mission	Objectives	Goals	Strategies	SSF*
To be the dominant food product company, supplying the most profitable domestic market segments.	Compete in profitable market segments	Identify and enter five new markets segments with high-profit potential by 1988.	Upgrade market research functions to identify high-profit potential market segments.	Effective market intelligence.
		Increase market share 15% in high-profit market segments where we are not the dominant supplier by 1989.	Develop a product line that fits the requirements and needs of the high-potential market segments.	New products.
			Expand product distribution network.	Market segment dominance.
			Product differentiation.	
	Be the low cost producer in our market segments.	Reduce total manufacturing costs by 10% by 1988.	Review and upgrade all labor standards.	High labor productivity.
		Achieve 3% return above the cost of capital by 1989.	Negotiate lower prices for raw materials and tighten controls over yields.	Low material costs.

*SSF = Strategic Success Factors.

The individual responsible for meeting the key performance indicators, in this example, would be the vice-president of manufacturing. He would receive information for measuring performance against these indicators and he would be judged by his performance against these indicators.

After corporate management has selected and defined the strategic success factors, it should develop a formal information plan that articulates the success factors at every level in the enterprise's information systems, from the top down. The information should familiarize users and information-processing professionals with the range of internal and external business information available to them. For example, just as strategic success factors and their associated key performance indicators are developed at the strategic-planning level, so operating success factors and their associated performance indicators should be developed for the operating levels of management.

RESPONSIBILITY FOR INFORMATION

In most organizations, no one person is responsible for information. A chief information officer should be appointed to oversee the merger of strategic planning and information processing. This position entails teaching management personnel to use strategic information, supporting the selection of the business strategies, identifying the strategic success factors, and building them into the information systems. While the chief information officer's role is clear, the best candidate for the position is not so easily identified.

The chief financial officer is a possibility. Until the 1970s, the CFO in most companies was the chief information officer. The only automated information was in the accounting system, and traditionally, the CFO was the keeper of the budget and of reports measuring actual performance against budget. This scenario changed when large amounts of operating information began to be kept in the operating departments and were no longer in the domain of the chief financial officer.

The head of information systems is another candidate for the chief information officer's slot. This person is potentially ideal except for existing dichotomy between information-processing personnel and other areas of the enterprise.

A third candidate is the head of corporate planning; planners are inherently information conscious. They enjoy the advantage of working closely with the CEO. The main drawback to this candidate is that most of the planners want to plan change instead of manage it.

Regardless of who are appointed chief information officers, they cannot serve as surrogate CEOs. Only CEOs can provide the authority and leadership necessary to meet the information needs of their firms. CEOs must motivate management teams to accept the CEO's goals as their own. Toward that end, they must conspicuously measure progress toward those goals. This last step, the conspicuous consumption of information, is the "engine" that mobilizes organizations to move in the desired directions. CEOs must be involved. Only they can define the direction of their organizations. Only they have the authority and leadership to change their organizations' concepts of ideal performance, introduce strategic success factors and induce their organizations to accept them as their own, and to motivate their organizations to change through their own conspicuous consumption of strategic information.

The most successful companies of the future will bridge the gap between information processing and corporate planning. The computer will be an essential tool in executive management's quest for information to execute strategy and in its selection of strategic success factors. The merger of strategic planning and information processing in the 1990s will finally create the environment in which the full potential of strategic planning can be realized.

NEED FOR INFORMATION PLANNING

Information technology is changing rapidly. Prior to 1980, personal computers were relatively unknown. In 1984, IBM projected delivery of one product, the PC, to exceed two million. By 1990, the U.S. Commerce Department projects the population of personal computers worldwide to be 100 million (see Figure 2-2). Microtechnology and the drop in costs of integrated circuits have made the personal computer affordable for almost everyone. It will replace the CRT as a data entry device for most applications other than a few high-volume applications such as credit card charge slip processing, or insurance premium processing.

Advances in systems and software such as decision support systems, end user

FIGURE 2-2   **MICROCOMPUTER SHIPMENTS IN 1982–85**

Worldwide Microcomputer Shipments (in thousands of units)				
	1982	1983	1984	1985
Personal desktop	500	2,250	4,000	5,500
Multi-user	18	125	200	350
Portable (notebook size)		100	750	1,500
Portable (luggable)		225	500	750

Source: "Personal Computing: A Challenge to Management," A Forbes Magazine Advertising Supplement (Advertisement no. 20), *Forbes*, May 21, 1984.

programming, the information center concept, all have brought changes to the way data processing is traditionally managed and viewed in the organization. Today, it is no longer data processing but information processing, and it must be managed jointly by top management and the chief information officer.

Walls built up over the years between users and computer people must be torn down and a new spirit of cooperation must be established. As new hardware and software improvements are announced, frequent meetings must be held between top management, users, and information-processing people to discuss developments that might help the company and to generate plans to deal with them. As key people in the organization are made aware of advances in technology, they will be able to think of uses for these developments which may not occur to the computer technician.

As Paul Williamson develops his strategies and goals, his team must think of the information and critical success factors needed to execute the strategies as well as the feedback needed to monitor progress against goals and objectives. By developing the strategic plan as a management team effort, all managers will understand the interdependencies. If the strategy is not feasible because of the lack of systems to provide the required information, the planners will know this in sufficient time to develop alternative strategies.

Another important reason for strategic information planning is the scarcity of skilled resources. There is no shortage of programmers today. There is an abundance of entry level, inexperienced programmers as well as those who still consider programming an art and refuse to adhere to control procedures and documentation standards. There is, however, a shortage of skilled, perceptive analysts and programmers who can communicate with users in common English and are genuinely interested in learning the business in order to develop workable solutions.

What is even more critical today is the shortage of experienced information-processing executives who can administer a large department, work with users to identify requirements, and communicate with top management to offer advice and guidance on managing information as a corporate resource. As the information systems department competes with other departments in the business for financial and human resources, the information systems manager must make tough decisions on the allocation of these resources. Since information systems is just one of many strategic business units within the company, resources allocated to it must come at the expense of another unit in the company. It is vitally important that the management of the information systems department get the message across that information is as valuable as a unit of production and should get its fair share of the corporate budget.

Perhaps the most critical reason for having a strategic information plan today is the proliferation of equipment throughout every organization. As users got fed up with the service provided by the data-processing department, many turned to other sources of processing to fulfill their requirements. Some, like UFB, went to a service bureau; many others bought minicomputers and microprocessors to develop small systems they could use themselves. At the same time, word processing started growing and required more powerful processors. Users saw the potential of linking word processing with data processing, or linking one word processor with another within the same organization. Companies with operations across the country saw the advantage of linking the word processors in each branch office together to communicate rapidly with each other. Three different technologies came together: the mainframe computer, word processors, and telecommunications. Acquiring a mainframe has always been the responsibility of the head of data processing. Word-processing equipment was the responsibility of the office manager and the head of the typing department. Telecommunications was the responsibility of the telephone company. When more lines were needed, you called the phone company and asked for their assistance.

The single event that brought the need to integrate data processing, word processing, and telecommunications to the attention of management was the rapid growth of the personal computer in business. Jerry, the vice-president of marketing at UFB, had been using a microcomputer to develop graphs showing market share and the results of promotional programs. Data on these topics were stored in the distribution department's computer. Since Jerry could not hook into that computer, he had to take printouts from the computer and type the numbers he needed into his microprocessor. If people like Jerry had been able to get the necessary information from the data-processing department, chances are that they would not have turned to their own personal computer or to minicomputers. The fact remains, however, that these computers, outside the control of the information-processing organization, have proliferated throughout every company. There is no way management can abolish them by decree; they must be linked to the company's mainframe so that managers can have access to information stored in corporate files without costly re-entry of data already captured in other transaction systems. Moreover, by allowing managers access to corporate data files, at least management will have consistent information upon which to base their decision making.

Businesses are starting to address this problem. Corporate information-processing departments as well as independent software companies have developed programs that will link personal computers and mainframes, giving more people access to the reservoir of information about customers, suppliers, and employees that every company accumulates. Instead of having to ask a programmer to get the information that is needed, a user can go directly to the source.

The links may create an entirely new set of problems for the information manager. Can users "mess up" the corporate data base if they can easily send files into it? Security problems also grow when personal computers are hooked into mainframes. An easily concealed five-inch computer diskette or three-inch cartridge diskette could hold a company's customer list or other valuable information. Greater communications capabilities will ultimately increase the cost of personal computers to a company. While the basic machine may cost under $5000, extra demands on the mainframe, additional software, more communication ports and lines, and more information-processing department time could increase the cost to more than $25,000 per personal computer. Nevertheless, practically all experts agree that the links are coming. They will make all the information on the mainframe more useful and more powerful than it has ever been. Equally important, it will make the need to manage that information more vital than ever.

Strategic information planning is more than determining how to use the company's mainframe computer to best advantage. It is integrating data processing, word processing, personal computers, communications, and office copying into an integrated system, and using that system to gain a competitive edge. Since UFB has done nothing in this area, Paul Williamson has the advantage of starting with a clean slate. There is no system to replace and he can plan an optimum system from scratch. How should he begin?

PROFESSIONAL APPLICATION COMMENT: APPLICATION OF STRATEGIC INFORMATION TECHNIQUES AT UNITED FOOD AND BEVERAGES

Paul Williamson is well aware that the attitude of his top management must change if UFB Canada is to remain competitive and continue to grow. Already, the problems caused by the recent years of acquisition are beginning to surface. Almost all of them can be attributed to the lack of anticipation, caused by the absence of corporate objectives and plans. In acquiring these companies, it may have been expeditious initially to keep them operating as separate divisions. However, it soon became apparent that there was a lot of duplication and inefficiency in using this approach. Each division had its own data-processing, accounting, and purchasing departments. Services that could be provided much more efficiently through a central organization were continued at the division level just to keep management of the acquired company happy. It was also interesting to note that many of the companies had been for sale because of problems with management, competitive position in the industry, or poor productivity. Yet the management team who could not solve those problems were kept on as divisional management after the mergers. It was no wonder then, that corporate headquarters insisted on doing all the planning for its Canadian operations, leaving only the execution of the plan and the monitoring of day-to-day operations to divisional management.

Paul was well aware that to remedy these problems, the company first of all had to develop a strategic plan to chart the direction to follow for the next five years: identify the strategic success factors, determine what resources would be needed to execute the plan, and identify the performance factors necessary to evaluate progress. This process might reveal that changes in organization and management personnel would be necessary to make the plan work.

Paul decided to start with a definition of the business functions performed within the company. He found that there were basically six major activities:

- Marketing
- Distribution
- Manufacturing
- Purchasing and procurement

■ Finance and control

■ Administration and support services

At the corporate level, Paul had a vice-president in charge of each of these functions except purchasing and procurement. This was performed by the vice-president of administration. Since Paul wanted to place special emphasis on planning and information systems, he moved the vice-president of administration to be vice-president of purchasing and procurement, and offered the position of vice-president of planning and information systems (replacing the vice-president of administration) to Michel Lozeau. The duties would be planning for all corporate resources, including information, and ensuring that all resources were available when required. The job basically was a combination of the traditional director of planning and the director of information systems. Michel found the concept challenging and he accepted Paul's offer. Paul also created the position of chief operating officer (COO) and had all the division presidents report to him. Paul had planned to work with the new COO to review the qualifications of each division president and decide where replacements were necessary. The new organization is presented in Figure 2-3.

With the corporate staff in place, Paul formed a planning task force consisting of the number two person in each of the divisions. He knew that all of these were young, dynamic people sent from home office. Working with the corporate staff, this task force would be charged to do the following:

■ Identify the objectives and goals for each business unit.

■ Identify the strategies for reaching those objectives and goals.

■ Identify the strategic success factors in each business unit.

FIGURE 2-3   **ORGANIZATION OF UFB**

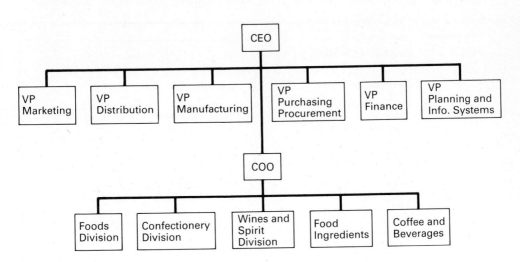

- Determine the critical individuals to be motivated.
- Select key performance indicators.
- Develop information for monitoring key performance.
- Document the procedure in a formal strategic plan for each business unit.

The divisional people were assigned to one of four groups (marketing, distribution, manufacturing, purchasing) depending on the key activity in their division. Paul, Michel, and the vice-president of finance worked in the area of staff resources, and information resources, as well as on integrating the efforts of the division teams.

The first step in developing the strategic plan was for the task force to identify the environmental, enterprise, industry, and company-unique success factors. These are presented in Figure 2-4.

Environmental restrictions have a major influence on the food-processing industry. Foreign competition from the U.S. and Western Europe is strong. The company's margins are low, so inflation represents a substantial factor. In addition, government regulations are important because of the flour dust created in milling operations.

The success factors that UFB and its competitors must consider include selecting market niches, providing competitive products within that niche, periodically purging their product line, and maintaining modern, labor-efficient facilities. These success factors could apply to almost any business: high labor productivity, minimum working capital, high-quality customer service, a motivated management team, and a return exceeding the cost of capital.

The second step was to develop a strategic plan which described the mission of UFB Canada, its goals and objectives, and the strategies to reach those goals. To avoid competition from foreign imports, UFB chose to focus on being the low-cost producer in the market niches selected. But because UFB valued employee satisfaction as much as profitability, the company's mission was twofold: first, to be the dominant supplier of food products to the most profitable segments of the domestic

---

FIGURE 2-4   **SUCCESS FACTORS**

Environmental

Foreign competition
Inflation
Government restrictions

Industry

Quality products
Low-cost production
Modern production facilities

Company-unique

New products
Stable work force
Market segment dominance
Low material cost
Effective market intelligence
Low-cost funds
Design for low-cost manufacturing

Enterprise

High labor productivity
Minimum working capital
High-quality customer service
Motivated management team
Return above the cost of capital

market, and second, to provide a high-quality work life for their employees. As a result, its objectives were to compete in profitable markets, be a low-cost producer, and offer a high-quality work life.

The third step was to select the strategic success factors. The task force's knowledge of the organization, coupled with a review of the corporation's annual reports helped it understand what was strategically valuable to the company. A series of interviews beginning with Paul and proceeding down the organizational chart also helped determine the strategic success factors. Key performance indicators and individuals were discussed. In a second set of interviews conducted from the bottom up, participants discussed the decisions and plans made to better understand the strategic success factors and operating success factors formulated for each organizational level. In this way, those factors constant throughout the organization were identified.

The more decentralized the company is, the fewer are the strategic success factors that apply to all units at all levels. In companies under centralized management, more strategic success factors are similar among different business units and executives. The strategic success factors important to UFB included effective market intelligence, development of appropriate new products, dominance in chosen market segment, high labor productivity, and low material costs.

The next step was identifying the individuals to be motivated to achieve these factors. A network of people from various levels of the organization was identified for each strategic success factor. It was found that many executives in the hierarchy were not part of the network of critical individuals because they were not vital to achieving that particular strategic success factor. These individuals were reviewed by Paul and the COO.

The fifth step was to determine and communicate the key performance indicators to the network of critical individuals. The key performance indicators had to be action oriented, capable of monitoring performance, and acceptable to management. Paul wanted all executives, regardless of their degree of interest or involvement in a strategic success factor, to assist in selection of key performance indicators, even though some of these executives would not be measured by the indicators. It permitted each executive to have a broader view of the entire operation, the factors critical for success, and the key performance indicators. For example, it allowed executives outside the purchasing area to understand why reduced material costs is an important critical success factor. At UFB, buying a few high-volume commodities at the right price is critical to the bottom line. In some cases such as flour and confection, the material represented 70 percent of the product cost.

The sixth step involved developing the information needed for monitoring performance. Information needs were determined by the key performance indicators, and where appropriate, modern techniques such as decision support systems were planned for development to supply the information. The availability of necessary strategic and operating information was addressed, and, when it was unavailable from existing source systems, the need for more systems was indicated. For the first time, Paul and the corporate staff found out the information available in the files of the division computer systems.

The final step was the conspicuous use of the information to motivate activity at all levels of the organization. The plan called for disseminating the information in group meetings, monthly newsletters, individual conversations, and other means of communication. While information summaries from the transaction systems were distributed to lower-level managers, the top executives benefited by receiving strategic information based on strategic success factors and key performance indicators.

After six months, Paul had three documents: a recommended strategic plan for UFB Canada with the necessary tools for monitoring execution of the plan; an information schematic for the company showing two levels of planning (strategic and operational) and the information needed to control and monitor plan execution (see Figure 2-5); and recommendations for reorganizing the company to eliminate or consolidate duplicate functions.

Paul was extremely happy with the results of the task force, especially with the recommendations for reorganizing the company. He had not asked for this recommendation, nor did he know that the members of the task force were working on it. It proved that they too recognized the duplications in the present organization and were not afraid to suggest changes. Furthermore, having recommended the changes, they would all work hard to see that they were accepted by the organization. All in all, Paul was quite pleased with how things turned out. Looking at the information schematic, Paul could see that a lot of thought and effort went into defining each level of planning and the information that would be needed at each level. It was apparent that quite a bit of thought has been given to each of the business units prior to convening the task force. The planning exercise had served as a catalyst to get these thoughts into the open and down on paper as strategic and operational plans. Most importantly, his management team were beginning to recognize the importance of information as a corporate resource. Paul was already beginning to think of ways to encourage early retirement for some of the existing senior executives so that this dynamic younger group could be given the responsibility for executing the plans they had developed.

The basis for good management is good planning. Through his planning exercise, Paul had applied the following principles of good planning:

1. He had allowed his management team (both corporate and divisional) the opportunity to define and develop plans for each business unit, thus widening their understanding of how the enterprise worked and the interactions among business units.

2. By including the new vice-president of planning and information resources as part of the planning team, he not only exposed Michel to other executives and to the requirements of their business functions, but he presented an opportunity for Michel to explain how information in each area would be needed to meet overall corporate objectives.

3. He allowed the planning team the opportunity to define overall corporate goals, identify the strategies needed to accomplish stated goals, develop the plans to carry out the strategies, and finally, identify how performance against plans was to be measured. The executives who worked on developing the plans and

strategies were now committed to executing them and taking responsibility for the outcome.

4. The planning process afforded division management a better appreciation of

- How operations of business units were linked together and the interdependencies and flow of information between business units. An example would be, distribution notifying marketing that a particular product was selling well, alerting manufacturing to increase production of the item, and letting finance know the financial impact of the increased sales.
- How basic transaction systems must capture source information once and supply this information to multiple business units.
- The terminology used in information processing such as transaction systems, and source data.

5. Most importantly, the planning process permitted division management to generate and provide information processing with ideas on how data should be captured and processing performed. This was the first step toward user acceptance of new systems.

Michel had quite a challenge ahead of him: How to design new systems using the latest in technology to provide the information required under the new strategic plan.

FIGURE 2-5   **INFORMATION SYSTEMS SCHEMATIC, CONSUMER PRODUCTS OPERATIONS**

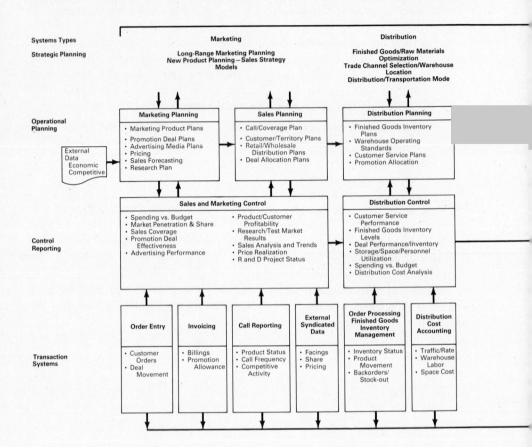

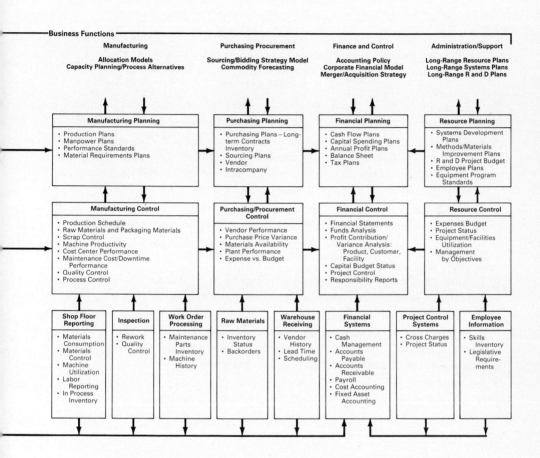

Business Functions

Manufacturing	Purchasing Procurement	Finance and Control	Administration/Support
Allocation Models	Sourcing/Bidding Strategy Model	Accounting Policy	Long-Range Resource Plans
Capacity Planning/Process Alternatives	Commodity Forecasting	Corporate Financial Model	Long-Range Systems Plans
		Merger/Acquisition Strategy	Long-Range R and D Plans

Manufacturing Planning
- Production Plans
- Manpower Plans
- Performance Standards
- Material Requirements Plans

Purchasing Planning
- Purchasing Plans—Long-term Contracts Inventory
- Sourcing Plans
- Vendor
- Intracompany

Financial Planning
- Cash Flow Plans
- Capital Spending Plans
- Annual Profit Plans
- Balance Sheet
- Tax Plans

Resource Planning
- Systems Development Plans
- Methods/Materials Improvement Plans
- R and D Project Budget
- Employee Plans
- Equipment Program Standards

Manufacturing Control
- Production Schedule
- Raw Materials and Packaging Materials
- Scrap Control
- Machine Productivity
- Cost Center Performance
- Maintenance Cost/Downtime Performance
- Quality Control
- Process Control

Purchasing/Procurement Control
- Vendor Performance
- Purchase Price Variance
- Materials Availability
- Plant Performance
- Expense vs. Budget

Financial Control
- Financial Statements
- Funds Analysis
- Profit Contribution/Variance Analysis: Product, Customer, Facility
- Capital Budget Status
- Project Control
- Responsibility Reports

Resource Control
- Expenses Budget
- Project Status
- Equipment/Facilities Utilization
- Management by Objectives

Shop Floor Reporting
- Materials Consumption
- Materials Control
- Machine Utilization
- Labor Reporting
- In Process Inventory

Inspection
- Rework
- Quality Control

Work Order Processing
- Maintenance Parts Inventory
- Machine History

Raw Materials
- Inventory Status
- Backorders

Warehouse Receiving
- Vendor History
- Lead Time
- Scheduling

Financial Systems
- Cash Management
- Accounts Payable
- Accounts Receivable
- Payroll
- Cost Accounting
- Fixed Asset Accounting

Project Control Systems
- Cross Charges
- Project Status

Employee Information
- Skills Inventory
- Legislative Requirements

CHAPTER 2   **DISCUSSION QUESTIONS**

1. What is the role of a management steering committee in monitoring a system development project? How do the user people on the committee evaluate whether the technicians are being realistic and truthful when they present progress and status reports?

2. What should be the salary of the head of information systems? Who should he or she report to? How can they learn more about the functional areas of the business?

3. Management has been disappointed with systems projects that are late, over budget, and not responsive to user needs. What can they do about it? Why does the information systems department, and its manager, get away with performance and results that would never be tolerated in other areas of the business?

4. Most companies do not have a person with responsibility for information. Should they? What would be the responsibilities of a chief information officer?

5. What would you do if given the task of integrating data processing with word processing?

6. Discuss the concept of strategic success factors in a business and indicate how information systems can participate in defining and using these factors.

7. Do you think most companies look at information needs from a "structured" viewpoint, that is, transaction processing, operating data, tactical data, strategic data? If not, why not, and if so, why have they not used the computer more successfully to capture and process the information?

3

TECHNOLOGY PLANNING

ISSUES

- What will future computers look like? Will they be significantly faster than those of today?

- What are knowledge-based systems?

- What impact will the move toward data base systems have for the corporation?

- Data administration—a function whose time has come

- The information center—a new lease on life

PROFESSIONAL APPLICATION

CITICORP

New York City's money center banks are known for their aggressiveness and competitiveness. Each is searching for its own niche; some, such as Morgan Guaranty Trust Company, have carved out their place in the arena as a corporate bank, serving the Fortune 1000 companies and foreign multinational corporations. Morgan does not handle personal accounts other than for individuals who happen to be executives with client companies or individuals with significant net worth. Banks such as Citibank and Chase Manhattan strive to be all things to all people, serving both retail and corporate customers. Others fall somewhere in between Citibank, the leader in consumer banking, and Morgan, the leader in corporate banking. Regardless of the strategy chosen to compete in the New York marketplace, all the large banks, Citibank, Chase Manhattan, Manufacturer Hanover, Morgan Guaranty, Chemical, Bankers Trust, and Irving Trust, are facing a rapidly changing banking environment. Electronics and deregulation have created major changes in the way banks have traditionally provided products and services, and accelerated the movement towards faster, better, more accurate delivery services. It has also helped propel an MIT-educated engineer and computer whiz, John Reed, to the top of the world's largest bank and holding company, the $150 billion Citicorp.

This case presents the technological challenges facing the banking industry in general, and Citicorp in particular. Planning for technology has become a vital part of strategic planning for most companies. At Citicorp, technology has been the catalyst for expanding into new services and the vehicle for devising innovative new ways to deliver these services to its customers. During the tenure of Walter Wriston as CEO, Citicorp grew at a rapid pace (see Figure 3-A) primarily because it aggressively applied new technology to traditional business areas. Reed is now faced with the task of leading Citicorp into a world financial services market where the distinctions between different financial institutions are blurring rapidly. Deregulation has allowed financial institutions to offer a full range of financial services. Every act of traditional banking is now a component of the information economy. Money is just a specially coded form of information. Rather than move gold bullion, we move bits and bytes across communication lines.

Some observers have suggested that the emergence of John Reed as CEO at Citicorp signals a new era in corporate management. The "technocrat"—a manager well-versed in electronics as well as the traditional business practices—may now take over other banks, financial institutions, and manufacturing companies. At Citicorp, the quest for the large scale application of technology, and the associated economies of such large scales, appears to be everything. Scale was never a factor in banking before automation. Automation has made scale important. Since the required investments in information systems are large, the greater the volume, the faster the payback, and the lower the ongoing operation costs per transaction. John Reed was one of the first to recognize this and during his career at the bank, he has actively promoted his concept of growth through scale and automation.

Citicorp has two satellite transponders for its own use. On earth, it has moved aggressively to become a common carrier and supplier of computing services. It is also developing a corporate-wide systems architecture to guide its interconnection of disparate data bases and computers. Building on its technology base, the bank has developed application software packages such as cash terminals for small local banks, helping them install and use the new services, and signing them up as correspondent banks in their local areas. Through this and other innovative practices, it has long circumvented laws restricting inter-state banking.

Economies of scale, as Citicorp has shown, can also be achieved by a process of acquisition and diversification into nonlending activities. In the late 1970s, the bank developed the five "I" strategy calling for emphasis in the areas of: institutions, individuals, investments, insurance, and information services. Reed and his predecessor, Walter Wriston, saw that the traditional wholesale banking business was changing, and that the impact of technology would force them to create new ways of doing business. In addition to the analysis that goes into strategic planning, the impact of technology would have to be factored into all future plans.

Wholesale banking (corporate banking) has always been the more profitable part of the bank's product mix. The wholesale bank's base of deposits from corporate borrowers has been eroding for the past decade. Rather than let deposits sit at fixed interest rates in banks over long periods of time, automation allows the creation of cash management networks and software. Citicorp foresaw that eventually banks would have to face the loss of their demand deposits to higher-yielding transaction

---

FIGURE 3-A   **CITICORP'S GROWTH UNDER WALTER WRISTON**

	1967	1984	Change
Total assets	17.5 billion	150.6 billion	+ 761%
Net income	103 million	890 million	+ 764%
Number of employees	26,900	71,000	+ 164%
Total loans	9.9 billion	102.7 billion	+ 937%

Source: *New York Times*, Apr. 21, 1985.

vehicles such as money market certificates, commercial paper, and certificates of deposit. In 1984, Citicorp depended on large deposits for 63 percent of its funding. Although its institutional banking group has settled into a pattern of no growth over the past three years, it still contributed 70 percent of the bank's earnings in 1984. Reed's problem is how to redeploy these assets away from structurally unattractive prime wholesale lending to more productive activities. He has chosen acquisition and diversification into computer-based services. That still leaves Citibank with the problem of where life-giving deposits will come from, and this is where the individual depositors come in.

It is almost axiomatic in banking that one cannot make money in retail services, especially when restricted by bank regulations to serving a local community. Even when that local community is as large as New York City, it is not large enough to generate sufficient volume through individual depositors to meet business loan demands. What is needed is the ability to access all the other individual depositors in the country. Wriston and Reed saw that because of regulation and geographical restrictions, a planned foray into computer services and the creation of a national branch-banking network would not be feasible. So, in the late 1970s, the bank decided to meet the regulatory and legal issues head on with the creation of a time-sharing services subsidiary, Citishare. The bank had been providing such services internally for years and it lobbied vigorously that it should be allowed to take the services to the open market. Reed argued that technological improvements in the delivery of financial services have enabled non-banks to compete with banks through money market funds and morgage pools. Additionally, the new information technology had made county, state, and regional boundaries artificial constraints. Citicorp claimed that only through deregulation could banks and non-banks compete on an increasingly equal basis.

Citicorp's plea to take the shackles off met with sympathetic ears among federal authorities, and Citishare's petition to expand the franchise of the bank on the legal and regulatory side so far has been successful. One could say that Citicorp both forced the issue of deregulation and created it to meet its own needs. At any event, by settling for nothing less than a free and unrestricted financial services market, Wriston and Reed probably saved the banking industry.

Reed, then in charge of Citibank's consumer banking push, saw that the bank's future lay with individual depositors, but he still had to reach them. In 1977, he boldly chose a direct and risky course by mailing 20 million credit cards throughout the country, and almost overnight the company became the second largest credit card issuer. More recently, Reed's innovative side surfaced in the creation of a sophisticated and ground-breaking network of automated teller machines in New York City and surrounding areas. Apart from the cost, the pioneering creation of new interfaces and the necessary resculpting of branches to accommodate the teller machines were greeted with skepticism by the banking industry. Now, after several years of red ink, the devices have proven themselves an unqualified success. Citibank's consumer banking business has grown substantially on Reed's technological bet. Reed's technology solutions have put pressure on other banks' brick-and-mortar branches, which are now vulnerable to a new competitor with lower-cost delivery methods. Branch banks flourish only because of their convenience. They offer little more than can be obtained through the use of credit cards and teller machines. Customers no longer depend on branches, but on technology. Citibank's need for more individual depositors also has led to the creation of an extensive network of consumer finance offices and the acquisition of numerous savings and loan associations nationwide. Wriston recently boasted that Citicorp already does business with one out of every seven U.S. households.

Also with the blessing of Reed, Citibank pursued an aggressive plan dubbed Project Paradise to install minicomputers wherever possible. The idea was to allow each user freedom in budgeting for and selecting computer services. They could use the services provided by the bank's central computers (operations), use an outside service bureau, or buy their own minicomputer. If each department was held responsible for meeting specific performance goals, then they should be allowed the freedom to select the resources which they thought could best help them meet those goals. Because Project Paradise was initiated at a time when user satisfaction with central operations was at a low ebb, most departments opted to move to minicomputers. This move unsettled IBM, among others, and prompted the industry leader to preview its Series/1 minicomputer to Citicorp many months before that machine was publicly unveiled. That did not stop Citibank from replacing a 370/145[1] mainframe with two dozen Interdata 7/32 minicomputers in the stock transfer department. It was a risk that did not work out too well: Citibank's stock transfer operations gained a reputation for excessive delays and costly mistakes.

To pioneer means to accept the fact that some projects will fail. The bank, nevertheless, tried its hand at almost any and all new computing and communications technologies. It set up a technology caravan at a Park Avenue office to which bank managers at all levels were invited to test different vendors' equipment. Several in-house technology teams were set up to evaluate and recommend hardware and software to the many departmental systems groups. Buy it and try it, was the edict from above. If it did not work, perhaps the next one would. This free playing technological adventure may have misfired. After several years of bragging, Citibank eventually grew reluctant to discuss Paradise, but the die had been cast. The bank would never be the same from a technological point of view. Management had had a taste of the power of computing and was not about to go backwards.

One former Citibank employee explains that Reed was brought in to make large investments in technology and delivery systems and have them pay off in the long term. Now that he is the top man, there is no reason for him to change his *modus operandi,* and his success will most likely be repeated. But because of the deregulated environment he was instrumental in creating, he can no longer afford to manage change at his leisure. The Bank of America, which among U.S. banks is second to Citicorp in assets ($118 billion), recently disclosed plans to spend five billion dollars on new technologies as well as on the maintenance of its old systems. That is as much as Manufacturers Hanover, Chase Manhattan, and Chemical combined will

---

1. See Appendix A for a description of the IBM family of computers.

spend. Reed can feel the hot breath of European banks as well, as they mount ambitious electronic banking programs.

Citicorp established an internal think tank, Transaction Technology Inc. (TTI), to design and test 'systems using the latest in computer and communication technologies. Until recently, TTI has been able to operate in a world of sliding deadlines. Today, the pressure to install a system rather than evaluate and test new technology grows daily. For the past two years, Reed and TTI have been trying to design software which would enable a combination of individual retirement accounts (IRA), deposits, loans, and the administrative procedures for branch management to function from one data base. This new branch banking system would be installed in the 280 branches in the New York metropolitan area. In 1983, the bank evaluated four potential vendors as suppliers of the workstations for the new software. Though no final decision has been made, TTI and the systems team were told to implement the software immediately on microcomputer hardware for 50 of the branches. This would be a pilot test and after modifying the system based on results of the test, the remaining 230 branches could be implemented later.

Citicorp has been attempting to pull together its IDMS data bases and data centers into a massive cash management network for multinational customers. The network would offer current economic, financial, marketing, and regulatory information 24 hours a day for multinational corporations that needed it and could pay handsomely. Senior technical staff on the project are arguing that standards, at least where the network must interface with the outside world, are essential. The bank has been using the seven-layer ISO network model and IBM's SNA as references. Analysts feel that the bank could adopt the ISO model, but push for the addition of two extra layers to cover dynamic storage management and relational data from information centers. It is also possible that Citicorp will adopt the $\times$.12 data exchange standard which defines nesting, segmenting, and loop structures for data so that it can be independent of the systems sending and receiving it. At any event, it seems clear that the bank's hit-or-miss approach to technology could be giving way to a more mature, planned approach. A pilot home-banking system expected to be unveiled shortly is the result of a four-year development effort. It was initiated as the result of a technology-planning session, meshed into the overall corporate strategic plan of Citicorp, and is now undergoing analysis for the best way to market the service. The conclusion from one of his former colleagues is that Reed, the engineer, is ready to make the transition to planner and marketer. He's "everything but a banker. Reed wouldn't know a foreign loan if he fell over it. But he's part of a team and will have to sell his ideas despite the wave of technology he's riding. I doubt they would have picked him if they didn't feel that he could become a banker too."

Technology planning has turned Citicorp from the second largest bank in the country to the largest and most profitable. It has helped to have a person like John Reed leading the effort and to have him, a technocrat, as the CEO. This case illustrates how technology can affect a business and an industry. It can be used as a competitive weapon or it can make those who ignore it obsolete.

As more companies accept the fact that information planning should be included in their planning activities at the strategic and operational levels, the first question that arises is how to deal with rapidly changing technology. Most strategic plans cover a five-year horizon. How do we know what technology will bring in the information-processing area five years from now? Information processing in 1985 is very different from that in 1980. Surely, by 1990, information processing will be considerably different from what it is today. If this is a given, how do we cope with changing technology and how do we plan for it?

Computers are doubling in speed roughly every two years. Network designers are developing glass-fiber cables that will be able to carry the same amount of information in one second that copper wire lines now take 21 hours to send. Computer scientists are also making computers more powerful and versatile by adding "dedicated" microprocessors that take on some of the smaller, routine tasks and lighten the burden on a computer's central processor. These chips perform such jobs as graphic displays and communicating with other computers or with peripheral units such as disks and printers. Dedicated microprocessing could make computers from two to ten times faster than today. The proliferation of these small computers will not decrease the need for the large "host" computers that store and manage all the data. In fact, the demand for storage and computing capacity in host systems is growing at the same rate—40 to 60 percent—as personal computers are selling. Computer makers are supplying more power in these large machines as well. In the fastest, most advanced machines called supercomputers, new designs call for "parallel" processing, which allows hundreds of microprocessor chips to work on one number-crunching problem at the same time. Complex software divides up the problem to be solved so that each chip works on a different part of the task simultaneously. This eliminates bottlenecks that build up in today's conventional computers built around one central processor that must do all the work sequentially.

As work on new computer design advances, progress is also being made on the basic silicon chips used to build logic circuits and memories. Lasers are now tracing circuits with lines finer than 80 millionths of an inch. Fine-tuning lasers to make even thinner lines will, by 1987, make memory chips commercially available that will store one million bits of data, four times more than today's circuits. To make even denser chips, engineers are using such creative techniques as digging "trenches" into the incredibly thin layer of oxide that coats the silicon chip. The walls of the trenches then provide more surface area on which to put the transistors that store bits of data. While the theoretical limits of silicon probably will not be reached for at least five to ten years, some companies are installing production lines to make chips from gallium arsenide, a chemical compound that carries signals faster than silicon. Scientists "grow" crystals for gallium arsenide atom by atom through a technique called molecular beam epitaxy. IBM and Bell Laboratories both stepped up their development work on gallium arsenide in 1983, deeming it more practical than the much publicized Josephson junctions which require an onerous cooling process. Scientists are already dreaming of futuristic computers that use beams of light instead of electronic signals to calculate. That is for the year 2000 and after.

Looking into the future, five to ten years on, change will be evolutionary rather than revolutionary. This chapter will discuss several key areas of change that will have an impact on the development of strategic information plans. These areas are:

- Advance technologies: large-scale integrated circuits, disk drives, supercomputers, and knowledge based or problem-solving systems
- Data base developments
- Data administration
- The information center
- Planning future systems.

ADVANCED TECHNOLOGIES[2]

Several areas of advanced technologies are commanding high interest because development work is being done on a competitive basis by companies in Japan, the U.S., and Western Europe. These areas, sometimes referred to as "fifth-generation" technology include large scale integrated circuits, advances in magnetic and optical disk drives, supercomputers, and problem-solving systems. They will have an impact on the technology plans of businesses and will be interrelated in any future system. The Institute for Computer Sciences and Technology of the National Bureau of Standards made the following forecasts for these key areas.

Large-Scale Integrated Circuits

Semiconductor devices are likely to continue at their recent rate of improvement for at least another ten years. The 32-bit and 64-bit RAM chips have been routinely available since the early 1980s and the 256-bit RAM since 1983. Prices of memory chips have declined, on average, by 35 percent every year. The decline was especially steep in the 1984–85 period due to an extreme oversupply in the market (see Figure 3-1). The four-bit microprocessor on which the pocket calculator is based

2. The forecasts summarized in the Advanced Technologies section of this chapter are from the National Bureau of Standards, "Future Information Processing Technology," a report by Arthur D. Little Inc.; and "International Conference on Fifth-Generation Computer Systems," Japan Information Processing Department Center.

FIGURE 3-2   THE FALLING PRICE OF CHIPS

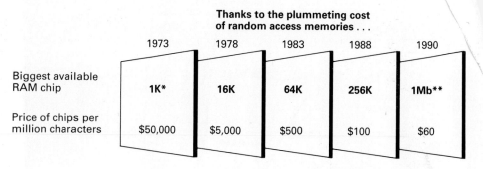

Thanks to the plummeting cost of random access memories ...

	1973	1978	1983	1988	1990
Biggest available RAM chip	1K*	16K	64K	256K	1Mb**
Price of chips per million characters	$50,000	$5,000	$500	$100	$60

... Demand for RAM chips is exploding

Annual sales, billions of dollars $0.06 .... $0.3 .... $1.8 .... $8 .... $10

Annual volume, billions of bits   8 .... 650 .... 28,000 ...... 800,000 1,400,000

*One kilobit equals 1,024 bits of digital storage capacity: **One megabit equals 1,024K.
 8 bits are needed for each character.

Source: *Business Week,* Apr. 2, 1984, p. 71.

communications applications and are available in prototype form for digital circuits, there is little doubt that they will enter widespread use. Cryogenic superconductor technology employing the Josephson junction continues to encounter engineering difficulties. IBM has discontinued several research projects using Josephson junction technology. With or without cryogenics, however, it appears likely that circuits with at least 20 times the speed of those in use today will be available by 1997. In planning for what future technology will bring for mainframe and microprocessors, we can conclude that they will be faster, smaller, and cheaper.

Disk Storage

Figure 3-3 shows 40 years of disk drive prices in terms of purchase price divided by capacity (cents per character stored). The historical points from 1955 to 1980 are derived from IBM's list prices for its largest capacity magnetic disk drives, starting with the 305 RAMAC in 1955 and ending with the 3380 in 1980. These prices fall on a remarkably smooth curve, and have fallen approximately 20-fold. The density

FIGURE 3-1   **THE PLUNGING PRICE OF MEMORY CHIPS**

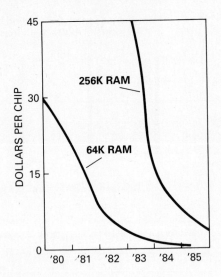

Source: *Business Week*, May 20, 1985.

now costs under one dollar and the 16-bit microprocessor (still the heart of m
personal computers) has dropped below five dollars. In early 1985, as new ch
making plants in Japan, Korea, and the United States brought additional capacity
stream at a time when the electronic equipment industry went into a slump,
imbalance between supply and demand caused the price of the 64K RAM to sell
less than 75 cents on the spot market, down from $3.50 at the end of 1984.

The rate of price decline will slow during the next ten years (see Figure 3-
This will happen not because the unit cost of manufacturing chips will stop declin
but because companies in the semiconductor industry will make heavy expenditu
to finance new production equipment. This may be the only industry where i
necessary to throw away most of the factories every five years or so and start o
with new ones that will probably cost twice as much.

The area of large-scale integrated circuits will be characterized by larger sc
(up to wafer-size) integration, narrower line widths that will reduce the size of ii
vidual circuit elements, reduction in defect densities, and improvements in the m
ufacturing art. These improvements, together with advances in cooling and packag
techniques, will bring about higher speeds of operations. New technologies us
gallium arsenide instead of silicon as a substrate will increase circuit speed b
factor of five. Since gallium arsenide devices are already used in high-freque

of storage on a leading edge disk drive now exceeds 10 million bits per square inch, and improvements are continuing through combinations of thin film heads, plated media, and a variety of engineering improvements ranging across a size scale from 3-inch floppy drives to 14-inch, large capacity Winchester drives.

Two major technological innovations are expected in the disk storage area: optical storage and vertical magnetic recording. In vertical magnetic recording, the magnetized domains are stacked perpendicular to the surface of the substrate, rather than horizontally as is the case currently. Vertical recording at 100,000 bits an inch has already been demonstrated in the laboratory and ultimate linear densities of over 400,000 bits an inch are considered possible. Corresponding area densities would be as high as 400 million bits a square inch in 1997, nearly a 40-fold improvement over today's level. It is not certain that such improvements are possible because considerable refinements will have to be made to the electro-mechanical assemblies in the drives to work at these extremely high recording densities.

Optical recording promises packing densities comparable to, or even greater than, those achievable with vertical magnetic recording; furthermore, they may occur first. Most approaches to optical recording, however, do not permit rewriting of data in the same place. Perhaps one or more of the several rewriteable systems under development will be successful, but it may not really matter. Archival and office

---

FIGURE 3-3   **DISK STORAGE EVOLUTION**

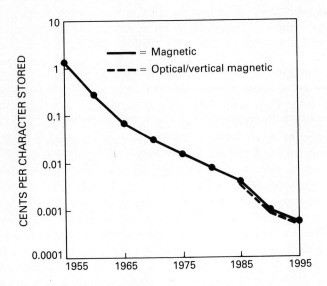

applications in which rewriting is not desired may be sufficient to provide ample market growth. It seems very likely that optical and vertical magnetic recording will coexist in different applications and configurations.

It appears certain that large data bases can be easily contained on very few disk drives, and the access speeds for retrieval will fall significantly from what they are today. The limiting factor will not be in the technology for recording on disks, whether vertical or optical. The limiting factor will be the drive itself, and the software to make use of the greater volume of data recorded on one disk.

Supercomputers

Supercomputers are high-powered processors with numerical processing throughput significantly greater than that of the largest general purpose computers. The definition of a supercomputer changes with time and the throughput capability of the largest general purpose systems. In 1985, supercomputers were systems that had a capacity approaching 100 million floating point operations per second (MFLOPS). Today, prototypes of computers with one gigaflops capacity (one billion floating point operations per second) have been built. It is important to define the term supercomputer with care because the popular publicity given to the Japanese fifth-generation computer project tends to lump together all development projects for advanced computers, even though they differ widely. Japanese research plans make no such mistake: funding and research project structures are entirely different for supercomputers and fifth-generation systems. The fifth-generation project is at the basic research stage, but supercomputer development is at the stage of final system design.

Japanese companies have been trying to surpass one another in setting supercomputer speed objectives. In July 1982, Fujitsu announced a machine it claimed would be capable of 500 MFLOPS. Two months later, Hitachi announced a machine rated at 630 MFLOPS. In May 1983, NEC announced a machine intended to run as a single processor at a speed of 700 MFLOPS, and as a dual-compressor at a speed of 1300 MFLOPS. This would exceed the speed of the Cray 2 computer which is expected to reach 1000 MFLOPS.

The speed of supercomputers has always been constrained by the degree to which the problems to be solved can be broken into parallel elements for simultaneous computation, because linear processes are constrained by the speed of the best components available. While these will improve 20-fold, there are customers who would like much greater improvements in computing speed. Their only hope lies in using multiple computing elements in parallel, but many problems insist on remaining linear. Thus mathematical algorithm and software development are intertwined with components and architectural development in the design of future supercomputers. It appears that the result will be hybrid systems, in which portions of an overall computational problem are converted into parallel form for processing in a specialized processor (at speeds of as much as 100 gigaflops by 1997), while the remaining portions of the job, including input/output, file reference, and scalar processing, remain separate and are delegated to functional processors optimized for each purpose.

The functional processors are interconnected by data and control buses, and the complex operates under control of a supervisory processor. Figure 3-4 schematically depicts such a system, with the "specialized processor" corresponding to the parallel processor of the supercomputer.

Figure 3-4 is labeled "Future General Purpose Computer System" rather than "Future Supercomputer System" because in fact most experts expect this type of modular design to be universal. In a supercomputer application, the general purpose computer system of Figure 3-4 would be equipped with a powerful specialized processor and relatively limited I/O and file storage processors. The application processors might be a set of generalized microprocessors for scalar and control functions. In a batch processing or data base application, however, the balance of size and capacity in the functional processors would be very different. The rather surprising

FIGURE 3-4   **FUTURE GENERAL PURPOSE COMPUTER SYSTEM**

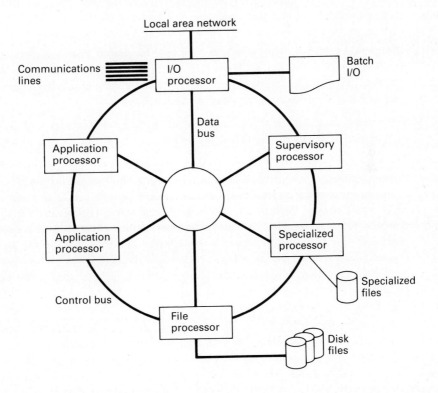

Source: Arthur D. Little Inc., from Frederick Withington, "Winners and Losers in the Fifth-Generation." Reprinted with permission of *Datamation*® Magazine. © Copyright by Technical Publishing Company, A Dun & Bradstreet Company, Dec. 1983, p. 206. All rights reserved.

conclusion drawn from this forecast, then, is that the supercomputers of the future will look very much like general purpose computer systems, varying only in the mixture of different functional processor types employed.

Knowledge Based or Problem-Solving Systems

Figure 3-5 summarizes an official description of the proposed Japanese fifth-generation computer as it was presented at the International Conference on Fifth-Generation Computer Systems in 1982. A comparison of this figure with Figure 3-4 shows how different the proposed fifth-generation architecture is from even advanced versions of general purpose architecture. The fifth-generation architecture is more a set of functions that the developers hope to distribute within some yet-to-be-identified set of modules. Figure 3-5 refers to several different technologies. Very large-scale integrated architecture is the subject of the semiconductor forecast presented earlier in this chapter. Except for the interface technologies, most of the rest are associated with the concepts of the so-called knowledge based, or problem-solving systems. These systems consist of three basic building blocks that together make up a new approach to the solution of complex problems. The building blocks are:

1. The knowledge base. This is a body of expert or agreed knowledge about a particular subject. This knowledge is represented in one of several formal ways: "if-then" logical rules, frames or scripts expressed in natural language, and as mathematical formulas or some other structured way.

2. The context data. This is the information that is built up by the system about each particular situation in which a problem arises.

3. The inference engine. This is the computer program that provides the strategies to draw inferences and produce solutions to the problems under analysis. These computer programs are specifically tailored to accommodate particular "knowledge representation" formats and user-friendly dialogues. The inference engine operates in two ways. First, it draws inferences about a situation as it is being presented; questions are generated automatically and are asked of the user. Second, the inference engine presents to the user the logical reasoning behind the solution it generates and any underlying insights or general advice that may be of use.

These three building blocks are all software, so they can be developed to run in conventional computer systems. The characteristics of the processing (relational, parallel), storage (very large and slow), and control (pointers, stacks), imply that specially developed hardware may be desirable. Before the usefulness of an inference engine can be established, a realistic knowledge base and context data must be developed for it. Hundreds or even thousands of definitions and relationships need to be established. Typically, two man-years of effort are required before even a demonstration model of a problem-solving system becomes operational. Optimists hope that a problem-solving system, once built, will be used by many people operating in

FIGURE 3-5   **PROPOSED JAPANESE FIFTH-GENERATION COMPUTER**

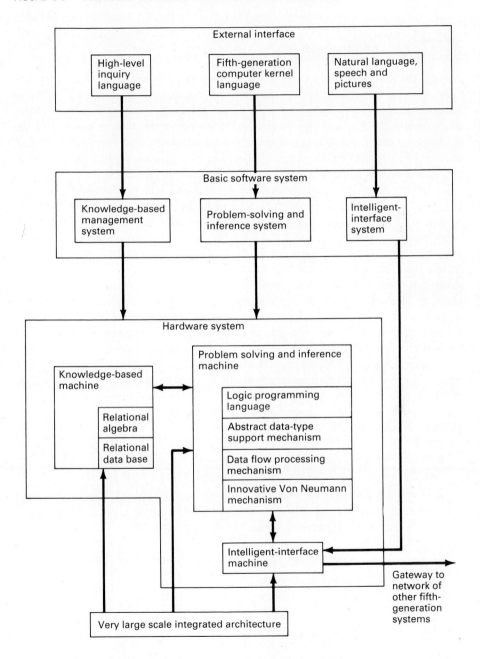

Source: Japan Information Processing Development Center, from Frederick Withington, "Winners and Losers in the Fifth-Generation." Reprinted with permission of *Datamation®* Magazine. © Copyright by Technical Publishing Company, A Dun & Bradstreet Company, Dec. 1983, p. 208. All rights reserved.

a similar professional area. Pessimists think use of the systems will be limited to their authors.

DATA BASE DEVELOPMENTS

Perhaps the most significant trend in the next decade will be the move towards data base systems. This move will create problems because of organizational structure rather than technology. Today, strategic planning is carried out by high-level corporate executives. They use this process to define the organization's position in the marketplace and in the industry. Specific strategic business objectives result from an analysis of the corporation's standing relative to its competitors. Plans are developed and information systems built for monitoring progress against plans.

Data base design is usually done by departments near the bottom of the organizational ladder. They are concerned with planning, logically structuring, and implementing the data bases that support the organization's information systems. In many companies, there is little connection between these two activities because of the separation of organizational levels. Nevertheless, the data base design process should take into consideration the strategic business objectives. The logical data structure of planned data bases must contain the data needed to develop tactical plans, to measure progress toward the objectives that are established, and to implement systems in support of specific business goals. The organizational gap between strategic planners and data managers must be bridged if management's direction of the business is to be supported by the company's computer systems.

Since most information system development projects involve the design of data bases, what can we expect from data base software in the next 10 years? The biggest change by far should be an expansion of the role of data dictionaries. At present, data dictionaries are quite limited in scope. The typical package is an "off-line" utility to provide services such as:

- Storing information about an organization's data, and where the data is used, (for example, reports, files, projects, people, departments).
- Selectively querying the above for information about the data base environment (for example, what file contains the field product number, what programs update the field department, what fields are accessable via the password Pay1223).
- Maintaining control routines, job control language (JCL), to run various configurations of the data base package.
- Maintaining "canned" data base procedures, usually for report writers or query languages.

While all of these are quite useful, it is clear that most of the data base package vendors are working toward a data dictionary that is truly integrated into the data base package. A pioneering effort in this area and one which serves as the model for today's development of integrated data dictionaries was a package developed by Arthur Andersen & Co. called LEXICON. This was an integrated data dictionary which defined each data element and its environment, specified validation requirements, editing requirements, and report formats. In defining a file using LEXICON, the user could automatically generate an input validation program, a file update program, an extract program, and a report generation program. LEXICON was developed before data bases became popular and used in large file maintenance environments. Its concepts are being applied today to generate data dictionaries integrated with its data base so that data can be described once for the dictionary and automatically used by the data management software.

Another area where major development efforts are occurring is the area of query languages, the migration toward true natural language query facilities. Ever since it was claimed that COBOL and FORTRAN would eliminate the need for programmers, end users have been promised natural language query facilities. Today, some packages claim to be user-friendly. Most of them provide minimal flexibility in data selection and display, thereby requiring minimal grammar constraints. By contrast, some packages combine extensive report-writing capability with true programming language facilities. These packages are not user-friendly and are suitable for use by systems personnel only. They are very useful in generating "canned" parameterized modules which can be stored in a library and called by nonsystems personnel with minimal technical knowledge.

Query languages today are used in the same way as data base packages. That is, application oriented files are being processed in isolation from the remainder of the organization's data. This is done in one of two ways: either additional indexes are created for production files, or a spin-off file is created from the production file for query purposes. The former creates additional overheads for the maintenance of the production files, the latter results in querying against an "almost up-to-date" file, not to mention the computer resources required to create the spin-off files.

Integrated systems, also known as "clustered systems", will be a goal designers will aim at in the next decade. Integrated systems are those that take a transaction from start to finish, ignoring the artificial boundaries placed by business functions. For example, a transaction, such as a parts order, affects the business in a host of areas. Ideally, the system will instantaneously note a change in inventory, record and print an invoice, update accounts receivable, notify shipping, and send instructions to the warehouse. This requires an integrated system with on-line update. The important criterion for most businesses is that all of this activity takes place at the moment of order entry. Today, all on-line applications do not update the data base instantly. Transactions entered on-line are queued and then the data base is updated at a later time. Integrated systems means that a company has to accept the concept of on-line transaction processing. They require a data base management system with relational capabilities that is built around the way a company works, not by application. And they require a task force of users and systems architects working in tandem to literally change the way information processing is currently performed. This task force must convince top management that it has to reexamine the traditional way of doing business because present business procedures are dictated by applications constraints rather than logical and coherent business practices.

The next decade should see the shift from file oriented systems to data base oriented systems, and a switch to integrated systems and the inter-application use of query facilities. It does not appear likely that we will see significant progress in data retrieval languages for nonsystems personnel. The major area of query language development will be in the area of combination programming languages and report writers designed to optimize the use of data base facilities by systems personnel. Since hardware will be faster, more powerful, and cheaper, our ability to store, index, and retrieve data should improve markedly. Performance criteria will become progressively less important and more and more companies will convert to organization-wide data bases. When this happens, it should become evident to corporate management that the major obstacles to the development of data base systems are organizational, not technical.

DATA ADMINISTRATION

With the growth of data base management systems, users are finding that an unintegrated approach to design and development has resulted in systems that have not met their expectations. In the early days, the data administration function was one limited to the development and maintenance of a data dictionary. The data administrator developed the rules and regulations for data entering the data base, standardized its name, and resolved questions such as who had authority to change the information, who owned the data, and who could use the data. Today, the data administration function is much broader, some companies have established the objective of data administration as being the managing of information as a corporate resource. As such, the data administration group should be the focal point for all the interfacing and communication between management, end users, and technical personnel. Their role is to translate business plans into data resource plans. They would use data models, business models, and other analytical techniques to structure the information needed to support corporate goals and objectives. In the process, they would evaluate user needs, weigh them against long-term data resource development objectives, assign individual priorities, present the priorities to the managment-steering committee for approval, and develop a data resource development plan based on the approved priorities.

In the past, system development teams have had to arbitrate disputes and disagreements between end users, often within the same department. The efforts of a data administration group would relieve the system development project of these responsibilities by securing agreement as to projects, data, and priorities prior to system development. As a result, the system development plans that are developed will have better user commitment as well as the full support of top management.

Data administration is more allied to the end user than to the information systems department. Because of this relationship, they are better situated to handle the issues of information ownership and data standardization. Resolving these issues requires an understanding of business processes as well as an ability to deal with organizational politics. Defining requirements for data base systems means bringing users and systems analysts together and providing them with direction in their analysis. Data bases usually deal with multiple disciplines and users and are therefore found to be complex even when structured analysis techniques or other analytical methods are used. The data administration staff, with their overall awareness of corporate business processes and data resources requirements, are likely to do a much better job of providing leadership here than anyone from the end user or information systems staff. Their business experience and substantial expertise are also likely to give them greater leverage in standardizing business procedures, always a thorny problem for the information systems department.

The existence of the data administration function also ensures that certain types of crucial tasks that are almost always ignored in data base development are addressed. These include: changing end user procedures, redirecting the channels of information flow outside the data base system, and modifying associated manual information handling tasks. On their own, information systems personnel usually fail in these tasks because they lack time, interest, and authority.

Finally, the issues of data security and privacy are as critical outside the data base system as they are inside. Although the technical data base administration function has made strides in attending to these issues inside data base systems, on the outside these issues have remained virtually untouched. Naturally, effective company policies and procedures for data security must include all stages of data handling and all types of data. The data administrator is ideally suited to attend to those outside areas.

Figure 3-6 presents the typical functions performed by the data administration

FIGURE 3-6   **FUNCTIONS OF THE DATA ADMINISTRATION GROUP**

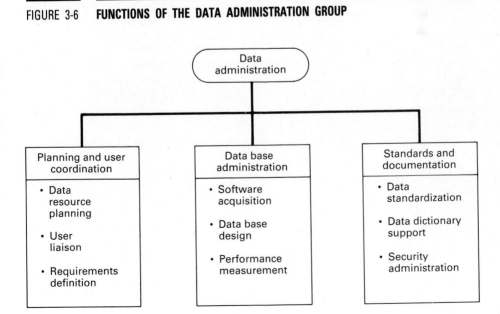

group. They can be divided into three main areas: planning and user coordination, standards and documentation, and data base adminsistration.

Planning and User Coordination

The objective of this area is to work with the users to define and plan their information requirements. Since the key thrust of using data bases is to achieve data integration, the system development plan must be compatible with a corporate business plan. Data administration develops long-term functional requirements from the corporate business plan which are then translated into business information models. The business information model in turn is used in the development of corporate data models and conceptual systems models. Based on the overall pictures produced by these different models, the data resource planning staff generates a system development plan in conjunction with key end users and the information systems department. Corporate data base systems are not only complex in terms of their components and interrelationships with other systems, but they are also constantly changing as the needs of the end users change. The data resource planning staff have the responsibility of working with management and the end users to ensure that these changes are planned and logically introduced into the corporate data models for inclusion in the developing data base systems.

Data administration should provide a forum where end users can come together and discuss their problems, procedures, and systems requirements so that their requests can be implemented in a uniform fashion. These discussions could lead to disagreement on procedures and priorities. The data administration group could arbitrate these disagreements and work with all the end users to achieve a satisfactory compromise. They could assist in negotiating data ownership and in communicating user requirements to the system designers. Most of the time, existing procedures reflect the limitations of conventional file systems. These procedures must be changed if data base technology is to be exploited to its fullest. The user liaison group must help end users examine their business policies and procedures in light of changed business requirements and new technology, and make the necessary changes. This process will produce some conflicts; the user liaison function has to make sure that they are resolved and that viable procedures are developed to support the corporate business objectives and goals.

Finally, the data base design and the associated system design reflect the quality of the end users' functional requirements as defined by the system analysts. The requirements definition methodology appropriate for data base systems is drastically different from those used for traditional systems. Data base design calls for the definition of end user data views in very specific and quantitative fashion during the early stages of the design phase. Defining requirements for data base systems means bringing end users and systems analysts together and providing them with direction for their analysis. Data base systems usually deal with multiple disciplines and are extraordinarily complex. The data administration group, having gained an awareness of corporate business processes and data resource requirements through its modeling activities, can provide effective leadership for these efforts.

Standards and Documentation

The responsibilities of the standards and documentation group are to develop policies, procedures, standards, and controls that are necessary for the development and maintenance of the data base. They are also responsible for communicating these standards to all users. The data dictionary is an automated tool that facilitates documentation and monitors the development of the data base. Management of the data dictionary is also a responsibility of this group.

Data standardization means defining each data element, its name, format, size, usage, validation rules, and other pertinent information. All of this is documented in the data dictionary so that it is available to users as well as systems developers. As crucial as this function is, it is difficult to implement because of corporate organizational barriers and the reluctance of users to share their data or lose control of it. Therefore, the data administration group must have the authority to enforce standards, including the standardization of presentation media (everything does not have to be printed), common reports, forms, and other sources of information.

The data dictionary will be increasingly used in the data base environment. It is a productivity tool not only for the data administrator, but also for all data users. The dictionary stores all the information about data elements, records, data bases, programs, reports, transactions, organization, processing rules, business functions, end user views, and other project details. It should be an integral part of any data base management system. An automated data dictionary, integrated into the data base software, is a necessity if a company plans on extensive use of data base systems. The key to successful data dictionary implementation is a training program that motivates data dictionary users. These are all responsibilities of the data administration function.

Storing the corporate data resource into one or several data bases requires some precautions. The security administration staff have to work with management and end users to get security and privacy standards for all the data elements, records, and files. Working with data base administration, security administration designs passwords and other controls. Some data elements require more restricted access than others. In order to maintain the controls on such data, and continually monitor their use, information ownership is established for each critical element. Once an information owner is established, that group is responsible for seeing that the data element is properly defined, and that its integrity and privacy are maintained in the data base.

Data Base Administration

Data base design provides the foundations for the integration of the corporate data resources. Data base administration is charged with designing an overall data base structure that is stable in the long term but at the same time meets the requirements of component systems. In the absence of such a centralized data base design function, each system would go its own way and data integration across applications would be impossible.

Acquiring a data base management system can be a time-consuming and frustrating task. They range from systems provided by a manufacturer for their specific product line (IBM's IMS system, for example), to a generalized system from a software vendor (ADABAS from Software A.G.). They also range in price from several thousands to upwards of $250,000. The criteria for selection should not be price or the number of features offered by the package. The only successful way to implement a data base management package is to first define the information requirements and the data resources needed to meet those requirements. Then, through model building, decide the functions the data base must perform, the technical requirements such as response time, data structure (relational, hierarchical, or network), and query language requirements. These requirements should be matched against the features offered by vendor packages. If possible, a benchmark test should be designed for the vendor to use on a specific package. After evaluating the test results, vendor support, availability of an integrated data dictionary, and the experience of other companies using the package, the package most fitted to the company's needs should be selected. The software acquisition group would perform these tasks.

Data bases are designed to optimize the use of physical storage and CPU processing time. Data base management systems are software packages enabling users to communicate with the data base. Since the data administration function bridges the gap between the users and the technicians in information processing, the group should also bridge the communications gap when describing how the corporate data resource will be organized and used in a data base. The data base design group relates user and business requirements to the technicians, assists in the technical design, and then communicates the results of the design to the users in a language they can understand.

Since several end users share a common data resource, and they all have to go through one data base management system to access their data, performance becomes a common concern. The fact that most data base management systems have on-line usage further complicates the performance issue. Because no one application has total control over system performance, the responsibility falls to the data base administration group to manage performance. This group works with the systems programming and operations staff in setting standards, procedures, and performance-monitoring techniques. They are also responsible for conducting reviews of development projects to ensure that data base systems being designed conform to corporate standards. For example, they may sometimes simulate the performance of a data base system during the design stages in order to ensure that the response time expectations of end users will be satisfied.

Organization Placement of Data Administration

If the data administration function has all these responsibilities, where should it be placed in the organization? The nature of its responsibilities indicates that it should be placed in such a way that provides a forum through which end users can express their frustrations, desires, and needs. End users must feel that the data administrator is responsive to them, and in fact, is their corporate representative on matters relating to information. Therefore, the data administration function should be independent of the other information system functions. In some companies, such as UFB Canada, the data administration department is placed on a par with the information systems department, both reporting to the vice-president of planning and information resources. Although they were successful, there is no conclusive evidence that this is the best arrangement.

Naturally, the data administration function should be placed high enough in the organization hierarchy so that it has sufficient authority to issue policies, enforce standards, and resolve conflicts. It must work closely with both user departments and the information systems department. The data administration function provides an organizational framework within which data base technology can be successfully employed for the benefit of its users. Among other things, the data administration function will embody the humanization of a technology that has frustrated end users because it has offered high promises but delivered less than expected performance. Many companies view it as a regulatory body, establishing rules, and standards, and guarding the contents of the data base. It is much more than that; in addition to the functions described in the preceding paragraphs, it has important responsibilities for data resource planning and data base promotion. Any technology, once mature, requires that more attention be devoted to education and enlightenment than to its own further technological exploration. Equally important are learning the environment in which it operates, speaking in its language, and understanding its problems. That is the situation in which users of data bases find themselves today. They must learn how to use the technology that already exists and productively plan its exploitation to gain a competitive advantage for the company. The data administration function can help them reach that goal.

THE INFORMATION CENTER

Technology planning involves more than predicting what will be available in the future with respect to hardware and software. Equally important is to anticipate the role of the user in the information-processing environment of the 1990s. In the past, as the backlog of applications awaiting development mounted, the concept of end user computing was formulated. This would involve providing the user with access to a computer via a terminal, user-friendly software packages, an easy-to-use query language linked to a report writer. Armed with these tools, users could develop their own programs to solve unique or one-time problems, thus reducing some of the application backlog. At this time, IBM proposed an information center concept where the user could call (via a "hot-line") to get assistance on the software package, how to make programming enhancements or modifications to the package, or how to use the terminal. An integral part of the IBM concept was that users had to do the programming and develop the computing solutions to their problems. The concept was implemented in several companies using generalized retrieval packages such as Easytrieve and Mark IV, and problem oriented programming languages such as RPG

II and RPG III. Success with the concept was limited to those companies where the information systems department extracted information the user wanted from corporate files, set up a separate file for the user, and then trained the user on using report packages to retrieve and format the information needed. This created a lot of work for the information systems group, much hand-holding by information center personnel, and not quite up-to-date information for the user, who quickly lost interest.

With the growth of personal computers in the early 1980s, the concept of the information center got a new lease of life. Now management was interested in using these microprocessors as tools for analysis and planning. Electronic spreadsheets and word-processing software made the personal computer something managers could use without much training. Once hooked, they wanted to do more. "Wouldn't it be nice if I could get information directly from the company's computer to feed into my spreadsheet program", or "Why can't I send the memo I prepared on my word processor directly to Jill's word processor without going through the interoffice mail?", or "I want to buy my own personal computer, which one is the best buy for me?" As these and other questions were asked, it soon became apparent that the information center concept, expanded to handle user problems would be an ideal solution. While personal computers were not included in the original IBM information center concept, the advent of personal computing has meant that the information center now has a new role. Instead of the notion that users must do their own computing, the role now is to provide the users with full support in helping them reach a solution to their computing problems.

Individual users should be able to choose any viable computing alternative as long as the user department is willing to pay for it and the overall solution is compatible with the company's information plans and objectives. This was the approach taken by Citibank in initiating Project Paradise. In adopting this approach, it is important that the information center educate the users about the companywide and long-term implications of their computing decision. User computer activities such as matching of user requests for information with the appropriate computing alternatives, user training, computer equipment acquisition, and software package selection, need to be managed so that the end result is an integrated system compatible with the company's mainframe hardware and corporate information plans. The new information center should be the focal point for managing these activities.

The information center can play a vital role in helping the company manage a new technology, personal computing. An opinion survey[3] taken in 1982–84 of 52 information systems managers about problems encountered with personal computing indicates several areas that may present significant costs to an organization. The managers were presented with a list of possible problem areas and were asked to indicate, on a scale of 1 to 5, their level of concern with each problem:

1. not concerned at all
2. a little concerned

3. Guimaraes, Tor, "The Evolution of the Information Center." Reprinted with Permission of *Datamation*® Magazine. © Copyright by Technical Publishing Company, A Dun & Bradstreet Company, July 15, 1984, pp. 127–28. All rights reserved.

3. concerned
4. very concerned
5. extremely concerned.

The problems identified by the managers, ranked in order of concern are as follows:

4.8. Lack of a company plan for personal computing

4.7. Lack of user education regarding a companywide and a long-term perspective about personal computing

4.6. Poor maintainability of user-developed systems

4.6. Unnecessary high costs to the company due to users learning by trial and error about lack of compatibility with mainframes

4.5. General lack of communication between the information systems department and users

4.4. Overwhelming growth of user requests for assistance from the MIS department

4.3. Unnecessary high costs to the company due to users learning by trial and error how to use available software packages

4.2. Contamination of corporate data on the company's mainframe

4.2. Mismatch of user applications to other possible user computing alternatives, such as mainframe packages or the traditional approach for systems development

4.2. MIS department has image problem with personal computer users

4.2. Lack of equivalent or better (more user-friendly) mainframe software packages to compete successfully with microcomputer software packages

4.2. Lack of adequate training on such things as products, and computer concepts

4.1. Unnecessary high costs to the company due to users "reinventing the wheel" in systems development

3.9. Lack of user knowledge or concern about microcomputer data integrity measures such as a file backup

3.8. Lack of integration of micro/mainframe data exchange and control

3.7. Inability of mainframe computing to compete with personal computing in terms of cost/benefit in certain areas

3.6. Lack of control over user-computing resources utilization by user department management

3.5. Lack of adequate support from hardware vendors

3.2. Lack of adequate support from software vendors

3.2. Lack of control over user-computing resources utilization in user departments by the MIS department

3.2. Personal computing is further straining MIS department relations with users

3.2. Lack of centralized management over corporate data resources to support user personal computing

3.2. Lack of appropriate staffing to identify and service potential information center customers

3.1. Lack of user concern about personal computing equipment security

3.1. Information overloading due to too many vendors and products in a given area: micros, software packages, local area networks

2.9. Lack of integration in MIS management of personal computing and mainframe user computing

2.9. Lack of user interest in personal computers

2.6. Unnecessary high costs to the company due to users learning by trial and error about lack of compatibility with other micros

2.3. Unnecessary high costs to the company due to users learning by trial and error how to negotiate with vendors

2.1. Measuring the level of user computing activity

1.7. Unnecessary high costs to the company due to users learning by trial and error about lack of compatibility with microcomputer peripherals

Many of the problems cited above can be corrected by the information center if they are brought to its attention. For example, most information centers have a "help desk" to which users can go for advice and assistance on computing problems. The people at the desk are trained to supply answers to technical questions or to direct the individual to the right place for the answer. Another useful function performed by the information center is the dissemination of information. Many organizations have grown so large that organizational subunits and the people in these units are unaware of what is going on outside their own units. This knowledge isolation leads to unnecessary costs. A critical task of the information center is to collect and disseminate information about available computer resources (equipment, user developed systems, software packages, and data), that can be shared. This requires the centralization of knowledge about all company computing activities, including personal computing.

Planning for the acquisition of personal computers and their use in the corporate environment, as well as planning for the information center and its role in the company should be part of the company's technology plan. Future user information requirements can, to a considerable extent, be satisfied by more than one alternative. The planning of any one alternative will affect the others. For example, if the information systems department does not know that a signigicant number of users will be acquiring personal computers instead of using the terminals attached to the company mainframe, mainframe capacity planning will be significantly inaccurate. The role of the information center should be to provide mechanisms to make prospective computer users aware of all the alternatives to personal computing, and to match the users' requirements with these alternatives.

Future developments in the information center/personal computer area would include the following:

■ Personal computer users will substantially increase the demand for data resources as well as for personnel to help them select processing alternatives.
  The role of the information center will be expanded to supply this support.

■ The trend toward substantially more powerful and user-friendly data base management systems for microcomputers will continue, even though mainframes
  will remain the dominate store for corporate data. Again, the information center
  must help the user decide whether to use the personal computer as a terminal
  to access data from the corporate mainframe, or to offload data from the mainframe for processing on the microcomputer.

■ The most important change in data management will be the increased level of
  direct service to personal computer users. Dispensing information on data item
  availability, access requirements, and costs will become a major component of
  the data administration function. Many information systems departments may
  want to include data items on outside data bases as part of their service responsibilities to their user departments.

■ Finally, new methodologies will be available to help users define their information requirements. Having users define their own requirements is more efficient than asking users to try to communicate their requirements to an analyst.
  When the user needs help, the information center is there to supply support.
  This is particularly important in the short term to overcome user reluctance to
  communicate with the information system department because of their low
  credibility with the user community.

PLANNING FUTURE SYSTEMS

Computer users are entering a rapidly changing, high-risk period that will require
careful planning and close supervision. The changes include the growth of microprocessors, providing end users with computing power, installing automated office systems, and implementing integrated telecommunications networks. Some years hence,
large and small computers will be everywhere and, to a great extent, they will be
interconnected via networks. The big questions are: What will be the structure of
these future systems, and how will users get from their present computer environments to these new ones?

　　What is needed is a coherent plan for guiding the migration of computer power
to end users. The components of such a plan would include processors, networks,
services, and standards.

Processors

Based on our earlier discussions of advanced technologies, it appears that there will
be three levels of processors, each with their associated information storage. (1)
Single user systems such as today's microprocessors. These will operate in a stand-

alone environment or as terminals connected to the mainframe. In addition, some single user systems will be connected through a local area network. (2) Multiple user systems will serve local groups of users through terminals, much as today's minicomputer systems. They will provide backup for the single user systems as well as more powerful computational requirements and data base management facilities. (3) Remote mainframe systems will provide the heavy-duty computing, corporate data base management, remote batch processing, and communication management (message switching) for the smaller processors on the network. For most organizations, these are represented by today's centralized mainframes.

Networks

The network architecture for the immediate future will consist of two levels: (1) Local networks will provide high-speed information transfer as well as linking several single unit processors to a multiple user system. This would provide the single user systems with access to hard disk storage for shared files and main program libraries. (2) Remote networks will provide connections among the multiple user systems and the mainframe system.

Services

Using the networks will be three types of services: (1) Terminal access: all terminals on the system should be able to access each other as well as the next level of processor. (2) File transfer: users will have the ability to send and receive files and have read-and-write privileges at both ends of the transfer. (3) Computer mail: the originator of a message will have read-and-write privileges only at the point of origin, not at both ends as in file transfers.

Standards

Two major types of standards will be required: (1) operating systems and (2) communication protocols. The corporate standards on operating systems should be designed to minimize the barriers to the transfer and use of programs and data. Ideally, a selected operating system should run on more than one vendor's equipment. An example of this kind of standard, UNIX, might be preferred for the single user systems, and MVS (IBM and plug compatible computers) the standard for mainframe systems. Standard protocols will be needed for terminal access, file transfers, and computer mail. The ISO 7-level protocols or IBM's SNA could be chosen to perform these tasks.

The task of getting there from where we are today could involve the following steps: (1) Select the standard operating systems and communication protocols. Encourage compliance with these standards by the operating units of the organization by offering more support to those units who do comply. Develop a phased implementation plan to convert all existing systems to these standards, as well as enforcing these standards for all new systems. (2) Begin developing or acquiring the network interfaces for communicating from single users, to multiple users, to central mainframes. These interfaces should provide for both terminal access and file transfer. (3) Select appropriate computer mail services. These services will determine whether mail transfer facilities are to be located on the multiple user systems or on the central mainframe, or even on a commercial network service. In any case, user interfaces for mail services should be available on all systems.

These are highlights of an interesting approach to the structure of future systems. The situation today is still fluid, but starting to crystallize. Microcomputers, local networks, data base technology, data administration, the information center, all these and more show signs of convergence toward standard approaches. By setting standards, establishing the processing and communication environment, and incorporating these into a corporate information plan, management can truly view information as a strategic resource to be used successfully as a competitive weapon. We can finally bridge that gap between users, management, and data-processing personnel through technology planning and by providing end users with the computing power to do what they have wanted to do since the birth of computers.

PROFESSIONAL APPLICATION COMMENT: CITICORP'S TECHNOLOGY PLANNING

Some may say that technology planning at Citicorp for the past 20 years has looked more like a "try everything" scattershot approach than a coherent strategy. While there may be some truth in this, the strategy was designed to increase the bank's competitive position in the long run, by increasing the use of technology to reduce the delivery costs of bank services. How to make the most effective use of technology was the experimental part. Citibank invested heavily in technology. By pioneering the development of automated teller machines and automated cash dispensing terminals, a hugh sum of money was poured into automated facilities for retail banking, an area which other bankers claimed could never be profitable. Now that Citibank is profitable in this area, others are rushing to automate their retail operations. The experience gained by being a pioneer is now applied to developments in other areas. But Citicorp obviously is taking a big risk. Many companies that have strayed from their main business have suffered costly failures, particularly in high technology. Diversification of any sort will challenge Citicorp's managment skills. Most executives joined the bank because of their interest in banking rather than high technology. Will they have the talent to run several different businesses? Evidently John Reed has the confidence that Citicorp can effectively manage the largest bank in the world as well as the related high-technology areas in information processing. If he is correct, Citicorp will have gained a competitive edge over its rivals that will be very difficult and expensive to overcome.

CHAPTER 3   DISCUSSION QUESTIONS

1. What do you think of the Citibank approach to microcomputers and microprocessors—"buy it and try it"? What are the advantages and disadvantages of letting departments and managers learn new technology through trial and experimentation?

2. With the rapid growth of microcomputers, an estimated five million installed in 1985, are the days of the mainframes numbered? Will we be able to do most of our processing on two megabyte microprocessors?

3. Why has the use of data bases not caught on in the past? Data base software has been commonly available for the past 15 years, yet few data bases are in existence and fully operational. Why?

4. Who should own the information in a data base? What responsibilities does ownership entail?

5. How does the data administration function help in data base development and what role, if any, should the user play in data administration?

6. Describe the role of the information center. How should it be staffed and what career paths are there for those working in an information center?

7. What conclusions can be drawn from the list of concerns information systems managers have regarding personal computers?

8. With technology changing so rapidly, is planning for future systems really possible, or should one react to new technologies as they become commercially viable and economically affordable?

4

SYSTEMS PLANNING

ISSUES

- Information systems managers as agents of change

- Why is systems planning more important today than ever before?

- The need for an information strategy

- What are the issues top management should address in managing

  information resources?

- Should the information systems effort be centralized or decentralized?

- The role of steering committees

- Applications planning

- Developing the overall information systems plan

THE INTERNATIONAL BANK

Jim Long sat in his office reflecting on the tough past six weeks. He was the head of the international department at the American International Bank (AIB). Six weeks ago, the chairman of the bank called him into his office. A bulletin had just come over the bank's wire indicating that a military *coup d'etat* had taken place in Portugal. The new military dictator had frozen all foreign assets in Portugal as well as imposing strict currency controls to keep capital from fleeing the country. When the chairman heard about this, he asked Jim a perfectly logical question: What was the bank's exposure in Portugal, in terms of loans to Portugese businesses, and its foreign currency exposure? It had taken Jim over a month to get the information, and even then, he had to admit that it was not very accurate. AIB did not have an integrated information system in the international department. Each overseas branch had its own small computer to keep track of its customers and handle the daily operations of the bank. Jim had to call each branch and ask them to manually search their records for loans to businesses based in Portugal, loans denominated in Portugese Escudos, loans backed or guaranteed by assets in Portugal, and other exposures in Portugal such as deposits in other Portugese banks and foreign exchange exposure. Since the branch records were by customer rather than by country of risk or by currency, the branches had to manually check each customer account to determine whether any loans met the search criteria. This had taken several weeks to compile and recheck for accuracy.

Jim seemed to recall a monthly report which presented exposure by country and currency but when he asked his data-processing department about the report, he was told that the report had been discontinued over six months ago when no-one expressed an interest in it during the department's annual survey of reports distribution. During this survey, a listing of all reports prepared by the computer center was sent to all departments. Each department then checked the reports they would like to continue to receive. The reports which only one or two users indicated they wanted were not distributed for a period of three months to see if the users asked for the reports when they did not get them. If no-one complained about not getting these reports after three months, they were permanently discontinued. This technique had eliminated over 35 monthly reports with a saving of several hundred hours of computer time to prepare and print the reports. Unfortunately for Jim, the country-of-risk report and the foreign currency exposure report were two that no-one indicated they used regularly and had not been missed when the data-processing department stopped producing them. In checking with his people in the department on why these reports, which should have been of vital concern in reviewing the international loan portfolio, were not used, he was told that they never reconciled with the department's manual records, so their accuracy was always suspect. Moreover, the reports were also one calendar quarter behind, so that the first quarter report issued in March was for information collected as of December 31. Jim had asked for a meeting with the director of data processing, Pamela Lawrence, to see what could be done.

The American International Bank is a money center bank specializing in wholesale banking. It has a small but prestigious client list. AIB concentrates on meeting the needs of the American multinational company abroad by providing all the services the company can get in the States. With 11 overseas offices, (London, Brussels, Paris, Zurich, Frankfort, Milan, Tokyo, Hong Kong, Kuala Lumpur, Singapore, and Kuwait), AIB structured its branch offices to provide a full and complete range of banking services to its corporate clients. The special relationship built between the bank and its clients was based on close personal ties between bank management and client management. Each branch manager and account representative met with officers of client companies monthly, just to let them know that they were constantly in the minds of their bankers. For example, when the *coup d'etat* took place in Portugal, all of the bank's clients doing business in Portugal were visited by AIB officers who personally briefed them on the coup, and discussed the potential impact on their business with them. This type of personal relationship had worked effectively for the bank, making it one of the larger and more profitable wholesale banks in the U.S.

Because the bank's success was built on personalized service to its clients, branch managers had almost total autonomy to manage their branches in the manner that would be most satisfactory to their clients, considering local customs, services expected, and government regulations in the host country. AIB headquarters issued policy statements, kept control of credit policies, foreign exchange trading policies, currency exposures, and the general credit worthiness of its clients. Each branch manager had the authority to operate within these policy guidelines. The 11 branches reported directly to Jim Long. The relationships between Jim and his branch managers were excellent. He had complete confidence in their judgment and was kept informed through monthly reports as well as phone conversations on any major transactions. Jim made semi-annual visits to all the branches and quite often would accompany the CEOs of major clients when they went abroad to arrange for a merger or acquisition. During these trips, Jim made sure that the local branch manager accompanied him on all client visits. Often the company being acquired would be so impressed with this type of client service that if the deal fell through, AIB got the target company as a new client. Once every quarter, each branch manager visited headquarters in New York to review clients, discuss plans, and exchange ideas. Jim would try to schedule three meetings so that as many managers would be in New

York at the same time as possible. This afforded a chance for the managers to meet and exchange information about mutual clients. All in all, the working environment at AIB was competitive but cordial, and one of trust and mutual respect among management personnel.

Each of the branches had a computer. These ranged in size from an IBM 4300 system at the London office to minicomputers in all the other offices. London was the most automated of the overseas offices because it was the largest and had a thriving trust operations and a merchant banking business (securities transactions). The other offices used their computer to maintain the branch financial records, bank ledgers, and information needed to prepare government regulatory reports. Other than monthly statements, clients records were kept by each individual account officer on a manual basis. With the exception of London, all software development was done by people from the head office data-processing staff. Analysts and programmers would go to the branches, help them define requirements, and design and program the systems for them. One person in the local office was designated to operate the minicomputer as well as maintain the system. This involved collecting inputs from the originating department, supervising the data entry clerk(s), running the program, checking the results, and distributing the reports. If problems arose, New York was called for help. This arrangement had worked well until recently. The local office people did not have to worry about systems development or operations, they got to say what they wanted and resources were sent from New York to implement a system for them. The costs were all absorbed in New York. The data-processing people in New York were happy because they got to design individual systems in Europe and the Far East, had few restrictions as to how the system was to be designed, and could be as creative as possible. Moreover, since the work was done on site, they lived on expenses, vacationed in the glamorous resorts of the world, and enjoyed the first class travel. The London office had its own staff of analysts and programmers.

Since 1980, competitive banks had started to offer computerized banking services to clients. Corporate cash management services, debit card services, and computerized financial management services were offered by competitors to lure accounts away from AIB. Initially, AIB used the approach of "personalized services" to off-set the "impersonal machine services" offered by competitors. But branch managers could see the day when they would need to make greater use of the computer as a competitive tool. While this had been the subject of discussion at several of the quarterly meetings, nothing was done because no single branch wanted to be the first to automate fully. In addition, they all knew that to automate would require a significant capital investment which would impact the bank's bottom line and consequently, their bonus. Most of the branch managers felt that AIB's strength was in the personal relationships built up with their clients over the years. They knew what was going on with their clients and could anticipate their financial needs through monthly visits, not through reviewing computer listings. The pressure to automate was not there.

An incident took place when the branches were compiling their report to Jim on their exposure to Portuguese businesses which changed their complacent feelings about automation and "shook-up" the head office. AIB had long been the lead bank for one of Europe's leading automobile manufacturers. Recently, a new line of credit for $50 million was arranged with the bank. Each branch was notified of the new line which was $25 million more than the old. The auto company went to each of the six European branches and drew down $20 million at each branch. Since the company was a good client of the bank, none of the branch managers had reason to question the transaction. Individually, it was well within the $50 million line of credit. The automobile company had a plant in Portugal, so each branch reported to head office what the exposure was. This was when head office noted that the company had borrowed $20 million from each branch, for a total of $120 million, well exceeding the credit authorization. Not only was this an embarrassment to the bank, but it created an awkward situation with its client company. How could this happen? Because of the autonomous nature of each branch, there was no coordination of all activities by client. Since the automobile company went to each branch and drew down $20 million, each branch could have no way of knowing that this transaction was being repeated at each of the other European branches. Eventually, when the monthly loan reports were compiled in New York, the situation would be identified, but not until then. This affair, coming shortly after realizing how difficult it was to get exposure information by customer, created a crisis atmosphere at the board of director's level, with several directors demanding that the bank take immediate action to get more up-to-date and accurate information to monitor and control its overseas transactions.

When Pamela arrived in Jim's office, Jim had already decided to seek her advice on how to automate customer information in the overseas branches. Jim wanted to be able to pull up an electronic file on a customer's current account balances, loans outstanding, foreign exchange positions, and other data anywhere in Europe and eventually around the world. This information would enable his officers in Europe to know which of the bank's products to push, and would give them more complete information to assess a customer's creditworthiness. Tracking a total relationship with a client was not possible now. With this new system, Jim wanted each branch to have access to the total relationship with a client, regardless of where the client did business. Better controls would prevent clients from overdrawing their lines of credit. Since foreign currency trading accounted for a large part of the bank's operating income, Jim would have liked to electronically track each trader's buy-and-sell positions by currency. As a result, the head trader at each branch could instantly detect any unauthorized trades and spot when an individual exceeded a specific limit.

"Can we do all of this, Pam?" asked Jim.

"Sure," replied Pamela, "but we'll need to do some planning first. In a sense, we are lucky. We have a minimal investment in systems in Europe. Each branch has its own system, all need upgrading, both from a technical and user perspective, and we have been thinking about how to approach you in developing an integrated information system for our international operations."

"It sounds like you might have some ideas on how to go about doing this. What information do you need to get started?" Jim asked.

"There are some basic decisions the bank has to make before we can start planning on how to develop the system you want." Pamela answered. She then listed the following problem areas for Jim to consider:

- What strategy does the bank plan to follow with regards to its overseas branches? Will there be more openings in the next five to ten years? Will the services offered overseas stay much as today or will there be some major changes? What are the key success factors for an overseas branch, and how does the bank intend to track performance against these factors? What information is needed to help branch management remain competitive and keep ahead of the competition?

- How does Jim plan to elicit support for an automated information system from the branch managers? Who will sponsor the project? Will the costs be allocated to the branches? Who will identify and sign-off on the requirements and scope of the system? Will the branches have a common system, or will each branch be able to tailor a system to meet their unique needs, or will it be a combination of both?

- Will there be one central computer to serve all six branches in Europe? If so, where should it be located? If a centralized system is selected, will this create problems in the area of cross-border data flow? Can the Zurich branch, for example, store client information on a computer located outside Switzerland, or will this run into conflict with Swiss banking laws? The same question could be asked of all the other countries in Europe.

- If a decentralized system is selected, how will the branches be linked to each other and to head office? Will multicurrency accounting be installed or will the present dual-currency system be continued? Even with a decentralized system, will software be centrally developed? If so, where? Where will the software be maintained, and who will maintain it? Will the hardware for a decentralized system be centrally procured?

- Is the bank willing to experiment using microcomputers linked to mainframes and using relational data bases for integrated processing, or does it prefer to remain with more proven technology such as terminals linked to mainframes using hierarchical data base systems?

"Whoa," Jim yelled. "You really started me thinking with questions of a policy nature, now you're getting far too technical for me."

Pamela laughed: "Sorry, I wasn't intending to snow you, but as you can see, my staff have been batting this problem around for a long time. There are many more problems, some business related, others have to do with costs of designing and implementing so enormous a system, and of course there are the very technical problems, such as satellite communication, terminal response time, and compatible operating systems. We didn't even know how to get started, so I am just delighted you called so that we can think this project through. Jim, my suggestion is to pool our thoughts and prepare a presentation for the executive committee. You can tell them why such a system is needed, and what the benefits would be for head office and the international department, and I can tell them, in non-technical language of course, the current state of the art, what can be done, and what the alternatives are. If we can get the executive committee to set some directions, we can begin by developing a systems plan for the new system. My only reservation is: To what extent should the branch managers in Europe be involved?

Jim replied: "I think that is an excellent approach. As for the participation of the branch managers, I would think that it is an absolute necessity. Without their 100 percent involvement, the project will fail. The problem is how to get them to participate without ordering them to do it."

"We could form a planning task force, or steering committee, composed of the six branch managers to 'brainstorm' an information system for the European branches," Pamela replied. "We could tell them that the CEO wants us to consider automating the information needs of the branches and to coordinate this with the information needs at head office. We want their opinions on what is needed as well as how to go about developing such a system."

"Yes, we could give them a few weeks to think about it, check with their people, and then have a meeting in London or Paris to start the ball rolling. I like the idea very much. Well, Pam, it looks like you and your staff will have to start educating us on what a computer can do for the international department. What do I have to know before I can participate effectively in developing a system plan?"

"Well Jim, the best starting point is to think about the questions I raised and how you think we can get the answers. You will learn a lot just by thinking things through as we decide on system objectives, such as scope, timing, costs, benefits. I just hope we can keep up with you." Pamela replied.

Jim was excited about the project and after Pamela had left, he started to think: How did one go about developing a system plan? How could he get the branches to participate both in the planning and in the execution of the plan? How much would all of this cost? How long would it take?

After more than 25 years of experience with computers, some corporations are still encountering unhappy surprises with their computer installations. These surprises are frequently the result of failures in system planning. Unfortunately, there are many information systems managers who have not adopted the techniques of strategic planning and management control that are widely used in their corporations. Excuses for not planning are numerous. They include frequent changes in hardware and software technology, rapid personnel turnover, constant changes in system requirements, and unexpected user demands. All of these factors are indicative of the changing environment in information systems. What many managers fail to realize is that they themselves are agents of change; consequently, they should help plan how those changes will take place.

In the preceding chapters, information planning was described as the process for determining the information needed to support the business strategies of an enterprise. This process starts with a statement of the corporate goals and objectives, defines the strategies to meet those goals and objectives, and concludes with the information needed to measure progress against goals and objectives. All of this is defined in very broad terms. For the information systems department, one of the most important documents generated in this planning process is the information schematic showing the various levels of planning: strategic, operational, and control; the types of information needed at each level; and the transaction systems required in each business unit to capture the required source data (see Figure 2-5).

NEED FOR SYSTEMS PLANNING

The information schematic becomes the master plan for the information systems department. It serves as a road map for developing specific systems and shows how those systems will fit together. Too often, in the past, the lack of a systems plan has led to fragmented applications, all standing alone and gathering redundant information from different sources. The result was inconsistent information which led to the mistrust of information coming from "the computer." While coordinating and integrating development efforts is a worthwhile goal, systems planning is required for many other reasons.

Increasing Costs of Systems

Computer costs have been falling since the 1960s. As the cost of hardware started its dramatic drop, total costs have also been declining, although at a decreasing rate.

Today, total costs for applications are rising again, due to the increasing costs of people to support existing systems and develop new ones using advances in technology. A turning point has been reached. Today the biggest cost element for an application is people. People represent at least 80 percent of total information systems costs, and even more if proper weight is given to the cost of user involvement (see Figure 4-1). The cost of hardware will continue to drop as a percent of total costs, but the increasing labor costs will raise total costs more than the savings from reduced hardware costs. The president of Honeywell Information Systems said at a recent conference that software development costs (people costs) are rising so rapidly that he foresees the day when manufacturers will sell software and give the hardware away. A firm in Kingston, Ontario provides a legal retrieval service for lawyers. Any lawyer subscribing to this service can access a data base and look up legal precedents for the case he is working on. This firm supplies each subscriber to the service with a free IBM personal computer to use for terminal access. Additional terminals are provided at cost. Since system development is labor intensive, management cannot afford to have large development projects, or any project for that matter, fail. One tool to help reduce failures is the development of a sound system plan.

FIGURE 4-1   **COSTS FOR A "TYPICAL" APPLICATION (LARGE ORDER ENTRY SYSTEM)**

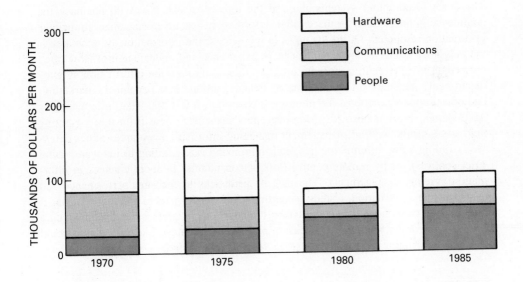

Technological Advances

The pace of technological advances exceeds the ability of many businesses to keep up. The developments in chip technology and integrated circuitry have led to rapid changes in computer technology, communications, office automation, and factory automation. These changes have led labor unions to fight for jobs made obsolete by technology. Many computer specialists are afraid that their jobs will be overtaken by technology, that they are falling behind technically. To keep up to date requires a level of training that many organizations are unable or unwilling to provide. Many businesses are falling behind as well. The majority of businesses today have outdated computers running outdated applications designed in the late 1960s and 1970s. Management practices are based on the 1970 environment of large central processors handling high-volume applications on a batch basis. Some of the best people leave for companies in the forefront of technology so that they can get technically updated. Companies not in the forefront of technology fall farther and farther behind, to the point where they cannot benefit from technology without taking great risks, such as redesigning their entire application portfolio. Increasingly, a business cannot incorporate the most modern and efficient manufacturing processes without up-to-date computer systems. Those who let their information systems departments fall behind are endangering their companies as well.

Lack of Management Support

The crisis in computer systems starts at the top. Most executives do not have the confidence in their ability or that of their information systems management to manage information resources. Of all the areas in a business, the information systems area is the only area where top management lacks experience and understanding. How often are people in an executive training program rotated through the information systems department? Yet they all spend time in finance, production, personnel, marketing, and other support functions. Technology is changing so fast that what little managers have learned is soon obsolete. Moreover, few managers come from the computing field. As a result, we find management managing information resources either defensively (going slow, minimizing budgets, minimizing risks, failing to innovate, using strict controls), or by remote control (lots of consultants, frequent changes in information systems management). The lack of yardsticks to measure performance and results in the information systems department has made matters worse. If management would treat the information systems function as it treats other business functions, that is, ask for a plan and measure performance against that plan, a start could be made in bringing information systems resources back under control.

Backlog of Applications

Recently a survey was conducted in Toronto to determine what the backlog of applications awaiting development was among 10 large companies. Most replied that they had a two-to-three year backlog of approved applications. Not included were applications in the systems area, for example, installing data management software, communication systems, upgrading operating systems. Two companies said they had a five-year backlog, and one company estimated over 100 man-years of work to implement everything in their systems development plan. There is no question that the backlog of applications awaiting development is large and growing. Businesses are creating and approving new computer projects faster than they can implement existing applications. Not only can businesses not keep up with the demand, but what is being produced is still not done within schedules and budgets. There have been few productivity improvements in programming. Most departments are slow in adopting productivity aids and in installing proven design and progamming methodologies. Soon the price of a medium-size computer will equal the salary of a good programmer. Information systems management must learn new techniques for managing development resources or the backlog will continue to grow and users will increasingly find ways of meeting their systems needs by going around their departments.

Rigid and Inflexible Design

Not only is the backlog of applications awaiting development growing, but the applications in use today are also proving to be inflexible and difficult to change. Few information departments are changing their production systems to take advantage of advances in technology and changing user needs. A large part of the "computer problem" stems from the poor products produced in the past. Change is costly, difficult, and time-consuming. The reasons are varied: documentation is not current, it is not a data base system, it was written in assembly language, it is too complicated to change. Whatever the reason, there is general dissatisfaction with the adaptability of information systems to changing requirements. Yet flexibility is the crucial element of these systems, especially when you consider the high cost of development, the lead time for implementation, and the useful life of the system (five to ten years).

Obsolete Applications

Many of today's standard applications were developed in the 1960s. They need replacing today when all resources are committed elsewhere and the backlog of new applications is growing longer and longer. They need to be replaced because requirements have changed, more controls are needed, and they could be made more responsive and efficient by redesign to take advantage of new technology. These will be large efforts, they will add little to the company's profit or to its competitive position. Where should these projects go on the company's system plan?

Each of these problems is serious. There are many other problems. To address them, the business organization must have an information strategy, a system plan that charts direction for information systems. This chapter describes how to manage information resources by developing both an information strategy and a system plan.

If information resources are the key strategic factor in a business enterprise, then surely top management should be involved in managing these resources. Yet we find that top management is not involved, or it concerns itself with things like steering committees, approving new projects, reviewing the status of projects under development, selecting hardware vendors. These activities are important, but they are operational activities and not the issues for top management. Top management should spend its time addressing four important issues in managing information resources.

1. How should information resources be organized and deployed?
2. How should information resources be controlled?
3. What strategy should be used in collecting and processing data?
4. What strategy should be used in keeping current with technology?

The policies established by addressing these questions will set the framework within which systems planning can proceed.

ORGANIZATION PLANNING

One of the first questions facing top executives is how to organize the information systems effort. If there already is an existing department, is it properly organized and located to meet the changes in technology and methodologies? The major question in the organizational issue is that of how to deploy information resources. Should they be centralized, decentralized, or a combination of the two? In the past, hardware costs heavily influenced how the data systems department was organized. Because of high hardware costs in the 1960s, most organizations consolidated their systems resources in large data centers. In contrast, rapidly falling hardware costs, improved telecommunication costs, and the introduction of the mini- and microcomputers in the late 1970s permitted organizations to distribute their systems power. The factors influencing the final decision on centralization versus decentralization include management control, advances in technology, the way information services are provided, and organizational fit.

The Case for Centralization

By centralization today, we mean a central hub with a distributed network. Few companies planning for a new organization in the 1980s will stick with the old traditional data center where all work is submitted through batch remote job entry terminals or on-line data entry systems, processed, and distributed to the end users. The growth in personal computers compels information management to provide a link-up with the central or host computer through a communication network. The advantages of a centralized approach include:

1. The need for management control. Management can exert more control over the information systems environment through a centralized system. Moreover, the ability to attract to quality people by providing an environment of research and advanced technologies, the development of sophisticated systems, and the ability to manage and control these resources in a cost effective manner is a compelling reason for a strong central unit. A single large host computer permits a more professional, more economical, and higher-quality operation than a series of small independent units. Better backup can be provided through multiple processors at a single site. Should the CPU fail in one system, pushing a button can switch the network to another system. On the other hand, an environmental disaster could cripple the entire system.

2. Available technology. Some users only need large-scale processing capacity on an occasional basis. This can be provided to them through a central facility more economically and effectively. Technology has made inexpensive computer power available to most users through personal computers or stand-alone minicomputers. The business environment will see individual users meeting their information needs through their own systems, accessing data in a central system, and using the central processor for large linear programming models or mathematical calculations that require large computing capacity. Moreover, many companies see an opportunity to manage aggregate computing more effeciently, thereby reducing hardware expenditures. By providing inexpensive microcomputers to end users and linking them to central computers, management can control both the host and the micros.

3. Control of data. Another reason for centralized organization is the ability it gives management to control access to corporate data files. Direct access to large data bases in the past was limited to applications such as passenger reservation systems, credit card authorizations, and other critical real time systems. With the sharp reductions in storage and processing costs, users with less critical applications can now access the corporate data base economically. This has permitted the growth of decision support systems where managers can extract information from the corporate data base, combine that information with their own files on their personal computer, perform manipulations and generate information to help them in their daily decision making.

4. Staff motivation. The large staff that is required in a centralized computer center provides an opportunity to attract qualified technical staff and keep them challenged. The opportunity to work on a variety of problems, to do research, and to assess how new technology can be applied to the company's business functions will keep technical people motivated. Having these skills will reduce the risks when the company embarks on new applications applying the latest in technology. Since these skills are always in short supply, consolidating them in a central unit to serve the whole corporation is a much more effective use of scarce resources than deploying them in the field. Finally, a large group of scarce resources at the hub permits more comfortable adaptation to the inevitable turnover problems. Losing a few people in a large group is less disruptive than losing a few people in a small group.

5. Organizational fit. Whether to decentralize or centralize the information systems activities will depend to a great extent on the corporate management philosophy. If a company exercises decentralized management, with its operating division granted a high degree of autonomy, then perhaps a decentralized approach to information systems would be preferable. In most companies, computer hardware was introduced centrally. In many cases management felt that even with centralized control, they had little influence over the information systems department. To permit decentralization of the function would just add to their control problem. If the corporate structure is centralized control, then the information systems function should be organized with a central hub to ensure organizational fit.

The Case for Decentralization

With the advent of microprocessors, the case for putting systems power and data into the hands of the users with little or no systems power at the hub has grown considerably. The major reasons for this are:

1. User control. Dissatisfaction with past service from the central facility has increased user desire to have local control over both processing and data storage. Locally-managed files provide quick response and permit local users to know deviations from plans before central management does. This gives them an opportunity to analyze the variance and take corrective action before management questions them on something about which they have not yet been told. Also, by being removed from the varying workload demands on a centralized computer, users have better stability in response time and can control the scheduling of work on their computers. They are no longer at the mercy of corporate priorities and workload fluctuations. With the distribution of processors, the company as a whole is less vulnerable to a massive failure in the corporate data center. Companies that are completely dependent on computer systems, for example, nationwide credit authorization centers or banks with nationwide teller networks, are already finding it desirable to set up two or more large data centers and to split the work between them so that should one fail, the other could run the essential functions.

2. Technology and costs. Prior to 1980, the high costs of central processors and storage precluded many organizations from distributed networks. However that is no longer the case today. The percentage of hardware costs as a part of the total information system budget has dropped sharply. Personnel, telecommunications, and other operating and development costs have risen. The efficiency of hardware is no longer the controlling issue it was a decade ago. These factors, and the explosion of user needs for on-line access to data files that can be generated and stored locally, make a strong case for decentralization.

3. Location of data. Many users have little need to access data generated by other departments. Also, improvements in telecommunications now permit users to access other locations as easily as accessing a central facility. Companies in this situation may find it uneconomical or undesirable to manage all data by central access, especially if the ability to access and relate data is not necessary to corporate strategy. A nationwide chain of home improvement centers, for example, found it necessary to access information at its nearest warehouse or the next closest home improvement center to determine availability when it was out of stock on an item. It had little need to access data at the head office, but a continuing need to access information at adjacent stores. A decentralized system linking all local home improvement centers would be a good organizational fit in this case.

4. Quality of life. Most corporate headquarters are located in metropolitan areas. Moving functions away from the urban environment to more rural settings can reduce stress and employee turnover. In addition, at the subsidiary or division level, information systems staff are closely linked to the user organization. Plans can be implemented to move technical people into user organizations and user personnel into the systems department. This interchange of personnel opens new career growth opportunity, reduces the number of "dead-end" jobs, and enhances relations between user and technical departments. The location of a central hub data center in a rural or suburban area would provide a better quality of life for the people in the information systems department, but would not afford the interchange of ideas and people with user organizations.

5. Organizational fit. In many businesses, the distributed approach is a better fit based on organization structure and management style. This may be particularly true for companies with highly decentralized structures and those that are geographically diverse. Most large multinational corporations find it more manageable to decentralize their information systems facilities to local countries with local control. Communications with headquarters can be made through communication link-ups.

Deciding on the appropriateness of a particular kind of organization structure for information systems, the hardware, and the data configuration can be very challenging. There is no optimum solution. Each organization has to develop its own structure based on corporate strategy and management philosophy. However, all but the most decentralized organizaitons have a strong need for central control over standards and operating procedures if the mistakes of the past are not to be repeated. While changes in technology permit distribution of the execution of significant portions of hardware operations and data handling, decisions on how to develop and operate systems should be centrally controlled and monitored.

CONTROL PLANNING

The second element of information strategy is control planning. Top executives must plan who will control which aspect of information resources, how control will be effected, and how performance will be assessed. Some key issues to be addressed in this area are:

- Who plans and approves applications and sets priorities?
- Who selects and approves new technology?

- How are budgets set, and who determines spending levels?
- How are make-or-buy decisions made, and by whom?
- What financial controls are used for the information systems department?
- How is performance measured?
- Who sets corporate-wide standards and policies and how are they enforced?
- What is the role of computer auditing, and how is it used?

Each organization will address these questions in different ways. Most companies will place responsibility for budgets, applications, standards and technology with the information systems department. Priorities for developing applications are usually a joint decision between the information department and user groups. Monitoring performance and control is a function of management. The key question is: Who ensures the effectiveness of the company's information systems? If the answer is the information systems department, then they should be given the responsibilities and authority to do the job properly.

Steering Committees

Some organizations like to make great use of steering committees. Experience has shown that committees are useful to get a consensus of opinion, to keep management informed and involved, and to communicate the impact of systems on many departments. They are rarely successful as a device for managing a project or department. Essentially, the steering committee acts as a board of directors. It does not make the day-to-day operating decisions, but establishes priorities, controls expenses, and makes policy decisions. While the corporate board of directors works to expand an organization, quite often the information systems steering committee works to limit and control information systems expansion. When the decision is made to limtit costs, the committee creates for itself the problems of allocating a limited and expensive resource and resolving the political problems arising from contention for this resource. There are two types of steering committee: the permanent steering committee, responsible for the overall guidance of the information systems function, and the project-steering committee, responsible for the successful completion of a specific project.

Permanent steering committees. If a permanent steering committee is to be used, the president or CEO should chair the committee and all executives whose departments use information systems services should be on the committee. The head of information systems should also be a member. The major functions of the committee would include the following:

- Determining the appropriate level of expenditure and capability for the information systems department based on the company's strategic and tactical plans
- Approving specific proposals for the acquisition of major hardware/software

- Approving long and short range information system plans
- Determining whether specific projects are to be undertaken based on criteria such as expected return on investments, business value to the company, impact on competitive position, impact of internal organization, conformity with corporate plans
- Determining project priorities
- Reviewing and approving cost allocation methods
- Reviewing project progress
- At specific decision points, determining whether projects should be continued or abandoned
- Resolving territorial and political conflicts arising from the impact of new systems.

Because these duties require on-going attention, the permanent steering committee should meet regularly, preferably on a monthly basis.

Since the permanent information systems steering committee is composed of the top executives of the company, the two biggest benefits of these committees are: (1) resolution of political and economic conflicts at the highest levels without making the information systems manager the person in the middle, and (2) interaction between top executives and information systems management. This latter benefit has a corresponding risk: the information systems manager is exposed to the evaluation and judgment of the executives. This exposure is only a danger for the incompetent; a well prepared, effective information systems manager should welcome it.

There is agreement that the biggest problem with a permanent steering committee is poor attendance. The people who should serve on the committee are the executives with the greatest demands on their time. Three strategies can help improve attendance: (1) The president or CEO should be chairman and should stress the importance of regular attendance. Without this support the committee will fail. (2) Good staff work is required by the information systems manager. Presentations should be clear, precise, pertinent, and should avoid technical jargon at all costs. Visual aids should be developed carefully and in a uniform format. Status reports and proposals for new projects should be distributed in advance. (3) Meetings should be brief and businesslike. Top management appreciate subordinates who recognize the value of their time and who act accordingly.

There are potential disadvantages associated with the steering-committee approach. Occasionally, a steering committee may act precipitously and make a decision or take action that is counterproductive. This action can be very difficult to reverse and the effect can be widespread. Good staff work, proper education, and occasional lobbying can help avoid this pitfall. "Analysis paralysis", otherwise known as "the stall", can also hamper the committee. Committees sometimes avoid difficult decisions by recommending further study. The solution to this common problem is to define a specific goal and a means for achieving it prior to entering the meeting. The member making a presentation should specify the decision or action desired and structure the presentation so that it leads logically to a conclusion or a specific recommendation. Finally, the committee can start out with noble objectives such as setting high-level priorities and establishing policies, and wind up immersed in picky little details at the lowest operating level. Or, worse yet, the steering committee not only steers, but it also designs, builds, modifies, maintains, and often wrecks the information systems function by gradually assuming full management responsibility and turning the information systems manager into a highly paid, highly frustrated clerk. These things usually happen when the top executives lose interest and delegate someone from their organization to take their places at meetings. The persons delegated are usually those with nothing to do and not vital to the department operations. They can create havoc at these meetings. The only thing to do is to disband the committee and have a long talk with the CEO on the future of information systems within the corporation.

If a company already has an executive or management committee whose function is to provide overall policy and planning guidance to the organization, a permanent information-steering committee is not needed. The management committee can perform this function. In this case, the committee's involvement must be limited to matters of major significance such as approving the corporate information resource plan, establishing spending levels, and resolving major conflicts between user departments.

Project-steering committees. The project-steering committee is a board of advisors to a specific project. The chairman is usually the executive in charge of the user group that initiated the request for the project. Committee members should include executives from other groups in the organization that may be affected by the system, managers of the user functions that will be involved with the system, the information systems manager, and the project manager. The functions of the project-steering committee include:

- Reviewing and approving the schedule for project tasks and segments
- Monitoring project progress by reviewing periodic reports from the development team
- Ensuring that the resources required for successful completion of the project are available
- Resolving territorial conflicts among users and among members of the development team
- Making major systems design and budgetary decisions
- Providing management direction to the project manager.

The success of the project-steering committee depends mainly on the clear understanding that its head is directly responsible to corporate management for the successful completion of the project. Project-steering committees provide benefits to both the information systems manager and the user department. By giving the user executive total responsibility for the successful implementation of the system, the responsibility of the project manager is restricted to the proper area, providing the required system support functions. The user also receives benefits. Steering-committee reviews provide greater assurance that the system design specifications meet user requirements, that adequate acceptance testing is performed, that the proper resources are available at the right time, and that a workable conversion schedule is planned. In addition, the costs of the project are more visible, allowing more effective control of project expenses.

Steering committees can be a useful tool for organizations experiencing problems in coordinating information systems activities with corporate plans and objectives. Before deciding to use a steering committee however, top management should consider alternative solutions, such as changing the reporting relationships of the information systems function. If steering committees are created, information systems managers will need all of their managerial skills to work effectively with them. A steering committee should be used only if the CEO feels that it is the only way to establish an increased awareness of the information function within the company. It should not be used to diffuse responsibility so that should something go wrong, no one person would be responsible.

Management Control

Control should be exercised on the information systems department just as controls are placed on the marketing, manufacturing, or engineering departments. These departments all submit departmental budgets and operating plans to management where they are reviewed, changed, and approved. Appropriate resources are committed based on the operating plans and the departments then are responsible for executing the plans. Management monitors progress against the plans and asks for explanations of variance. As economic conditions change, the plans are updated and resources reallocated. Why can management not use the same techniques in controlling the information systems department? It can, as soon as management realizes that programming is not an art, and that programmers are not eighteenth-century craftsmen.

Control issues will become more important as companies experience the full effects of changing computer economics and proliferating technology. Divisional data centers may then become inefficient compared with large corporate controlled host computers and networking that can achieve more significant economies of scale, not so much for equipment as for people. At the other extreme, many will find microcomputers spreading rapidly throughout their organizations. Some of the proposed applications will be unjustified, and control challenges here will be even more severe than when minicomputers began to enter the business world. Key professional and managerial employees will be lost to the company for days, if not weeks, as they ''play'' with their personal computers. The $2500 purchase cost will escalate as the organization adds equipment (another disk drive, a better printer, a color monitor, more memory), and buys software, lots and lots of software. Next will come requests for access to the corporate data files, and soon the company will find transaction systems being built with no ties to divisional or corporate information systems. The company will wind up with hundreds of fragmented systems each serving a single user. This could happen if management does not get information systems back under control and start managing its information resources properly.

APPLICATIONS PLANNING

Organization planning and control planning establishes the environment in which the information systems function will operate. Applications planning and technology planning provide the specifics of what the information systems function will do for the next five years. When most people refer to a systems plan, they usually are referring to an application plan and a technology plan. The objective of an application plan is to avoid a wild development of applications and systems that are responses to the users who yell the loudest or who have the most pull. The technology plan spells out the direction the company is moving in hardware, office automation,

FIGURE 4-2   **PROJECT PLANNING FLOWCHART**

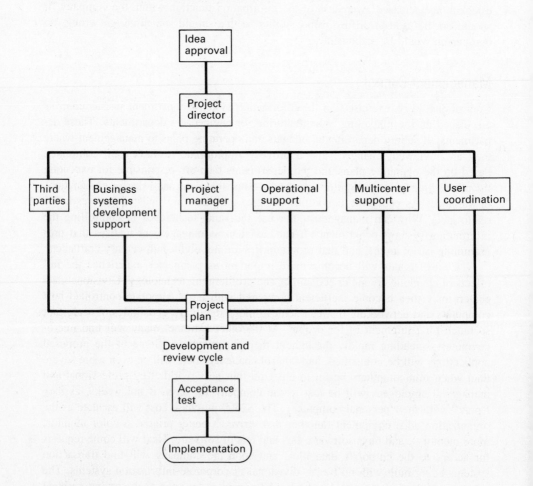

and telecommunications. If the hardware plan calls for IBM mainframes as host computers and SNA as the communications network architecture, then word processors and personal computers purchased by managers and people in user organizations had better be IBM compatible.

Systems planning implies the development of a master plan consisting of the following:

1. An application development plan for the short-, mid-, and long-term periods
2. The resources required to execute the applications development plan
3. The optimum sequence of development
4. A plan for the integration of systems under development
5. A plan for integrating applications being developed into existing systems.

A commonly used technique to develop a systems plan is to use the information schematic and develop a portfolio of projects and a resource allocation policy to rank projects for development (see Figure 4-2).

Portfolio of Projects

Each company should have a list of projects to be developed. These projects should include:

- Replacements for applications currently in use, but in need of redesign to meet changing requirements, or in need of updating to take advantage of new technology
- Major revisions to existing applications
- A backlog of applications approved but not started
- Proposed applications generated by the latest review of the information strategic plan
- User requests for immediate service
- New opportunities to gain a competitive edge in business arising from changing technology.

Resource Allocation Policy

With limited resources and a large backlog of applications awaiting development, a resource allocation policy is needed to take the comprehensive list of projects and rank them in order of priority for development. This is done after feasibility studies have been completed to ensure that the projects are feasible both technically and economically. The criteria for setting these priorities could include the following:

- Is the application essential to the company's business? (for example order entry system, passenger reservation system)

- Is it a prerequisite for other applications? (for example data base prior to application implementation)

- Is it a custom development project, an application package, or a user developed system?

- Is there a quick payback? Does it generate savings, or does it enhance a company's profitability? (economic feasibility)

- Is technology available? (technical feasibility)

- Can the user organization absorb and use the proposed system? (organizational feasibility)

- Is it compatible with other systems and applications or is it a stand-along system? (If it is a high-priority stand-alone system, it could be developed outside the information systems organization.)

- What are the time and resources required?

- What priority is assigned to that project by the user organization and by the management review committee?

Using this list of criteria, a corporate management committee or the permanent steering committee can work with the information systems department to assign priorities to each project. For example: user departments may defer their projects until data base software is installed so that they can have a data base system. Similarly, the accounting department may defer its general ledger system until the feeder systems (such as payables and receivables) have been completed so that there is no need for the manual feed of information into the general ledger. The top-level committee can discuss priorities and alternatives and come to conclusions and guidance for the information systems executive. The information systems department can offer suggestions for uses of existing technologies and reasons for sequencing projects in a particular way. Again, a byproduct of these meetings is further understanding of computers on the part of the users, and better understanding of the business on the part of information systems personnel.

After fitting a development schedule to the application plan, information systems now can determine when hardware and software will be needed and can develop the required hardware and software strategies. A clear definition of the strategies, objectives, and policies of the information systems organization is needed before systems planning can begin.

Objectives are the results to be achieved by the information systems organization. Strategies are the actions to be taken to achieve the objectives. For example, an objective may be to develop information systems using the latest state-of-the-art technology. A hardware and software strategy must be developed to accomplish this objective. Policies are the guidelines or procedures to be used in carrying out strategy. For example, a hardware policy for determining computer capabilities is to ask all vendors to submit to a benchmark test of their proposed equipment. Some typical information policies are:

1. **Planning policies**
   Information system planning responsibilities
   Description of the planning process
   Defining the scope of plans
   Procedures for monitoring, reviewing, and updating plans
   Defining resource allocation schemes

2. **Organizational policies**
   Mission, objectives, and goals of the information systems organization
   Organizational structure of the department
   Location of the information systems unit in the organization
   Responsibilities of the information systems unit
   Duties and rsponsibilities of departmental committees
   Security practices
   Interface between information systems and user departments
   Auditing the information systems function

3. **Personnel policies**
   Recruiting and career progression
   Education and training
   Career development practices
   Performance evaluation and promotion
   Salary administration

4. **Hardware policies**
   Determination of computer capabilities
   Centralization versus decentralization
   System architecture
   Communication standards
   Systems integration policies (data and word processing)
   Compatibility and standardization of equipment

5. **Software policies**
   Software selection and acquisition
   Language standards
   Operating systems
   Hiring of outside contractors and consultants
   Methods of financing software
   Methods for software development (centralized, decentralized)

6. **Application development policies**
   Systems development standards
   Documentation standards
   Use of external consultants
   Initiation, approval and release of applications
   System and acceptance testing
   User training

The Master Plan

Once the information systems department has established its objectives, strategies, and policies, and developed a comprehensive information plan based on the company's long-range strategic plan, it is ready to document the results of the planning process. The master plan provides the framework for the short-range (annual) planning process and all detailed project planning. As in any planning document, the master plan should include the following:

1. **Objectives and strategies.** The company's long-range objectives, strategies, priorities, and information needs are restated. The overall objectives of the information systems department are presented, together with a description of how the department is organized and structured to meet corporate information needs.

2. **The current posture of the information systems department.** A summary of the current hardware, software, applications, and staffing situations, the systems and applications under development, and the resources required to run the department are given. Capacity utilization of existing facilities are presented to give a complete picture of the current information-processing environment.

3. **Financial plan.** The projected expenditures for the information systems department over the next five years are presented on an annual basis. It would be helpful to categorize the expenditures by major resource groupings, that is hardware, software, people, training, facilities, outside support. Some corporations like to show total annual information systems costs as a percentage of total revenue or total sales in comparison with other support costs.

4. **Support plan.** The hardware and software requirements are presented on an annual basis for the next five years together with the personnel, by job classification, required to support these requirements.

5. **Operations plan.** The hardware deployment strategies and operating philosophies to be used over the next five years are described. The plan for integrating all information resources in the corporation is outlined: that is data processing, word processing, communications. The people and facilities required to provide operational support and the resources needed for production and support of development projects are listed.

6. **Staffing and organization plan.** A five-year projection of the total personnel requirements by major type of activity: application development, software development, system maintenance, operations, training, administration is given.

7. **Application development plan.** A listing is made, by priority, of the applications to be developed over the next five years. The time schedules and expenditures for each application are included as well as a brief description of each project, the benefits, and the risks involved.

The Short Range (Annual) Plan

Since the information master plan covers a five-year period, the final planning task is to develop the short-range or annual plan. This plan is concerned with the performance targets and the specific tasks, schedules, and budgets to achieve short-range objectives. The time horizon is usually one to two years and is generally equivalent to a department annual plan. The top priority projects from the master plan make up next year's annual plan. In addition to the projects identified in the master plan, which is a result of a lengthy planning process and feasibility studies, two other types of projects have to be included in the annual plan:

- Enhancement projects: small changes to existing systems to make them more useful to the users
- Maintenance projects: changes to existing systems due to changes in requirements, changes in technology, or to correct original design flaws

The annual plan is updated once a year. Sometimes use is made of rolling plans in which a plan is prepared every quarter or semi-annually. The new planning period is added and the one just completed is dropped. Contrary to the development of the master plan, where user personnel and top management are involved, the annual plan is primarily an activity performed by information systems personnel. The annual plan would contain the following:

1. **Departmental objectives and overview.** A brief statement is given of the objectives of the department and the assumptions upon which the annual plan is based. It also should provide a management summary of the annual plan including major expenditures, overall resources needed, major acquisitions of hardware and software, and the total annual expenditure.

2. **Development and maintenance plan.** This section describes all applications to be developed during the year in terms of objectives, resources needed, development schedules, milestone dates, and completion dates. Major maintenance and enhancement activities are also described in this section.

3. **Operations plan.** This plan describes the workload by major application of all work areas in the operations function: data entry, computer rooms, output quality control, data storage, data transmission. It shows all the resources needed: people, equipment, materials, to handle the workload.

4. **Technical support plan.** This plan describes the activities and resources needed to provide technical support to the information systems department. It includes such activities as hardware performance evaluation, installation of system software, system software maintenance, communication network administration, data base administration and support, maintenance of development standards and methodologies.

5. **Standard practices program.** This section describes the plan and resources

needed to implement standard practices: standards in design, programming, development methodology, data, security, and auditing.

6. **Staffing and organization plan.** This section shows the major changes in the organizational structure of the department required to meet changing demands for services. It summarizes the total demand for personnel by project and support units. It also outlines a plan to acquire the needed resources.

7. **Education and training plan.** This section outlines a plan of action for developing necessary skills in existing personnel as well as for new hiring.

8. **Site plan.** This section is on new facilities or improvement to existing facilities showing uses, dates available, and major construction projects.

9. **Research plan.** This is a section which describes research activities to maintain currency in technology and the application of that technology to users' information needs.

While the nine sections in an annual plan may appear to be a lot of work with some duplication from the master plan, it should be remembered that each section would be prepared by various people in charge of specific functions within the information systems department. The head of research, or education and training, or software maintenance, would each prepare their own annual plan. Collectively, they would become the departmental annual plan upon which the managers would be measured and evaluated.

PROFESSIONAL APPLICATION COMMENT: PLANNING AT THE AMERICAN INTERNATIONAL BANK (AIB).

Using the heightened interest in international banking because of the political activities in Portugal, Jim Long, head of the international department of AIB, lobbied with the bank's CEO to reevaluate the bank's customer information requirements. While he could initiate a project to develop an integrated customer information system for the international branches, the information collected abroad should be used by corporate banking to develop a composite picture of a customer's banking relationships domestically and overseas. Domestically, the existing systems were developed in the early 1970s and rather fragmented. There was a current accounts system, a loan administration system, a trust system, a cash management system, and the financial reporting systems for internal and regulatory reports. None of these were integrated so that if information was needed for one client, one would have to go to each system separately to extract the information. These were file systems with no on-line inquiry capability. There were batch extract programs to pull information on each customer account from the appropriate file. Since each of these domestic systems generated reports by customer on a monthly basis, corporate banking would compile all the

reports for one client as the customer profile. Both the CEO and the head of corporate banking agreed that this would be the ideal time to reevaluate the bank's information needs and start planning on replacing existing systems as well as developing new ones for the overseas operations.

A small planning task force was created to do the preliminary work on how to approach the task of defining information requirements for the bank. The task force was chaired by the CEO and included the heads of the international department, corporate banking, and information systems. This group of four prepared an agenda for a five-day planning conference at Greenbriar, a resort in West Virginia, to be held over a long holiday weekend. The top executives from the bank would attend to develop long-range corporate goals and objectives and define the information needed to execute the strategies for meeting stated long-range objectives. Moreover, priorities would be agreed on for system development at this planning conference. To accomplish as much as possible over the five-day period, staff work was done in advance to prepare detailed schedules and agendas for the meeting. The participants would be divided into work groups with specific problems to solve. Leaders of these discussion groups would have background information prepared together with the relevant facts and statistics. Recommendations from each group would be presented for discussion, modification, and adoption by all the conference participants. The four-member planning task force identified six areas of vital concern to the bank and circulated exposure drafts describing the challenges and opportunities in each area to the appropriate departments. The departments would have time to develop their thoughts and recommendations prior to attending the planning conference. Since the planning task force included the top executives in the bank, there was no fear that this effort would not receive the highest priority within the department, or that participants would arrive at the Greenbriar conference unprepared.

Because of the staff work and planning that preceded the conference, the results were predictable, the conference was very successful. So much enthusiasm was developed for automated information systems that Pamela Lawrence had to constantly remind the audience that everyone could not be satisfied overnight. Priorities would have to be placed on systems to be developed, and systems would have to be implemented on a phased approach. Pamela pointed out that the information systems staff had no experience in developing systems using the latest state-of-the-art technology and would need help. They were competent analysts and programmers and knew the bank's business very well but they definitely were not up to date technically. On the plus side, they had the trust and confidence of the users, since they constantly helped users enhance existing systems to meet changing banking requirements. The recommendation of the planning conference was to bring in a consulting firm that would help Pamela develop the systems on a joint basis with the information systems department. The consulting firm would provide the leadership and direction, as well as technical competence. AIB would provide the manpower to do the design and programming. Planned properly, this would enable a transfer of knowledge from the consulting firm to the bank as the projects proceeded so that by the completion of the work, bank personnel would be updated technically and would have gained by working side by side with the consultants.

Pamela readily agreed with the recommendation and got permission to engage the consulting firm in time to develop the master plan for information systems. This plan, along with the specific project plans were approved by the management committee, and the board of directors. Even though the bank was decentralized, with much autonomy granted each operating division and branch, it was decided that the focal point of the new information system would be the client. All activities that a client had with the bank should be available centrally. Moreover, activities of all related clients should be identified, so that subsidiaries of large conglomerates could be grouped with the holding company to describe a complete banking relationship and total exposure. This concept led to the development of a centralized system with the client data base at the hub and feeder systems at the branches. Each branch would have access to the client data base through land and satellite communications. The account manager for Toyota in Tokyo would have knowledge of the account balances and loans outstanding of the Toyota factory in Tennessee, as would the U.S. Toyota account manager in New York. Head office could monitor total exposure by customer on a worldwide basis.

Because of restrictions placed by foreign governments on the transmission of data for processing across national borders, Pamela decided to have each country process its own data and transmit information to the central hub for consolidation into the corporate client data base. Since this procedure was viewed as sending information for consolidation by the U.S. parent company, foreign governments did not object to this type of cross-border data flows.

Three hubs were established to collect and process information from the worldwide branches. The central hub would be in New York, linking all domestic branches and London and Singapore. The international hubs would be in London, linking all the European branches, and in Singapore, linking all the Asian branches. London and Singapore would always have the latest version of the client data base maintained in New York for clients with international activities. In addition, any branch could make an inquiry against any client in the data base. For example, if the Paris branch inquired against the data base in London for a client profile and the client was not in the London data base, Paris could then inquire against the New York data base for the information. This could be a client of the bank about to start an international operation in Paris, or a client going to the Paris branch to transact some business with a French firm.

Systems development proceeded in parallel in New York, London, and Singapore. Each location had specific systems to design, test, and pilot. Personnel were assigned to these projects from all offices so that at the completion of the project, each office would have someone familiar with the system from working on it. Systems development proceeded with the use of a standard development methodology so that there was consistent generation of documentation as well as uniformity in work segments, tasks, and steps. The data base selected had an integrated data dictionary, and a data administration function was established to design and control the data base. Standard hardware and software architecture was selected and all branches converted to the prescribed architecture. A policy was established that all office automation equipment and personal computing would be compatible with the main-

frame hardware, would use the mainframe communication network architecture, and would be compatible on a worldwide basis for electronic mail.

The design and installation effort was monitored by the bank's management committee meeting on a monthly basis. Reports were given to the board of directors on a quarterly basis. A prototype system was ready at the end of 24 months and the full system operational in 36 months. The cost of the project exceeded 26 million dollars. Account managers can now pull up an electronic file on their clients and determine their account balances: by branch and in total, loans outstanding, by currency, branch booked, country of risk, and guarantor, foreign exchange positions, cash management information, and the latest financial statements and credit reports for the client.

This professional application is a good illustration of the fact that a comprehensive information systems plan is essential to the effective management of information resources. The information plan is developed through joint planning sessions with top management to define goals and objectives, the strategies to meet those goals, and the information needed to implement the strategies. Information systems planning begins with the development of the information schematic for the business enterprise. This schematic shows the information requirement at each functional level for each business unit. The transaction systems required to supply the basic data for each business unit are also shown as are the interrelationships among transaction systems. Using the information schematic as a road map, a hierarchy of plans can be developed to supply the needed information.

System planning involves the development of a series of plans, each being more detailed, concrete and operational than the preceding one, until an annual plan is developed to specify the tasks to be performed in the coming year. While the responsibility for defining the corporate information needs rests with the top management of the enterprise, the strategies to collect, process, and provide the information is a responsibility of the information systems department working with user management. The next section of this book will be devoted to the activities in executing the system plan.

CHAPTER 4   **DISCUSSION QUESTIONS**

1. Many companies, especially smaller ones, do not do formal planning. Will they have to adopt formal planning procedures if they are to successfully implement computer-based information systems?

2. Discuss the value of reducing an organization's information requirements to an "information schematic." How difficult is it and how would one go about preparing an information schematic?

3. What impact will the rising cost of analysts and programmers (80 percent of total information systems costs) have on the development of future systems? What alternatives does management have?

4. Most systems in operation today have as their original design, the systems installed in the 1960s and 1970s. Do you think that these systems will be redesigned in the future to take advantage of advances in hardware and software technology? How can they be cost justified?

5. What is the trend in organizational structure for providing computing services in today's business—centralized or decentralized? What are the advantages and disadvantages of each?

6. Is the use of a steering committee, "passing the buck" for decision making and management to a group so that if the project fails, no one person can be blamed? The other functional areas of a business rarely use steering committees in their daily work, why must information systems rely on them?

7. Why can management not use the same techniques in controlling the information systems effort as it uses in controlling other departments? What are these techniques?

8. With a large backlog of applications awaiting development, how does management assign priorities and how often should these priorities be reviewed?

9. Is a master plan for information systems really that important? After all, how many businesses have formal plans that they rigidly follow?

5

SYSTEMS DEVELOPMENT

ISSUES

- How many major development projects should be attempted at one time?

- How to resolve conflicts between users and technical personnel during the systems development life cycle.

- Assigning priorities to projects

- Managing large development efforts

- The need for a systems development methodology and standards

- Breaking the systems development bottleneck

GLOBAL COMMUNICATIONS INC.

Global Communications Inc. (GCI) is a large communications utility. Half of its annual revenue of over four billion dollars comes from telephone operations and the remainder from the manufacture and sale of electronic and communications components. GCI operates 25 telephone companies in the United States and Canada. They range in size from 22,000 subscribers in Quebec to over 1,500,000 in southern California. While each company is an autonomous corporation in the territory in which it operates, it is tightly controlled by corporate headquarters in terms of strategy, policies, and financial management. All the company presidents report to an organization in corporate headquarters known as the service company.

Don Gault was vice-president of operations, in the service company. His responsibility was to provide policies and guidance to the telephone companies in the areas of operations and maintenance. A few days ago, Don was appointed head of a special project group to study the GCI Data Services organization and recommend improvements in the systems development area. What had surprised Don was that the assignment was for two years. Carl, the president of the service company, had given Don the following challenge.

GCI Data Services was the creation of a brilliant computer systems specialist with the Western Telephone Company. In the 1970s, her company was faced with the task of redesigning and upgrading some of its basic systems such as billing, payroll, customer accounting, and plant. All of these systems were originally designed as card-processing systems, converted to the 1401, then to the 360. These conversion processes were so lengthy and expensive that the next one would have to be the last; one last crack to get systems completely up to date and suitable for the needs of the Western Company for at least ten years.

Joan Callahan was the director of systems development at the Western Company. She had yearned for years to upgrade the existing systems, turn them into data base systems with real time, on-line facilities. She had difficulties convincing her own management of the need for this upgrade, and the data-processing management would not bring the idea to company management for approval and funding. Joan was told: "If you want to redesign every application in the shop, you had better come up with a very good justification for the expenditures and a good estimate of savings for the company. Otherwise, you are wasting your time. Management is under pressure to keep costs down; after the last two fiascos in conversion, they are really skeptical that we can do anything right. This is not the time to run to them suggesting another massive conversion. They are liable to fire you on the spot.''

Joan was convinced that if the company was to remain competitive, they had to upgrade their systems. After all, almost everything in the telephone company was automated and they simply were not keeping up with technology. But, what her boss said was also true. In the past, conversions from one system to another were not easily accomplished; everybody had that problem—lack of documentation, lack of understanding of the applications, lack of communications with the users, she could go on, and on, and on. This time it would be different. She had made sure that the current set of documentation was kept up to date. She knew what enhancements the users wanted and had their support to upgrade their systems. But, how could she sell the idea to top management, and even tougher, to the service company?

Her own people gave her the answer. They had told her to ''cool it''. ''Every company has the same problem. Some day management will wake up, find themselves behind their competitor and initiate a crash project to catch up. Isn't that how it's always done?'' Every company had the same problem. That was it. That was how she was going to convince management. The systems at all the telephone companies were developed within a few years of each other. All needed upgrading to use new technology and systems techniques. Instead of each company redesigning its own systems, why not design the 'ultimate' system for use at all the telephone companies. Why not; there should be no differences in the systems for payroll, billing, customer service, plant, and construction in each of the companies other than differences in such things as local taxes and deductions. All of that could be table driven and designed into the system. Instead of designing 25 payroll systems, one could be designed for use at 25 companies. The same was true for all the other applications. The savings would be tremendous.

Joan started to explore her idea with others in the department. ''Good idea, but who is going to do it? The Western Company certainly isn't going to fund developing programs for all the other companies. Where are you going to find the people for such a massive project? Where are you going to get computer time to test all the programs? Who is going to sell the idea to the other companies? ''Joan knew that before she presented her idea to management, if she ever did, she had better develop a plan and a strategy for executing the plan.

The concept for developing common business systems was a sound one. Joan was surprised that no one had thought of it before. She could get enough people if each company contributed systems analysts and programmers. But then, where would they be located? No single company, not even the Western Company had the space to house a large development organization of several hundred people. Furthermore, where would they get the computer resources to mount such an effort? Each company had enough difficulties finding computer time to do their own program testing and maintenance. Yet each company was but a division of the corporation, some large, some very small. If the divisions did not have their own computer resources, what would they do? The solution became obvious.

A corporate data center—that was the solution. One data center to develop programs for all the telephone companies. Programs would be operated at the company's own computer center, but developed at a central location—centralized development, decentralized operations. Joan liked that. She tested this new idea with her associates. They liked it, but it had one flaw: the service company was deliberately kept small so that when its expenses were allocated to each operating company, the regulatory commissions governing each telephone company would not complain about the size of the corporate overhead the company had to absorb. To increase this overhead by creating a corporate data center would probably not be acceptable to either the service company or the telephone companies. What if the companies paid for the system development services? Would they still complain? The answer was no; then it would be a make-or-buy decision, but not through the service company. It would have to be an "arms length" transaction to satisfy regulatory commissions. In the past, many of the telephone companies had gone to outside services to get systems developed quickly. Usually they were not that successful, but that was the fault of the company, not the software house.

Joan came up with another idea: set up a separate company to provide development services to the phone companies. They would buy all development services from this new company and operate the new systems at their data centers. As she discussed this new idea with her associates, someone said, "Why just development, why not everything?" Create a computer utility, supply all data-processing services to the telephone companies—systems development, maintenance, operations, everything. Each company then, would not have to worry about running a data-processing operation. Everything would be taken care of by this new company, including supplying the computer. As they debated the merits of this concept, it soon became obvious that there could be significant economies in consolidating hardware. Right now, each company had its own computer. Instead of replacing each one with a newer one, why not consolidate them into several large data centers, each with large systems that could serve several companies? The end result would be five or six regional data centers, each serving four to five companies. The expense of running 25 different data centers would be reduced significantly. Each company would pay for data services based on usage. Those with high volume would pay more. The savings from hardware alone could pay for the establishment of the new company. Since the new company would provide data services to all telephone companies, it was to be called GCI Data Services, Inc. (GCIDS).

Joan did her homework. She prepared an organization plan describing the mission, objectives, and goals of the new organization, how it would be organized and staffed, where regional data centers would be located, the proposed location of a headquarters for GCIDS and its centralized systems development activities, and the financial projections for the first five years of operations. She also projected the savings to be realized from a realignment of the computer operations for all telephone companies. Joan then tested this document with the data-processing people at Western, and with their approval, presented it to the management of the Western Company. They were impressed, made some suggestions for improvement, and the concept was presented to the service company.

With projected annual savings of over $10 million from the reduction of data centers from 25 to 7 and additional savings in systems development costs for the next five years, the service company approved the concept and started building the new organization. A company president from one of the telephone companies was asked to head up the new company and give it guidance during the start-up phase. Joan Callahan was appointed director of Business Information Systems. Business Information Systems (BIS) was the name given to the project to develop common business systems for all the telephone companies. The organization chart for the new company can be seen in Figure 5-A.

Basically, GCI Data Services had two missions: to develop common business information systems; and, to manage and operate the regional data centers. Since the largest computer center and system development group was in the Western Telephone Company, GCI Data Services headquarters and its system development organization would be located in southern California. They would have their own building and computer center for program development and testing. In addition, the new computer center would serve as backup for the Western Company's computer center. Regional centers located at an existing telephone company were created to serve a group of companies in the region. Their mission was strictly operations and program maintenance. There would be no systems development at these companies, therefore, the number of people needed was significantly reduced. All system analysts and programmers who were rated above average were given an opportunity to transfer to California to work on the new BIS project or to a regional data center to work on program maintenance. The timing of these moves was flexible since the companies would need programmers until new systems were developed and came on-stream. It

FIGURE 5-A   **ORGANIZATION CHART—GCI DATA SERVICES**

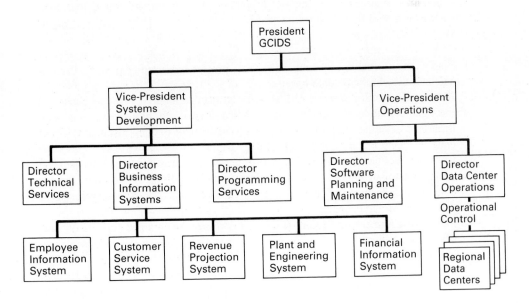

also provided an excellent opportunity for the company to reduce staff through attrition since once the plans were announced, many people who did not want a transfer anywhere would look for new job opportunities.

When Don Gault was appointed head of the special task force, GCI Data Services had been in existence for over five years. The operations side of data services was doing very well. The concept of regional data centers improved service to the companies because of new, large scale equipment and installation of on-line data entry devices. The expected savings did materialize and the phone companies found data-processing costs declining while service was improving. The systems development side of GCIDS was not doing well at all. Of the five major projects, all were significantly behind schedule, none had been completed. Since development costs were charged to the phone companies, they all had a large cost on their books with nothing to show for it. For example, costs were allocated to each company based on its size. The Western Telephone Company had been charged over one million dollars for the development of a payroll system that was not completed. It would be most embarrassing to the company if the regulators were to ask why a payroll system should cost one million dollars to develop when the most expensive payroll application package on the market sold for under $100,000. Would it take 10 times the cost of the package to modify it to meet any unique requirements of the Western Company? Worse yet, the company would have to admit that the system was not finished and that they did not know when it would be finished or what the final costs would be.

All of the other companies were facing similar problems and the complaints about waiting (and paying) for five years without seeing any results were beginning to pour into the service company and GCI corporate headquarters. Don's challenge was to find out why things were not happening and to take appropriate action to make things happen in the systems development area.

When Don and his staff arrived in southern California, he found that Joan Callahan was ready to brief him on the status of BIS projects. There were five major projects:

1. Employee Information System (EIS). This project consisted of payroll, Personnel, and the employee data base.
2. Revenue Projection System (RPS). This project monitored revenue generated through telephone operations and matched them with projections generated through a revenue requirements program. Settlement of long-distance toll revenue was also included in this project.
3. Customer Service System (CSS). Customer service was the largest project, an on-line customer inquiry system tied into customer billing and accounts receivable. It also included customer records, turn-ons and offs, directory services, and other service changes.
4. Plant and Engineering System (PES). This project maintained records on outside plant, central office equipment, construction, maintenance, and engineering.
5. Financial Information System (FIS). This project maintained financial records

such as budgets, general ledger, regulatory reports, financial statements, and the accounting transaction systems.

In addition to these five major projects were Special Projects, a group working on user requests that had to be performed to keep existing programs and systems operational. These included regulatory changes, and required updates to existing programs. Each project was organized as shown in Figure 5-B.

User consultants were non-data-processing people assigned by the companies to assist the development team in understanding the business requirements of each application. The phone company with either the highest interest in a particular system, or with a reputation of having a good system in that functional area was asked by the service company to assign someone knowledgeable in that functional area to Data Services to assist in the design of the new system. In effect, he became the user representative for that particular project, and the final word on functional requirements going into the project. Depending on the size of the project, there could be several user consultants on one project. In the Customer Service System, there were seven consultants, each working in a different area, for example billing, inquiry, and receivables.

System analysts were drawn from the other telephone companies and assigned to projects based on their background and experience. The programmers who were transferred to southern California were primarily senior programmers specializing in software development. Because of the abundance of programmers in the southern California labor market, the company decided not to move applications programmers in from the other companies unless they had special knowledge of a specific application or were above average programmers. The system analysis staff was dominated by people from the Western Telephone Company. The Western company became a regional center, but all of its analysts and most of its programmers were transferred to GCI Data Services.

Don started his assignment by interviewing the key people in system development: project managers, user consultants, senior analysts, technical specialists, software developers, and programmers. He asked them to describe what their jobs were,

---

FIGURE 5-B   **BIS PROJECT ORGANIZATION**

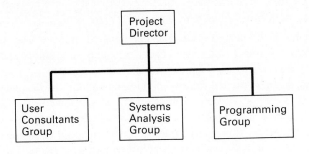

how they did the work, what direction they got, and what problems they met in doing their work. Don let them talk and get their frustrations out into the open. After talking to the people on the BIS project, Don visited several telephone companies to talk to the BIS liaison people and to company management. As a result of these interviews, the findings were as follows:

1. In every project, there was a history of inability to define the scope of the project, what was to be included, and rules for processing information received. Quite often, user consultants could not agree among themselves as to the scope. Each defined scope as what his company wanted, and designed the system based on his own background and experience.

2. System analysts were extremely frustrated in that they could not get an answer as to who was supposed to be designing the system. They thought that they were the designers of the system. They found themselves to be the "documentors," writing down what the user consultants wanted in the system. Not only did the user consultants state what they thought the requirements were, the also told the analysts how to process the data to get the required information.

3. User consultants were older people, experienced in telephone operations. The average age was 51 years. Almost none had experience in data processing. While their knowledge of the functional area they were assigned to was strong, much of it was based on personal experience gained many years ago when they worked in that area and might not reflect the current thinking of management or current technology. They strongly felt that their role was to design the new application based on their background and experience.

4. The system analysts were generally a younger group, with an average age of 27. Most were single and willing to relocate to the "swinging" area of metropolitan Los Angeles. Their experience with the telephone companies averaged around 5 years. They were told prior to joining GCIDS that they were the "cream of the crop" and hand-picked to participate in designing the "ultimate" in business information systems. They found that they had to take orders from "old has-beens" who had been transferred to the BIS project because local management did not want them in their old company but could not fire them because of their seniority and longevity with the company. The system analysts argued incessantly with the older user consultants on how things were to be done. It was their argument that the consultants should only state what had to be done, the analysts would decide how it would be done. These arguments resulted in no agreement on project scope or processing concepts.

5. The results of the design effort was documented in a set of systems specifications. This document was sent to each company for approval and sign-off. If a company disagreed with the specifications, they had the opportunity to indicate the changes they wanted before granting approval. So far, no company had approved a set of system specifications as presented. All had requested changes, adding new features, questioning why some features were included, making statements like: "this would never work in our company", or "it's not the way we do it now; to change would be too big an effort." System analysts

seized on these comments as proof of the stupidity and incompetence of the user consultants. Consultants blamed the analysts for the poor design of the system and the way the system was documented. As time dragged on, the specifications were becoming technically and functionally obsolete and were being changed to take advantage of new equipment, software, and technology. Five years after project initiation, not a single system specification had been approved by all the telephone companies.

6. In reviewing the specifications, Don Gault found that the format and organization was different for each application. He discovered that the project manager dictated the format for the system specifications based on his experience. He also found that there were no standards or procedures for system analysis, design, or documentation. The way a project was developed was up to the project manager, an experienced data-processing professional with over 10 years experience. The only two requirements imposed by Data Services were that a feasibility report be prepared that presented the economics of the application (cost/benefits, why needed, benefits to the company, benefits to the customers), as well as an estimate of the time and costs to develop the system; and a system specification report for user review and sign-off. Programming was not to begin until user sign-off had been obtained.

7. Programmers had not been working on the BIS applications since there had been no user sign-offs. Instead, they were working on installing software such as IMS, VM, and query languages. They also were attending a lot of schools to learn the latest in system software from IBM, how to use the software, and preparing common routines using the new software that could be used by all BIS applications, for example on-line editors, file maintenance routines, data dictionaries, data management systems, data extractors, and report generators. Unfortunately during the past five years, many new software systems had been released, therefore a lot of the training and work done by the programmers five years ago was now obsolete, thrown out, and replaced by newer system software and operating systems. These programmers became very valuable to other data-processing organizations in southern California and were able to command very high salaries because of their knowledge in the latest software and operating systems. The turnover rate was extremely high. GCI Data Services had a reputation of being the best "training center" for systems programmers in North America. They even had their own diplomas made up to look like a university diploma.

Don Gault also found that the budget for systems development—BIS applications—was running at around five million dollars a year. Very little was being produced, morale was low, no-one accepted responsibility for a task, and everyone pointed a finger at someone else when a task was behind schedule or discarded and restarted in a new direction. Management at the telephone companies were extremely concerned about the costs of the entire effort and the lack of delivery of finished products. Clearly the situation was completely out of control and something had to be done quickly.

For the manager of information resources, the management of the system development effort propably presents more problems than any other area. The GCI Data Services professional application presents the following issues for discussion:

- Did GCIDS try to do too much at once? How many large development projects can be undertaken at one time?
- How do you resolve the inevitable conflicts between users and information systems personnel as to who runs the project, who defines requirements, establishes the design, and has responsibility for the success or failure of the project?
- How should a major project be organized, managed, and executed?
- How should priorities be assigned to projects?
- What can be done to break the systems development bottleneck?

This chapter will discuss these issues and others in the systems development area. The GCI professional application presents a classic problem in systems development: large projects, schedules running late, overruns in costs, failure to communicate, antagonisms between users and systems personnel, failure to perform and deliver. Even more significant is the willingness of top management to allow the situation to exist for over five years before taking action. There is no way management would tolerate problems of this magnitude in the manufacturing, marketing, or finance areas and allow them to continue for five years. Yet this was not a unique problem or one caused by poor planning or inadequate resources. The concept of GCI Data Services was well planned, executed, and sound. All of the resources requested to develop systems centrally and operate them at regional centers were granted to GCI Data Services. Projects under development were initiated with a feasibility study and followed the classical system development phases: feasibility study, requirements definition, system design, programming, implementation. The effort had top management support, adequate funding and resources, experienced people, user participation, adequate documentation, and followed traditional development approaches; why didn't it work?

ATTEMPTING TO DO TOO MUCH

Even with virtually unlimited resources, did GCIDS try to do too much at one time? This issue addresses the problem of how many large development projects to undertake at one time. Large projects absorb a tremendous amount of man-hours not only at the analysis and programming levels, but also at the project management level.

Even more importantly, large projects require significant user involvement and commitment to ensure that current needs are being addressed. If the projects affect different parts of a user organization, and the resources, both user and systems, are available to undertake the project, then there should be no limit on the number of large projects that can be developed concurrently other than people and money. The key to success in a large project is the time it will take to complete the project. Unless the project can be completed in two years, management should look carefully at the effort.

Two years is about the maximum time that interest levels can be sustained with the users. The user is heavily involved in the feasibility phase. They are asked to contribute resources and time during the requirements definition phase and system design phase. During programming, the users are asked to develop new procedures for submitting inputs and processing outputs. They have to retrain their clerical and management people to use the new system. Unless all of this can take place within a two-year period, it would be extremely difficult to sustain the interest of the user and maintain credibility that the new systems would ever be developed. But even more important than sustaining user interest is avoiding changes in requirements and technology. Any project that requires more than two years to complete faces the risk that user requirements will have changed from those defined in the system specifications or that new technology in software design will have rendered the present design obsolete. For example, many companies have spent four to five years designing and installing a data management system using a hierarchical data base only to find when it was completed that the ''new'' relational data bases would provide information for decision support systems much more easily than the installed hierarchical design. The problem at GCI Data Services was not attempting to develop too many systems at one time, but was the fact that each system was too large to be completed within a two-year period. The better approach would have been to ''modularize'' the systems, developing them by releases, with the first release containing the essential requirements and each subsequent release adding more sophisticated features. We will discuss this concept further when we discuss alternatives to the traditional system development procedures.

RESOLVING CONFLICTS BETWEEN USERS AND SYSTEMS PERSONNEL

How does one resolve the inevitable conflicts between users and information systems personnel as to who runs the project, who defines requirements, establishes the design, and has responsibility for the success or failure of the project? Another major flaw in the GCIDS concept was serving too many masters at one time. It is feasible to design common business systems that can be used at all telephone companies. But to try to do this by satisfying the requirements of each company before implementing the system is virtually impossible, as they found out. Getting agreement on anything with three or four people involved is difficult; getting agreement on design specifications from 25 companies is impossible. The better approach would have been to select one company as the pilot company, design the system to fit its needs, get the system operational, then make modifications to install it at the other companies if modifications were necessary. The company selected as the pilot would be the one which really wanted to have the new system. They would pay for the development costs, but after the system was completed, the could sell the application to other companies and recover their initial investment. This provides incentive for the system to be completed in the first place, and incentive for the sponsoring company to ensure that the design was flexible enough so that other telephone companies would buy the software after it was developed and tested. Under this concept, the company most interested in the application gets to be the pilot for that application. Those who are not interested, do not have to pay for the development or buy the application from the developing company until they are interested in updating that particular application.

As part of this issue is the question of project management: Who should run the project and what tools are available to help the project manager? On large projects of the type being developed by GCIDS, it might be advantageous to have "co-managers" for each project: a project manager from the user organization, and a project manager from the systems organization. Depending on the phase of development, one or other would be the project manager. During the feasibility study and the requirements definition phases, the user would have responsibility for project management. During the system design and implementation phases, the systems organization would be responsible. Since overall responsibility for developing systems is a responsibility of the information systems organization, their project manager would have ultimate responsibility for the success or failure of the project. It would be his responsibility to work closely with the user project manager to ensure the project's success. If this working relationship was not possible, one or other, or both, should be replaced.

GCIDS tried a new and innovative approach to developing common business systems. Their problem was deciding on how these new systems were to be designed and built, what tools would be used and who would use them. "Tools" would include languages, development methodologies, structured techniques and processes used in developing systems. For example, COBOL, structured diagrams, strategic systems planning, are all examples of current systems development tools. GCIDS used tools that were common to systems development in the 1960s—classical systems life cycles, common file maintenance routines, report generators. What they needed were tools that could be integrated across the system development process. An example would be the Systems Development Tools Portfolio developed at the Bank of America and shown in Figure 5-1.

Tools in the portfolio are partitioned into three levels: strategic level tools, management level tools, and operational level tools. This partitioning, based on R. N. Anthony's classic business organization model[1] is particularly appropriate since an important motive for employing the systems development portfolio of tools

1. Anthony, R.N., *Planning and Control Systems: A Framework for Analysis,* Harvard University Press, 1981.

FIGURE 5-1   SYSTEM DEVELOPMENT TOOLS PORTFOLIO

Operational Level Tools

Item	Phase
Cost/Benefit	Feasibility
Structured analysis (context)	Feasibility
Structured analysis	
Functional specifications	
Language	
Automated tools	Analysis
Word processing	
Data dictionary	
Data modeling	
Walk-throughs	
Security	
Design documentation	
Structured design	
Language	
Automated tools	Design
Configuration	
Data dictionary	
Prototyping	
Walk-throughs	
Interactive programming	
Program documentation	
Quality assurance	
Structured programming	Programming
Procedural language	
Nonprocedural language	
Code inspection	
Unit test	
Integrated tests	
Test kits	
Modeling	Testing
Test generators	
Quality assurance	
Planning preparation	
Change control	
Education	Implementation and enhancement
Communication	
Quality assurance	

Management Level Tools

Item	Category
Security	
Budgeting	
Methodology	
Estimating	Project management
Risk assessment	
Project tracking	
Project accounting	
Data stds admin	
Logical DB admin	Information resource administration
Data dictionary	
Database management systems	
Physical DB admin	Database administration
Tuning	
Documentation	
Global data modeling	
Practices	
Audit	Standards administration
Data	
Change management	
Documentation	Quality assurance
Technical	
Testing proc audit	
Performance plan	
Career development	
Performance appraisal	Human resource management
Salary administration	
Skill assessment	
Additions	
Post mortem	Service queue management
Prioritization	
Reporting	

Strategic Level Tools

Systems
Capacity
Info resources
Organization
Human resource
Planning
Steering committee
Architecture

Reprinted by Permission of *Datamation*® Magazine. ©Copyright Technical Publishing Co., A Dun & Bradstreet Co., Aug. 15, 1984. All rights reserved.

is the promotion of the management of systems development activities like any other business activity.

Strategic level tools are used to plan for systems development. They tend to be long term in focus, address issues on a broad scale, and consolidate many detailed variables such as human, financial, and technological resources. These tools are used to set the organization's systems development direction. Strategic systems planning, human resource planning, and steering committees are examples of tools found at this level.

Management level tools help managers direct their resources in the direction established through the use of strategic level tools. Typical management tools noted are project-tracking techniques, performance review procedures, and setting project priorities.

At the operational level are tools used by those involved most closely in constructing a system. During each phase of a typical systems life cycle, several tools are available to the systems professional. Historically, tool development at this level has received the most attention. Structured design, walk-throughs, and higher-level languages are examples of systems development tools at this level.

Using these tools requires that an organization think through its mission, objectives and goals, and then develop an information resource plan as well as the techniques and structure for meeting corporate goals. Had GCIDS done this, it would have found that each telephone company had different objectives and goals depending on its stage of development and its market environment. They had different priorities, different management orientations. They would have discovered before starting the major business projects that these requirements would render the task of designing common systems difficult, if not impossible, to achieve.

ORGANIZING, MANAGING, AND EXECUTING MAJOR PROJECTS

In addition to the individual selected to manage each phase of the development effort, successful projects depend on three things:

- A project team that possesses the skills to develop the system.
- A manager or management team that can integrate these skills.
- A development methodology for implementing the project.

Perhaps the most important of the three ingredients is following a proven methodology for implementation. Without it, we are dependent on the experience and work habits of each individual working on the project and we go back to the cottage industry method of crafting systems. A systems development methodology should address the following questions:

- What should be done in developing a system?
- Who should do it?

- How should the work be done?
- When should the work be done?
- How should the results be documented?

To put it another way, the systems development methodology should provide the project manager with the tools and techniques to plan, execute, report, and evaluate the development effort. The methodology should describe the work required from the time systems needs are identified to the time the system is retired. By focusing on "what" work must be performed during the systems development process rather than on "how" it is done, a stable environment is defined. Technological changes can be incorporated into the process by simply redefining how certain tasks within the life cycle of a system are to be performed. Each phase of a well-conceived systems life cycle includes all of the tasks needed to plan the subsequent phase, to provide management with the necessary information to evaluate the system at its present phase, and to approve proceeding to the next phase. Proper definition of the phases can forestall inadequate and premature estimates that can result in schedule overruns. A systems development life cycle helps management sequence work properly, ensures the effective use of people and assists in promptly identifying progress problems.

A typical system life cycle might have the following phases: strategic planning, information planning, preliminary systems design, systems installation, and production systems support. The planning charts shown in the following figures graphically portray the interrelationship of each phase in the life cycle and the major work steps within each phase:

- Overall approach (Figure 5-2)
- Strategic planning (Figure 5-3)
- Information planning (Figure 5-4)
- Preliminary systems design (Figure 5-5)
- Systems installation (Figure 5-6)
- Production systems support (Figure 5-7)
- Overview chart of the complete systems development life cycle showing key management checkpoints, quality assurance review checkpoints, and primary deliverables of each phase (Figure 5-8).

Strategic Planning

Strategic planning helps management to determine where the organization ought to be in three to ten years, to identify the resources it needs to get there, and to preview the mix of products or services at the end of the planning horizon. As the starting point in the management planning and control process, strategic planning provides the foundation for the development of systems to support the implementation of strategy. Strategic planning lends itself to a structured approach to setting objectives and developing strategies. The planning chart for strategic planning illustrates the comprehensive nature of the process (see Figure 5-3). As an enterprise finalizes its basic strategic direction, it is in a position to identify the information required to monitor the implementation of strategy and control the organization.

Information Planning

The system requirements of most organizations are complex and far reaching. The implementation of all necessary systems will typically take many years and will involve a significant investment. An information-planning project ensures that the systems being developed will meet the long-term information requirements of the organization. Information planning also provides management with the ability to establish the priorities of systems projects (see Figure 5-4).

One step within the information-planning phase is the project definition and planning segment. This segment defines the work plan for the preliminary systems design phase for subsequent projects. During an information-planning project, only high-priority projects are planned to the project definition level. Subsequent projects are defined to this detail immediately before the preliminary systems design phase. This phase defines and sets priorities for future application areas. It also defines, on a preliminary basis, the facilities, personnel and organization required to implement them. The following are some of the problems that occur in the information-planning phase and some potential solutions.

FIGURE 5-2   **OVERALL APPROACH**

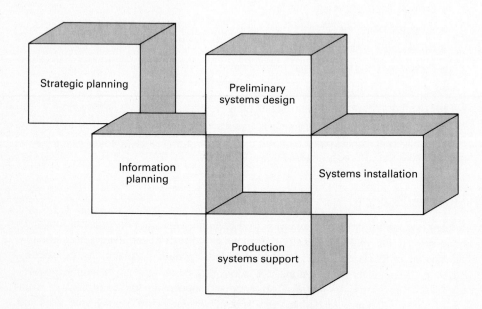

Source: Arthur Andersen & Company brochure, "Information Systems Planning Charts."

FIGURE 5-3   **STRATEGIC PLANNING**

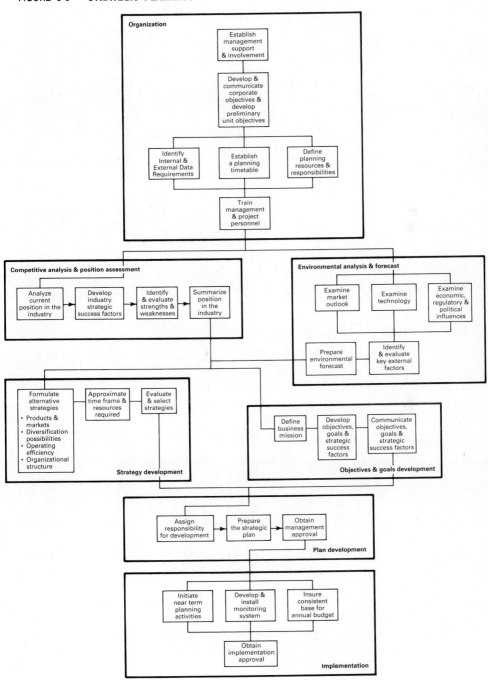

Source: Arthur Andersen & Company brochure, "Information Systems Planning Charts."

FIGURE 5-4   **INFORMATION PLANNING**

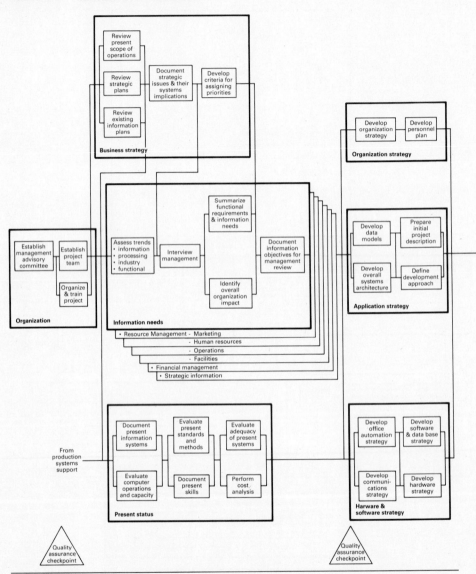

Problems:

■ Failure to relate the organization's business objectives to its information needs
■ Failure to recognize the management attention and emphasis necessary for the information systems organization to provide the required service
■ Lack of sufficient hardware capacity
■ Inability to meet processing schedules
■ Lack of project definition and scope.

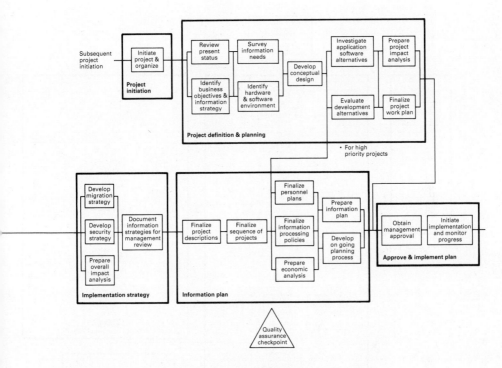

Source: Arthur Andersen & Company brochure, "Information Systems Planning Charts."

Solutions:

■ Determine current and future information requirements related to the strategic plans of the organization.

■ Evaluate current data-processing operations, systems, and organization.

■ Develop objectives for the organization's information systems department.

■ Develop overall systems strategy.

■ Develop strategies for hardware, software, and departmental organization.

■ Define each project in terms of scope, high-level systems concepts, overall project data model, work plan and estimated effort for the next phase, and approximations of costs and benefits.

Preliminary Systems Design

A preliminary systems design project comprises those steps necessary to establish systems features, functions, and priorities (see Figure 5-5). The work performed in this phase becomes the foundation for subsequent work during systems installation. Other names for this phase of work include: system specification phase, functional

FIGURE 5-5   PRELIMINARY SYSTEMS DESIGN

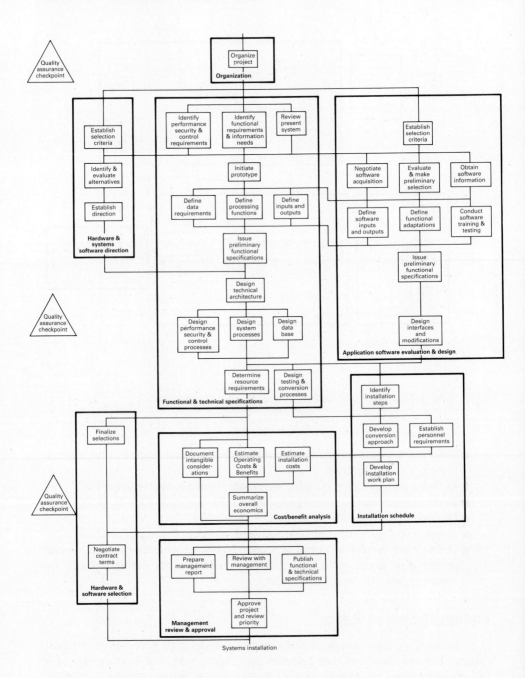

Source: Arthur Andersen & Company brochure, "Information Systems Planning Charts."

specification phase, or requirements definition phase. During this phase, analysts define the functional and technical design of the system in sufficient detail to ensure it will meet the users' needs. This work also provides an adequate basis to prepare realistic estimates of the effort, cost, and time-frame to implement the system.

A preliminary design will create the necessary information with the desired level of accuracy so that management, users, and information systems personnel can easily understand the major commitments required before beginning an installation. In this phase, management sets systems features, functions, and priorities, and the project team produces the information to support the major commitments an installation requires. The following are some of the problems and solutions in this phase.

Problems:

- Failure to understand fully how the system will work internally and from a user's viewpoint
- Failure of key management to agree on the capabilities of the system
- Failure to develop an accurate estimate of the cost of developing systems
- Failure to supply adequate personnel and hardware to install the system
- Unrealistic timetable for implementation of the system, resulting in missed target dates.

Solutions:

- Prepare a functional specifications report that includes a description of all systems functions, input and output descriptions, procedural flows, a listing of all data elements, performance criteria and security and control needs.
- Prepare a technical specifications report that defines the technical architecture, data base design (logical and physical), system processes, programs and modules, testing and conversion procedures, and hardware requirements.
- Prepare a management summary report that includes a summary of costs, resources required and benefits, summary installation plan, and recommended course of action.
- Obtain management approval and commitment for the system implementation.

Systems Installation

This phase of the systems life cycle requires the most significant effort. The systems installation phase involves the detailed design of the system, the installation of software, and the programming of the system (see Figure 5-6). In addition, the user must develop procedures to support the system, develop a conversion plan, test the system, check the results, and convert the system. The following are problems frequently encountered during this phase with their solutions.

Problems:

- Lack of accurate and reliable computer programs
- Failure to establish procedures necessary to implement and operate the system successfully
- Lack of documentation

FIGURE 5-6   **SYSTEMS INSTALLATION**

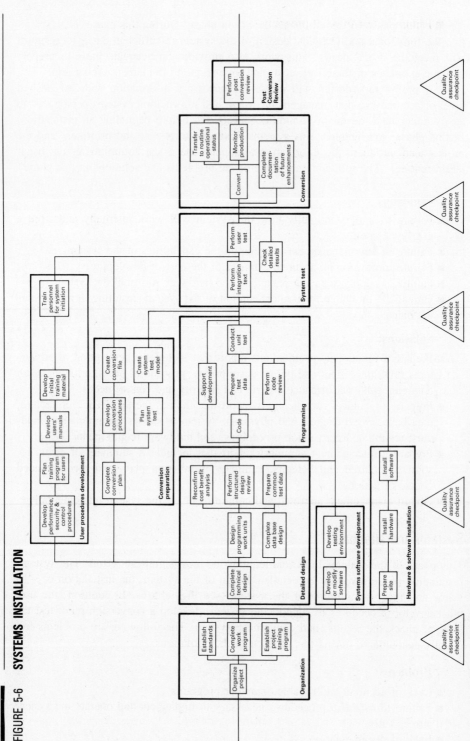

Source: Arthur Andersen & Company brochure, "Information Systems Planning Charts."

- Failure to test fully all programs
- Lack of trained personnel to operate the system.

Solutions:

- Develop programming specifications, including structure charts, module narratives, cross-references to logical and physical data base definitions, input form layouts, report layouts and screen layouts.
- Develop logically structured programs.
- Establish an appropriate environment for the system.
- Develop procedures manuals.
- Train user and operating personnel.
- Conduct comprehensive system tests and have users develop an acceptance test.
- Convert to fully operational systems.
- Develop documentation to support continuing system operations.

Production Systems Support

This phase begins after the acceptance of a system by its intended users and continues throughout its useful life. Proper support requires a project orientation for processing changes to a system and for periodic evaluations of accumulated changes to determine short- and long-term strategies for maintenance and replacement (see Figure 5-7). The following are typical problems arising during this phase with their solutions.

Problems:

- Significant portion of systems personnel are dedicated to system maintenance without apparent results to the organization.
- Failure to identify and control potential changes to computer programs and manual procedures
- Lack of management control over changes to the system
- Failure to document system changes.

Solutions:

- Implement an overall management control approach for this important function.
- Develop system modifications, including updated programming specifications and fully tested program changes. Train users in revised procedures.
- Prepare periodic status reports that include actual performance versus planned performance and an overall evaluation of the production system, considering such factors as user satisfaction and cost of operations.

Benefits of Structured Approach

There are many benefits to be gained from using a structured approach to controlling information systems projects. It enables management to relate the organization's objectives to its information needs. After assessing the effectiveness of information provided by its current systems and defining future needs, management can establish an overall strategy for hardware, software, and personnel. It can identify and set priorities for specific systems projects to meet its needs. This approach provides for

FIGURE 5-7   PRODUCTION SYSTEMS SUPPORT

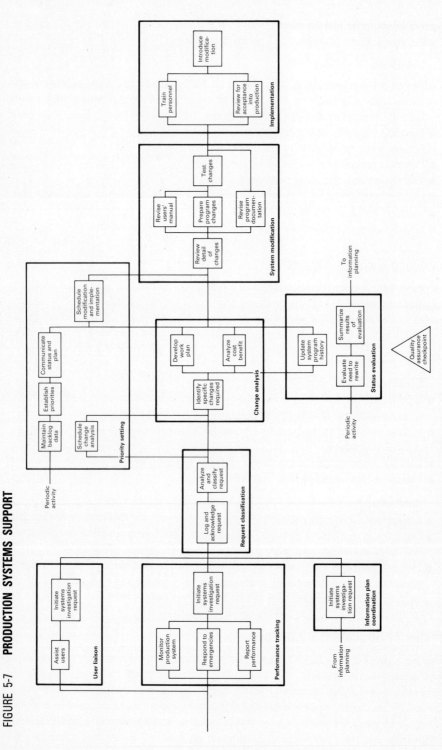

Source: Arthur Andersen & Company brochure, "Information Systems Planning Charts."

effective managerial involvement throughout the systems development life cycle (see Figure 5-8).

A structured approach not only identifies and documents what a system will do, it helps to ensure that all personnel responsible for using and operating the system understand and agree on how the system will work. It helps ensure that they understand what the installation effort and system operation will cost, the personnel and hardware resources required, and the timetable needed to implement the system.

During systems installation, this approach helps ensure the creation of accurate and reliable computer programs. Establishment of procedures for system operation, training of personnel in these procedures, and preparation of the necessary physical environment help make certain the effective implementation of systems.

The systems support function of a structured approach identifies potential changes to the system, computer programs, or procedures, and helps ensure that the organization properly and effectively implements these changes. Further, it provides management control over the cost, timetable, and sequence of changes in the systems. By assessing the quality of the structure and performance of the systems, it assists management in future information-planning activities.

A systems development methodology also helps an organization use people more effectively since it identifies work according to the skills required to perform particular tasks. Using this approach, an organization can gear its training to each specific task, providing a basis for developing a complete career development plan— from programmer trainee through senior project manager.

To be sure that we understand how a development methodology is used, let us look at Figure 5-4, the planning chart for "Information Planning." This phase of work is divided into 12 major segments as shown by the heavy lined boxes. Within each box are defined the specific tasks that have to be done. The positioning of the boxes shows the sequence for performing each segment. For example, the segments for developing an organization strategy, application strategy, and hardware and software strategy, can proceed concurrently, but cannot be started until the segment for defining information needs is completed. Similarly, within each segment, the tasks are shown in the sequence in which they are to be performed.

There are five tasks to perform in completing the "Information needs" segment:

- Assess the trends in information processing, the industry, and the functional area.
- Interview management.
- Summarize functional requirements and information needs.
- Identify overall organization impact.
- Document information objectives for management review.

These tasks are to be performed for each functional area—marketing, human resources, operations, finance, and development standards have been developed for each task. For example, if an analyst was given the assignment to: "assess the trends

FIGURE 5-8   **COMPLETE SYSTEMS DEVELOPMENT LIFE CYCLE**

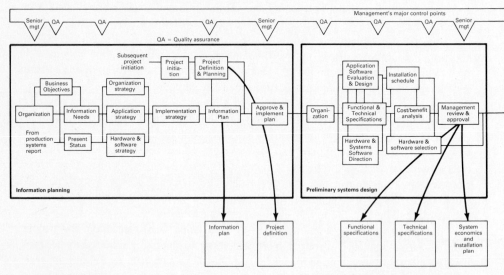

☐ Information Plan:
  ☐ Statement of current and future information requirements related to the strategic plans of the business or organization.
  ☐ Evaluation of current EDP operations, systems and organization.
  ☐ Strategic plan for the organization's EDP department.
  ☐ Overall systems development strategy
  ☐ Strategies for hardware, software and organization of EDP.
☐ Project Definition (each high priority project):
  ☐ Description of scope of project.
  ☐ High-level systems concepts.
  ☐ Overall project data model.
  ☐ Work plan and estimate of effort for next phase.
  ☐ Summary of costs and benefits.

☐ Functional Specifications Report:
  ☐ Description of all functions.
  ☐ Input and output descriptions.
  ☐ Procedural flows.
  ☐ Listing of all data elements.
  ☐ Performance criteria.
  ☐ Security and control needs.
☐ Technical Specifications Report:
  ☐ Technical architecture design.
  ☐ Data base design (logical and physical).
  ☐ System processes, programs and modules.
  ☐ Testing and conversion procedures.
  ☐ Resource requirements.
☐ Management Summary Report (System Economics and Installation Plan):
  ☐ System functional design overview.
  ☐ System technical design overview.
  ☐ Summary of resources and benefits.
  ☐ Summary installation plan.
  ☐ Recommended course of action.

Source: Arthur Andersen & Company brochure, "Information Systems Planning Charts."

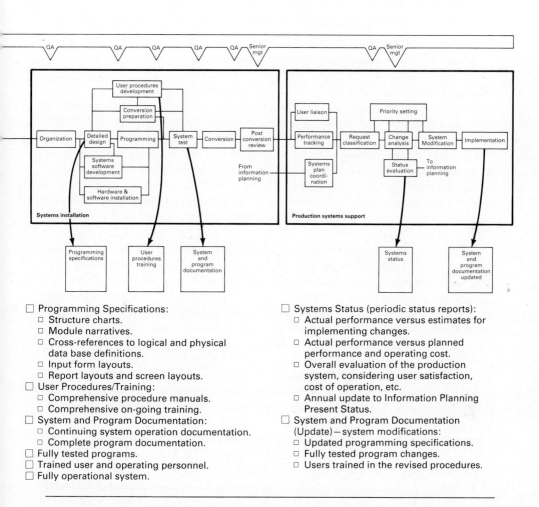

□ Programming Specifications:
  □ Structure charts.
  □ Module narratives.
  □ Cross-references to logical and physical
    data base definitions.
  □ Input form layouts.
  □ Report layouts and screen layouts.
□ User Procedures/Training:
  □ Comprehensive procedure manuals.
  □ Comprehensive on-going training.
□ System and Program Documentation:
  □ Continuing system operation documentation.
  □ Complete program documentation.
□ Fully tested programs.
□ Trained user and operating personnel.
□ Fully operational system.

□ Systems Status (periodic status reports):
  □ Actual performance versus estimates for
    implementing changes.
  □ Actual performance versus planned
    performance and operating cost.
  □ Overall evaluation of the production
    system, considering user satisfaction,
    cost of operation, etc.
  □ Annual update to Information Planning
    Present Status.
□ System and Program Documentation
  (Update) — system modifications:
  □ Updated programming specifications.
  □ Fully tested program changes.
  □ Users trained in the revised procedures.

in information processing, the industry, and the functional area,'' he could go to the
standard for this task and find the following:

■ The objective of the task: why it is necessary to perform this task?

■ How to perform this task: suggestions on reference material, sources of information, data-gathering techniques.

■ An estimate of how long this task should take: useful in estimating how long
this segment and phase of work should take.

- An indication of who should perform this task: analyst, user, or combination of the two.
- The requirement for successfully completing the task: the documentation required, format, forms to be collected.
- How to use the information collected in this task.

Thus one can see that for each task, the development standard is very comprehensive on how to successfully perform the task and pass the information collected on to subsequent tasks. Needless to say, preparing standards at this level of detail for each task in the system development process will result in a voluminous document. The Arthur Andersen methodology, Method/1, from which the examples used here have been taken, consists of seven volumes of documentation. Analysts are not expected to read the entire seven volumes. Instead, they refer to the planning charts to guide them in performing a phase or segment of work. If they want help on how to do it, they refer to the appropriate standard in the documentation, similar to looking something up in an encyclopedia.

Does having a methodology for system development guarantee that projects will always be developed on time and on budget? This is not necessarily the case since there are many installations with methodologies on their shelves, looking impressive but rarely referred to. Worse yet, many installations, in requiring that the methodology be followed, wind up following the documentation requirements and ignoring the substantive tasks of performing the work. At a major New York bank, hundreds of thousand of dollars were spent on a development methodology. Whenever a project was initiated, analysts went immediately to the documentation requirements to start working on the specification that was to be produced by that phase of work. The format of the output became the driving force, not the content of the report. They knew that approval came from having a specification produced exactly as specified in the standards. The content of the specification—whether it met user requirements, or whether it was technically feasible—was all secondary.

In summary, a systems development methodology is required to provide a proven, structured approach to developing systems. It replaces the artisan's approach of individual work habits, with proven methodologies. If used properly, it should reduce the number of projects that fail due to poor project management, poor estimates of the time and effort required, and the omission of key tasks that must be performed.

ASSIGNING PRIORITIES TO PROJECTS

The backlog of applications awaiting development is growing day by day. As new hardware providing more power at less cost comes on the market, users are starting to convert existing systems to new machinery and use new system software to improve throughput and efficiency. Problems arise when questions are raised such as: which system to convert by redesigning, which by straight conversion, and which new application to implement? How does an organization decide which information system gets top priority? The answers are not as easy as some might think.

Many executives will base priorities on "payback." Do an analysis of the payback period, they say, and implement the project that offers the quickest return on investment. Is the project offering the quickest return on investment the one that is most important for the business? Can it be implemented without first implementing a system software project that supplies the technology for operating the proposed project? Weight should be given to financial benefits, but other factors must be considered.

Another criterion might be to assign priorities by business objectives or the value of a system in meeting business goals, giving highest rank to those projects that further the goals of the business. Unfortunately, not all businesses have such clearly defined goals and objectives documented in a business plan. Moreover, most business plans identify objectives by business units or functional areas. How does one reconcile priorities among business units, especially in a multiline company? Does a corporate-wide financial information system rate higher priority than a marketing information system for the business unit that contributes most to the company's profit?

What about intangible benefits? There are many important benefits of a project that cannot be easily measured: better information for decision support, graphic presentations for better management understanding, improved operating systems to make applications more user-friendly. Rather than forcing all projects to be "benefits" justified, there are times when information projects can benefit the corporation in important but immeasurable ways. In fact, sometimes the intangible benefits outweigh the tangible ones.

Finally, some projects must have high priority assigned because of their technical importance. Management rarely understands why these projects are necessary. For example, after years of personal selling, the information systems manager of a large company finally got management to agree to converting to a data base system. He then tried to explain why additional funding should be granted to implement a relational data base rather than a hierarchical data base. Management lost all interest and the manager lost his project. What was an exciting and challenging concept to the manager was of no interest to top management. Had the manager sold management on how they could improve their profits or competitive position through a system that would provide them with better information for decision making, management would have sat up and listened. They would not have cared that the technique required for this was a relational data base. They would have approved whatever was needed to implement the project. As a result, smart information managers must sometimes obscure the main issue by creatively combining projects into a single, saleable package or by assigning resources to the technically important projects without higher management knowledge.

Complicating the issue is the question of who should set the priorities? Many large installations set priorities by submitting the project request to a steering committee which makes the decision. Since the steering committee is composed of representatives from all major functional areas, the decision usually becomes a political one, with one person supporting another in return for "future considerations". Moreover, arguments may be heated and the spirit of cooperation that the information system manager is trying to foster may be destroyed.

Another technique is to let the users set the priorities. Information systems management takes the attitude that the users have been presented with the projects. They know the requirements, feasibility studies have been performed, and they know the cost/benefits. It is up to them to fight it out and set the priorities among themselves. Unfortunately this approach always leads to two things: the losers will be so upset that they will find other ways to get their projects implemented, either by hiring consultants or by using microprocessors, or a service bureau. Or, they will bring the issue to top management to force a resolution in their favor. In this case, management will get information systems involved by asking them, since they are the experts, which application should be given priority. Clearly a "no-win" situation for information systems.

The best way to set priorities is to make them a byproduct of some formal planning process at the corporate level. During the annual planning exercise, corporate goals and strategies are established. The information needed to meet the goals and execute the strategies is also defined. Specific projects to provide the information can then be determined and priorities set for these projects after considering all the other projects included in the information systems department's development plan. Realistically, in most organizations the information systems manager must take the most active role in establishing priorities. He or she must try to reconcile conflicts between users in establishing selection criteria. Clearly, the decision must be based on more than just financial benefits. It is the task of the information systems manager to involve the people with the broad perspective in the decision-making process so that proper priorities are assigned.

Companies that have well-organized and well-managed information systems departments, operating with proven systems methodologies, will have little trouble setting priorities. More common are companies whose information systems are near chaos. Martin Buss, the director of planning for Philip Morris International, suggests the following steps for these companies.[2]

Step 1. Get Control of Data Processing

When a formal priority-setting process has not been adopted, a number of problems will probably already exist. One may well find individual staff members fixing priorities, a "them-against-us" syndrome, poor communications with users, and unilateral action by data-processing managers. Clearly, in such a situation, no approach can be effective. The newly appointed information-processing manager must first gain control by taking one or more of the following actions: establishing improved mechanisms for interacting with users, reorganizing data processing and hiring new staff,

2. Buss, Martin, "How to Rank Computer Projects," *Harvard Business Review,* Jan.-Feb., 1983.

creating some sort of computer-steering committee, and improving the information base for the outstanding projects.

Step 2. Document Systematically

Part of the problem in sorting out priorities stems from inadequate documentation of project requests. There may be several deficiencies: an outdated approach, randomness in the way projects are documented, deficient authorization procedures, or poor communication about projects within the information systems department and/or between users and management. As a result, the information systems manager may not have the necessary facts to evaluate and rank projects.

Proper documentation requires establishing the data required for various classes of projects such as data processing and office automation. Complete uniformity across all projects is unlikely because organizations will be at different stages in their use of technology. Managers may have to estimate data for some projects (prototypes, for example), while having a more solid base for accurately calculating costs for others. Some flexibility will, therefore, be essential. In addition, companies should develop standard procedures by which projects are identified and submitted for approval—allowing for different classes of projects—and convert informal outstanding project requests to the new procedures and standardized formats. Planners should describe not only the tangible benefits but also the intangibles, the fit with objectives, and the technical importance of each project. Management must insist that the new procedures for all projects be followed.

Step 3. Clarify Business Objectives

In an environment where business objectives may not be clearly stated, the information systems manager should take the initiative and attempt to state the business objectives personally for review by senior management. The purpose of this exercise is to place information systems projects in their proper business context. The information systems manager is looking for guidance on what the organization is trying to achieve and the nature of the key constraints. In looking at the first, he will want management views on such goals as increasing market penetration, reducing operating costs, expanding internationally, and accelerating product development. In looking into the constraints, such questions as time horizons, resources, and possible competitive responses will be important.

The best way to proceed is to combine judicious interviewing of business managers, division heads, territory managers, and others with a careful reading of internal documents and a quick review of the information processing of key competitors. The most critical element here is the interviewing of the decision makers. Although opinions will differ among the decision makers, they will almost certainly agree on the top three or four objectives. The information systems manager can build on these through discussions and review meetings with an appropriate high-level management group such as an operating or management committee, a policy committee or computer-steering committee. The result will be a consensus on the list of objectives which, although not perfect, can later serve as a guide for evaluating and ranking the information-processing projects in terms of their fit with company aims in step 7.

Step 4. Rank Against Financial Costs and Benefits

The prerequisite for this step is the classic analysis of costs and benefits on a project-by-project basis. Since the results for each project will differ, the manager must calculate the numbers under a series of assumptions concerning in-house development, subcontract programming, purchased package, and so on. The aim is to arrive at the optimum balance among the various means of putting applications into operation, not just the cost of carrying out the projects internally.

The necessary level of detail will depend on such factors as corporate policy, time, and the availability of information. Sometimes the only practical course may be to make gross estimates. Once the costs and benefits are known, the manager can show their relative priority status on a matrix showing projects with the highest financial benefits and lowest investment needs, to those with low benefits and high investment needs. Some may argue that this ranking is unfair since the major replacement projects, for example replacing the accounts receivable system completed in 1958, would require high investment with low financial benefits. Perhaps this is the type of project where a package is more suitable than custom development. The ranking allows management to look at all projects under consideration and consider alternative ways of implementing them. Often management finds that it simply does not have enough staff to do anything other than the bare minimum. Its alternative is to add staff or delay the projects. In any case, the information systems manager is able to do his job without unwarranted pressure to perform the miracles he had previously been expected to produce.

Step 5. Rank Intangible Benefits

A team composed of users and technical personnel should attempt to determine the intangible benefits for each project and assign a numerical value to each project so that the intangible benefits can be ranked in order of importance. These intangibles could include such things as: quicker information retrieval, improved image, better decision making, ease of use. The numerical values can be added to a total point scheme for the project.

Step 6. Rank According to Technical Importance

Some projects must be completed before others. System software must be installed before applications can operate under the software system. Information systems personnel can rank each project based on its technical importance and identify those that must be completed before others can use the system.

Step 7. Assess Fit with Objectives

Once business objectives are clarified, users and information systems managers can assess the quality of fit between objectives and projects. It is also possible to develop a quantitative approach in which a project's contribution to an objective is indicated numerically, with a maximum score of 10, for example, for a perfect fit.

Step 8. Summarize Priorities

The last step is to summarize all projects for top management. Using a grid or matrix, management can see at a glance how each project stands based on the ranking criteria. Moreover, with the knowledge of how different factors can affect priorities, executives can change the degree of emphasis given to each one depending on corporate circumstances. In hard times, for example, they might decide that only tangible benefits should be considered.

In this process of setting computer priorities, success depends on the interaction of three groups of people, namely, high level executives, users, and information systems managers. Each has an important role to play. Executives at the top must demonstrate a willingness to commit resources to approved high-priority projects. They should participate in setting the priorities and, in particular, in determining which aspect of priority setting should be most important in any one time period. They should also help clarify the business objectives so that the whole process can be related to the underlying needs of the company. Finally, they must be willing to exercise judgment and make decisions in areas that have not traditionally involved top management. The role of users is to commit themselves to the benefits stated in the cost and benefit analysis of each project and to involve themselves in the process so that the final decisions reflect a consensus. Particularly important here is an understanding of, and a commitment to, the intangible benefits. Information systems managers must lead the project and be responsible for its progress (see Figure 5-9). They must analyze the issues and develop the framework for setting priorities, then help top executives in decision making. As analytical and programming resources get scarcer and more costly, they have to be used more effectively by being allocated to high-priority projects. Identifying these by a structured approach will help the information systems manager and top executives think through the issues.

BREAKING THE SYSTEMS DEVELOPMENT BOTTLENECK

As indicated earlier, the list of projects awaiting development is getting longer by the day. A three-to-five year wait is not uncommon. This means that projects are waiting in line for two to four years, with the development taking one to two years. Furthermore, once development is initiated, 75 percent of the total cost is spent in defining requirements and developing functional and technical specifications. The power of programming languages and programming aids have reduced the coding and testing effort significantly. Nevertheless, something has to be done to break the systems development bottleneck.

Once user requirements have been fully identified and documented in functional specifications, many companies have turned to alternative strategies for systems development that modify the traditional approach specified in existing methodologies. Three such strategies include: application software packages, prototyping, and user-developed systems.

Application Software Packages

The idea behind the application of package systems is to enable companies to leverage the manpower expended in systems development by using the same software at several installations. It is exactly the concept employed by GCI in starting its Data Services organization. In fact, GCI was attempting to develop their own application software packages for use at all 25 telephone companies. Since the definition and design phases of the development effort involve a fixed cost that often exceeds 75

FIGURE 5-9   **STRATEGIES FOR SATISFYING INFORMATION NEEDS**

A. Internal MIS Development	B. Purchasing Outside Resources	C. End User Computing
Traditional Life Cycle Initial investigation Feasibility study/general design Detail design/prototype Implementation/prototype	**Contract Programming** Special skills Supplement corporate staff One-time requirements	**Ad Hoc Retrieval/Decision Support** Batch reporting On-line retrieval Simulation/modeling Data analysis Graphics
Prototyping Develop system without life-cycle approach Similar to research and development	**Time-sharing Network** Special software tools Immediate access Variety of packages	**Independent Systems** Data entry/gathering Department subsystems Production jobs
Purchased Appl. Software Follows traditional life cycle but detail design and programming are minimized	**Turnkey Systems** Integrated hardware and software package for specific purpose	**Personal Computing** Spreadsheets Communications Applications Files/list processing Word processing Graphics
Information Center Write ad hoc requests Consult Develop small systems		**Office Systems** Word processors Clustered systems Electronic mail Teleconferencing

percent of the total cost, this cost can be reduced by spreading it over many installations. The resulting economies of scale may reduce the unit cost of development to a small fraction of what it would have been had the system been custom built for a single user.

The growth of the industry supplying application software demonstrates the effectiveness of this strategy. The industry reached $100 billion in sales in 1985. Experts predict that companies in this industry will sell more than a million application software packages in the next 10 years. Today, there are application software packages for most common applications such as payroll, accounts payable, accounts receivable, general ledger, financial reporting, order entry, and billing. In addition, there are many more packages for data management, graphics, electronic spreadsheet, word processing, statistical computation, modeling, and manufacturing (see Figure 5-10).

Deciding whether to install an application software package is like the traditional make-or-buy decision. In most cases, the package will not fit the requirements perfectly. Management must trade off the cost of modifying the software against the cost of changing the existing procedures and/or organization to fit the package. When compared with the cost of custom development, modifying a software package and changing the existing practices and procedures to fit the system is a small inconvenience for the company to pay. The result is an up-to-date application which the user can use almost immediately. Most people in systems development predict that replacement of existing accounting and financial information systems will be by packages rather than by custom coding.

Prototyping

There are instances where a package implementation is not appropriate or even possible. This is particularly true when users' needs have not been, or cannot be, specified precisely. Prototyping is another innovative systems development strategy that is useful in such situations. The prototype approach to systems development exploits the advances in computer technology itself, through powerful high-level software tools made practical by inexpensive hardware. These technologies allow the designer to build "quick and dirty" systems in response to users' perceived needs. The systems are then refined and modified as they are used, in a continuous process, until the fit between user and system is acceptable. Since prototyping is an iterative process, the better defined the user requirements, the less time needed to refine the system. The key step in prototyping is to quickly develop a working model of the system, usually within a few days. Using tools such as time-sharing systems, data base management systems, high-level query languages, generalized report writers, and a library of other application software, the designer can put a basic system into users' hands quickly so that the process of refinement can begin. As users start using the system, they will still want changes made. The designer, working with the end user, will alter the system accordingly. Again, the emphasis is on fast response to requests for changes using the same high-level hardware and software tools.

As an example, the query language capability of many data base management systems can produce, within hours, data retrieval and reporting systems that would

FIGURE 5-10   Examples of Available Application Packages

Accounting	general
	banking
	tax
	trust

Accounts payable

Accounts receivable

Airplane reservation

Application development aids

Architecture

Banking systems

Bond and stock management

Bill of material processing

Check processing

Commercial loans

Computer-aided instruction

Computer-aided design

Computer management aids

| Construction | job costing |
| | accounting |

Conversion aids

Correspondence control system

Customer information file

Data base management systems

Data management systems

Demand deposits

Distributions systems

Document and text processing

Education

Engineering	electrical
	mechanical
	space

Financial	general
	control and planning
	management

Forecasting and modeling

General ledger

Graphics

Government	local
	federal
	state

Health care insurance

| Hospital | administration |
| | accounting |

| Hotel | reservations |
| | accounting |

Information storage and retrieval

Installment loans

| Insurance | general |
| | accounting and billing |

Job accounting

Job costing

Job performance measurement systems

Letter writing and mailing systems

Liability insurance

Library systems

Life and health

Loans	commerical
	installment
	international
	mortgage

Mailing and correspondence lists

Management sciences

Manufacturing

Modeling

Mortgage and loans

Order entry

Payroll–general

Performance measurement

Personnel systems

Petroleum industry

Production control

Preprocessors–computer language

Project control and planning

Property and liability insurance

Process control

Query languages

Real estate management

Remote job entry

Report generators

Resource management

Route scheduling

Sales and distribution

Savings systems

Scientific

Securities management

Statistical and modeling

Stock portfolio management

Tax accounting

Teleprocessing systems

Text and document editors

Time deposit accounting

Trust accounting

Utilities accounting

Word processing systems

take months to custom program. However, the cost of the data management system can exceed $100,000 and require a large scale computer system for processing. Moreover, the prototype approach largely ignores operating costs by concentrating on programming productivity. The system developed using the prototype approach will consume significantly more hardware resources than the same system developed traditionally using COBOL as a programming language, for example. However, it is becoming increasingly apparent that the trade-off between speed in development and operating efficiency is a profitable one. A number of companies have reported that the total systems development costs by the prototype approach are usually less than 25 percent of the costs with the traditional approach. These companies find that prototype systems will generally provide useful results faster than those that are traditionally developed. Furthermore, the systems that come out of an iterative design cycle in which users are involved are usually better received than those that derive from extensive, though one-time, design procedures.

The prototype approach stresses the importance of building a system quickly, and changing it quickly and easily. The way this is done runs counter to all our training to develop systems by carefully defining requirements, preparing specifications, and performing a detailed design before programming. We have always pointed to systems that have failed because programming was started before the requirements were finalized and documented in a set of user-approved specifications. The approach of development through experimentation is possible only because of the advances in software and the dramatic drop in the cost of hardware. The prototype approach is based on the assumption that, given a choice of possibly wasting either hardware resources or skilled manpower, one should waste the hardware. A manager steeped in the culture of managing large, expensive computer installations for operating efficiency may find this attitude difficult to adopt. Hardware costs have always been the most easily captured and controlled. The prototype systems development strategy is based on expending dollars on hardware in order to get the most from the people doing the development. With the current situation where the cost of developing an application is no longer hardware-bound but limited only by people and time, the prototype approach is well worth considering.

With prototyping and the use of application software packages, the assumption is that the information systems department will provide people to help the user select the package and make the necessary modifications, or that the department will work with the user in developing a prototype system. To avoid the delays inherent in using the scarce resources of an information systems department, one must consider strategies that eliminate the professional staff—that is, user developed systems.

DEVELOPING SYSTEMS BY END USERS

Systems departments cannot keep up with user demands for their services. Recently, end user computing environments have been touted as the way to cut through the applications logjam. An end user computing environment is one where the ultimate users of the system develop and program the system themselves, without the help of the systems department. Because of the increasing popularity of personal computers, more and more end users are finding themselves in a computing environment. Some companies think that this will lead to complete chaos, with noncompatible files all over the place, the loss of credibility for data collected by different departments, and a loss of control over information as a corporate resource. Others think that user developed systems will be the way to go in the future. They identify the following benefits:

- The ability to begin work on a system when it suits the users rather than waiting for the information systems department to free up time to help them.
- Development time will be reduced, especially for the definition of requirements and the logical design steps. Users know their requirements and do not have to explain it to systems personnel.
- More satisfaction with the end product.

There are several factors which must be present if end user development is to be successful. These factors include the following:

Relevant User Training

Walk into any end user environment and you will find a complete mix of experience, ranging from those from the shop floor to those with MBAs. They are likely to have equally varied levels of knowledge about computers. Training is needed to build a common foundation of knowledge among these users. They must be trained not only in the tools of the end user environment but also in computer fundamentals and the rudiments of system development. The objective is not to make systems analysts or programmers out of them but to provide the basic background in computers and systems so that they can work effectively on their computers. They can also learn this through experience and trial and error, as most people have done with their personal computers. However, from a corporate viewpoint, the time spent in a classroom will eliminate the loss time spent experimenting behind their desks. It is also essential to remember that for the end users, the computer is a tool, not a career. Interest in the machine lasts only as long as it assists them in their work. The courses should stress the things that will help them in their daily work.

Coaching

Even with basic training on computers and systems, there will be instances where users will need some coaching. For example, users might not be able to sign on by themselves because the terminals they used in class were already on. Another example is of a person who wastes a weekend trying to figure out how to store results temporarily while bringing in data from another file. To prevent these problems from happening, people variously called coaches, consultants, or advisors are needed. They are essential to a successful end user computing environment.

Evolutionary Development of Systems

End user systems tend to evolve through many versions. In a sense, they are proto-type systems developed on microprocessors. Quite often such developments are difficult for the traditional data processor to accept because it means users will not know their requirements until they see the system. This seems contradictory but can, in fact, be resolved through iterative development of different system versions. The emphasis changes from "What do you want to do with the data?" to "What data do you want?" It is reasonable to expect an answer from the first question, but management cannot answer the second without seeing the data. Since systems are being developed on an iterative basis, it is important that users see results and get a sense of accomplishment during the iterations. If all they are doing is running the same cycle over and over, they will get discouraged and give up. This means that end users must be involved, committed users. This commitment is particularly key to evolutionary development since early versions of the system may be rather rough and may suffer from such problems as program aborts, data exceptions, and logic flaws. In this phase, users must see progress toward a desirable system or their efforts will cease. This is also where the availability of a good coach will help immensely.

Appropriate Data Delivery Systems

In a successful multiple end user environment, expect a proliferation of end user data stores, along with the problems of synchronization and coordination with the original data source. A typical architecture defined for an end user environment consists of iteratively developed software, normally using a fourth-generation language. The system uses an end user data store usually developed for the specifics of the end user system; that is, one end user data store serves only one or a few end user systems.

The end user data store is maintained by a data delivery system. The data delivery system takes data external to the data store and puts it into a suitable format. Depending upon the tool, there may be a vendor supplied product that loads the data into the data store. Most systems have more than one data delivery system. The data source is external—it may be a transaction system, a corporate data base, or data supplied through an outside service. Given the wide range of possible sources, a data delivery system will probably be designed and implemented for each data source.

The data delivery system is one of the most complex components of an end user environment. It must handle all the typical problems of a transaction system such as data validation, extraction, reformatting, in a typically high-volume situation. In addition, it must address the question of synchronizing the end user data store and the data source. This alone can be very difficult when adjustments are made to the data source. A well-designed data delivery system is important to a reliable end user data store and, in the long run, to the viability of the end user environment.

Effective Use of Fourth-Generation Software Tools

Fourth-generation tools are prevalent in end user environments. They provide large productivity gains when requirements conform to the design assumptions of the product. They also provide productivity disasters when the data and architecture assumptions are ignored or misunderstood by end users and their coaches. These tools include such facilities as: non-procedural languages, interactive query facilities, report generators, screen formatters, graphics, statistical packages, financial packages, programming interfaces, data dictionaries, and security and backup routines. In using fourth-generation software tools, the important thing to remember is to fit the design into the capabilities of the tool. This means that instead of doing a data design, analysts should understand the fourth-generation language's underlying data design assumptions and fit their requirements into this design. In traditional systems development, the objective was to define requirements first, then find a language that met the requirements. Using fourth-generation tools, the aim is to understand the capabilities of the tool, then develop requirements around the effective use of that tool.

There has been enough experience with end user computing to know that there are no general solutions to all the problems. End user computing is one more way to get information to the people who need it. When considered with application packages and prototyping, end user computing provides another option for management to break the systems development bottleneck.

SELECTING A DEVELOPMENT STRATEGY

Given the fact that there are more applications awaiting development than there are resources to develop these projects, management is faced with selecting a development strategy that maximizes their return in their information systems. In the past, everything was custom developed (see Figure 5-11). While there were software packages available, two reasons were given for not using them: (1) we are unique and no package solution can meet all of our requirements, and (2) packages are too inefficient from an operating standpoint; we need efficient packages so that hardware resources are not wasted. Neither argument is valid today. Few applications are so unique that they must be custom tailored. If a software package is available, chances are that modifying the package will be faster and less costly than custom development. Second, hardware costs have fallen so dramatically that the argument for efficient coding has less validity than in the past. Furthermore, if these people really believed in efficient operations, all their programs would be coded in assembler language rather than in compiler languages to eliminate the inherent inefficiencies of a high-level language.

The following are some of the ground rules that might be followed in developing a development strategy:

1. Use application software packages whenever possible. This is based on the principle of not reinventing the wheel. Packages offer the benefits of quick installation, good documentation, user-training aids, and vendor support. A package, even with extensive modifications, will usually cost less than a custom system. Even if company practices have to change to obtain a perfect fit

with the package, it may well be worthwhile to make the changes so that the investment in custom design can be avoided. If the problem is truly unique, or the company's requirements dictate a unique approach to solving it, some sort of in-house development may be indicated.

2. If a package approach is not suitable, the next step is to identify the importance and impact of the proposed system. In other words, how important is this system to the company? Too often management equates importance with custom development. A passenger reservation system is certainly important to an airline; an order entry system is important to a distributor, yet both would probably use a software package rather than custom develop these applications. Management should rank by importance those applications where a package solution is not feasible: a sales compensation system based on differing commission levels and bonuses, a customer inquiry system accessing various records in the corporate data base, for example. The number of users should also be identified. Are these important applications to be used on a companywide basis or are they for a few users? Finally, are the requirements for the system clearly defined? Do the users know what they want? In-house development can then be considered for those unique applications that are important to the business of the company, are to be used by many users, and have clearly defined requirements.

3. Obviously anyone who submits a request for system development will consider the proposed application to be an important one. If it is to be used by just a few people, an engineering application for example, or if the requirements are

FIGURE 5-11   **TRADITIONAL SYSTEMS DEVELOPMENT MODEL**

Stage	Phase
Definition	Feasibility assessment
	Information analysis
Physical design	System design
	Program development
	Procedure development
Implementation	Conversion
	Operation and maintenance
	Postaudit

not clearly defined, a planning model for example, then the company should consider the prototype approach.

4. Finally, there are those applications that are required to help one person, for example a product manager wants some unique manipulation of data to display sales information graphically. These applications can be done through user developed systems, if the user is willing to commit time and effort to learning and using the computer.

In summary, managing information resources will become much more important to management than in the past. Information systems management must change their orientation from providing all computer services, including systems development and programming, to working with users in developing their own systems through prototyping or through the use of fourth-generation software (see Figures 5-12 and 5-13). By sharing the workload with the users, information systems will find that they have more time to install the sophisticated operating systems, system soft-

FIGURE 5-12   **PROTOTYPE MODEL FOR SYSTEMS DEVELOPMENT**

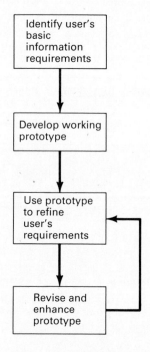

Source: Reprinted by permission of the *Harvard Business Review*. An exhibit from "Breaking the Systems Development Bottleneck" by Lee L. Gremillion and Philip Pyburn (March/April 1983). Copyright© by the President and Fellows of Harvard College; all right reserved.

ware, and data management systems, required to provide the users with an environment that can support both the traditional systems development methods and the more advanced techniques of prototyping and end user computing. Through a combination of all three strategies, the corporation will at last begin to reduce the backlog of applications awaiting development and start to manage its information resources more effectively.

PROFESSIONAL APPLICATION COMMENT: SYSTEM DEVELOPMENT STRATEGY AT GCI DATA SERVICES

To regain control of the Business Information Systems projects at GCIDS, Don Gault had to initiate some action that did not sit well with management and analysts. About the only thing that was completed was the definition of requirements in each of the functional areas. Although all telephone companies had not signed off on the functional specifications, the discussions with each company had solidified the requirements to the point where each company knew in precise detail what features were essential and which could be deferred for each application. Don had the companies rank the features by priority for implementation, noting those features that were essential to the system. Using the priority lists, a composite was developed for each application. Don then asked the systems group to match the composite features list with available application software packages to determine fit. Although everyone told Don that it would be impossible to use an application package because no single

FIGURE 5-13 **SELECTING A DEVELOPMENT METHOD**

Properties of a project			Suggested method
Commonality	Impact	Structure	
Common	Broad	High	Package
Uncommon	Broad	High	Traditional
Uncommon	Broad	Low	Prototype
Common	Limited	High	Package
Uncommon	Limited	High	User developed
Uncommon	Limited	Low	User developed

package met the requirements of all the telephone companies, Don found that packages in the payroll, personnel, and general accounting areas met 60 to 75 percent of all essential requirements.

Before deciding to use the packages, Don asked each company to identify the one application they would like to see implemented first at their company, or the most critical need at their company if more than one application was involved. He then asked the company if they would be willing to pay for the development of that application with the understanding that once the application was installed at their company, they could sell the application to other companies. The other companies would buy the application and pay for the modifications to be made by GCIDS. Moreover, by volunteering to develop the pilot application, the telephone company could select an application package and have it modified rather than incur the expense of custom development. To further entice the companies to fund the development of an initial application, the service company agreed to write off some of the development costs on the books of the participating company.

When the companies received this proposal from Don Gault, most volunteered to sponsor one application for development. Since this was much more than anticipated by Don, several projects had more than one sponsor, and they agreed to resolve differences in requirements. Packages were decided upon in the payroll, personnel, accounts receivable, accounts payable, general ledger, and financial reporting areas. The existing customer service system at one of the telephone companies was used as the core of an expanded customer service system, reducing the programming significantly. The other applications were unique to the telephone industry and were to be custom developed unless a phone company had an up-to-date system that could be modified to incorporate current technology.

Those who were looking forward to custom developing the latest state-of-the-art systems were disappointed, but could not argue with the logic of selecting packages and using a pilot company for modifying the package in light of their inability to produce systems in five years. Since the functional requirements were now a responsibility of the pilot company, all the user consultants were returned to their home company. The pilot company directed the effort to complete the functional specifications (working with their co-sponsors in some cases) and presented a set of priorities to GCIDS for implementation. If a package could provide more than 50 percent of the essential requirements, it was to be used as the basis for development.

A system development methodology was installed and all development work, whether custom developed or package modification was performed according to the development standards. All projects were implemented in releases, and no single release could take more than a year to develop and test. By the end of the first year, each telephone company had at least one system to convert and install. At this time, they discovered that the process of developing new user procedures and training personnel to use the new system was considerably more work than anticipated. In hindsight, they realized that they could never have implemented all the BIS systems as originally proposed even if GCIDS had met their original schedule. Equally impressive was the reaction of the companies to applications installed at other installations. Seeing the new systems operational and comparing these with the existing systems at their own companies gave incentive to purchasing these systems from the developing company and installing them at their own company with minimal modifications. It appeared that Don Gault's plan to accelerate systems development through extensive use of packages, and company sponsorship of custom projects worked well. With each company experiencing new systems and getting information they had not had before, Don took advantage of the momentum to suggest that the low-priority applications which applied to a few users in each company be developed through prototype or user developed systems. The engineering departments in the companies leaped at this suggestion and started to learn how to do prototyping and develop their own system. GCIDS sent out consultants to help these departments and found that they now had analysts located at each of the companies on a year-round basis. As the use of personal computers grew at these companies, the on-site consultants formed an information center organization that help users with their personal computers as well as with user developed systems.

Looking back at it now, Don was pleased that he could turn around the systems development effort by installing methodologies and procedures, and offering alternatives to custom development of all applications. For his effort, Don was rewarded by a promotion to the presidency of one of the telephone companies in the Midwest.

CHAPTER 5   DISCUSSION QUESTIONS

1. Joan Callahan at GCIDS was hoping for a chance to redesign all corporate information systems, a last chance to upgrade everything. Was she being realistic? Do systems last for 10 years without major changes? What time span is realistic when estimating the useful life of a system?

2. Upon encountering the situation at GCIDS, if you were Don Gault, what would you have done and why?

3. Comment on the concept of GCIDS. Did they try to do too much at once? They had ample user participation; why did it not work?

4. Define the responsibilities within a systems development project. Who should be the project director? How should a project be organized?

5. Where many applications are competing for development resources, how should priorities be assigned?

6. Does forcing designers, analysts and programmers to follow a system development methodology inhibit initiative and creativity? Do you think that a structured approach to design and implementation should be rigidly adhered to? Why?

7. Will prototyping be the way to design all systems in the future? If so, why the concern with development methodologies and structured techniques?

8. How does one decide whether to use a package, custom design, or use end user development techniques in meeting system requirements?

9. As the price of hardware falls and the major cost of system development is people, do you foresee the day when users develop their own systems and analysts and programmers are no longer needed, especially in view of the poor performance of analysts and programmers in the past?

6

PRODUCTION SYSTEMS SUPPORT

ISSUES

- Do information systems have a definite life span?

- How can system life be prolonged?

- What steps should be followed in the maintenance process?

- Programmers hate maintenance work—how can this problem be resolved?

- Factors to consider in replacing systems

CLAIMS ADJUSTERS, INC. (CAI)

Claims Adjusters, Inc., known throughout the insurance industry as CAI, offered a unique service: independent claims adjusting. For those companies that were self-insured, they offered their services on an annual contract basis. For example, several large car rental agencies and bus lines are self-insured. Should an accident happen to one of their vehicles, they would call on CAI to send an adjuster out to adjudicate the claims. Similarly, when insurance companies needed claims-adjusting services because they did not have an adjuster in that particular area, they would call on CAI for services and be billed on a time-and-material basis. When disasters struck, CAI adjusters would be mobilized to work for all the insurance companies with policy holders in the disaster area. To offer this comprehensive service, CAI had a staff of adjusters located through the U.S. and Canada working out of regional offices and their homes in the more remote areas.

CAI installed their first computer in 1967, and IBM 360/30 to do the accounting applications and management reporting. While automating these applications relieved the heavy manual workload in the accounting department, the applications did not address the heart of the business, namely keeping track of the location and individual workloads of agents, and client billing. Since CAI agents were located throughout North America, and traveled extensively to the site of accidents, it was essential that CAI keep track of their location and assignments so that as new requests for service came in from insurance companies, the closest agent be sent to settle the claim. It was this fast, efficient service that made it more desirable for insurance companies to use the services of CAI rather than maintain their own staff of adjusters. It was economically feasible for CAI because they served hundreds of insurance companies and could keep all their adjusters fully occupied at any point in time. Management had always wanted to have some type of computerized system to monitor the location of adjusters, their workload, and their schedule so that assignments could be made more efficiently. When several agents could be assigned to one job, an optimization model could be run to pick the best adjuster, based on travel, workload, billing rates, and experience.

Another top priority need of management was to have a unique billing system.

CAI's billings to some of the large insurance companies ran into the hundreds of thousands of dollars annually. These insurance companies wanted their invoices to contain unique information in specified formats. Some even went as far as to demand a specific number of copies of a certain color for their invoices. CAI tried to accommodate these large clients whenever possible by preparing their billings manually. Because of the complexity of the billing system, CAI always had a problem of unapplied cash, that is, checks from clients that could not be matched with the invoice being paid. While CAI could match it with the client account, they could not match it against the exact invoice or invoices the client was paying. Because of this, the next billing would remind the client of a past due invoice which the client had already paid. This led to ill-will and a client service problem. At one point, the unapplied cash amounted to over five million dollars.

In the early 1970s, the situation got to the point where CAI management decided that it had to automate the billing system and the agent assignment system, in that order. Moreover, they wanted both to be on-line so that queries could be made against the files to answer any customer questions or requests for service while the customer was on the phone. The IBM 360/30 could not drive the on-line system so an order was placed for the 370/145. Since both the agent location and billing systems were to be on-line simultaneously, the design and coding were quite complex and efficient code had to be generated to minimize file access and message response time. Both systems were coded in assembler language for optimum efficiency. The billing system provided complex generalized report formatters to design customer invoices in any style desired and translation routines to generate magnetic tapes in a code format compatible to their customer's computer system so that billing tapes could be sent directly from the CAI computer to the insurance company's computer system. These tapes were generated so that they could be fed directly into the customers accounts payable program, and they also provided the accounts payable department with an audit trail to ensure that they were not overbilled for services. Fourteen insurance companies participated in this program.

The agent location system allowed agents to call in their time and expenses, receive instructions for further assignments, and leave word as to where and how they could be reached. Since many agents would do this from their hotel rooms at night, CAI had automatic telephone answering and recording service 24 hours a day. During the day, the system would handle overflow calls so that agents would never get a busy signal. At night, the agent would leave his message and the time for the home office to call if they needed to talk to him. During office hours, these messages would be entered into the computer's on-line system. The system kept track of where all the agents were, their assignments and scheduled workload, and had an optimization model to send agents to the next job. In addition, time and expenses called in by the agents automatically generated a transaction for the payroll system. The time and expenses were checked against time standards for the type of adjusting work to make sure that they fell within normal limits. Area supervisors were notified when a particular agent consistently fell outside these limits or submitted expenses that were not reasonable.

The design of both the billing system and the agent location system was complex and pressed the state-of-the-art techniques. Management devoted a great deal of time to defining the requirements, including working with the major clients to design the billing tape interchange. Since CAI had a relatively small computer staff, most of the work was done by outside consultants assisted by IBM systems engineers. CAI made sure that it had one person involved in each application area so that they could form the nucleus of the department when the project was completed. Both systems were operational in 1977, having undergone a year of production testing. 1978 was spent fine-tuning the system, incorporating changes requested by the users during the 1976–77 test period. Also, a major emphasis was placed on updating all documentation in 1978 so that when the consultants and IBM left, CAI would have complete up-to-date documentation. By the end of 1978, both systems were running smoothly and all outside personnel had completed their work with the company. Needless to say, the cost of design and implementation, done primarily under contract with outside firms was expensive, over two million dollars in outside services alone. Management also recognized that neither the location system nor the billing system generated revenue for the company. It made the company more efficient in the field, gave them the ability to respond quickly to service requests with the closest adjuster, and eliminated problems in billings and unapplied cash. All of these improved service and reduced customer complaints, but it did not generate additional revenues directly. As management turned its attention to marketing, it hoped to amortize the cost of the computer system as quickly as possible and keep the costs of data processing to a minimum. One way of doing this was to reduce the information systems staff and put a moratorium on new systems development work. The company felt that since it had all the systems it needed for the immediate future, there would be no need to maintain a large data-processing staff. A few people to maintain the system should be adequate. Both the consultants and IBM tried to convince management that adequate staffing had to be maintained to make enhancements to the system, to handle changing requirements, and new user requests. Management's reply was that if the system was designed properly, there should be no difficulties in making any changes to it. The systems department was reduced to a manager and four analyst/programmers. Management felt that five people to maintain the system was unnecessary, but decided to go along with the consultants' recommendation that at least this minimum level be maintained until the workload indicated that a further reduction could take place without impact on system maintenance.

Sam Levine was one of the consultants' assembler language programmers on the implementation project. He was very good at programming, quickly grasped the logic of the application, and came up with some innovative ideas on how to handle some tricky technical points in the system. The people at CAI liked to work with Sam because he was always patient and had time to explain what he was doing to the client members of his team. While he was not the team leader, client people felt comfortable talking with Sam, he never made them feel stupid or inferior. As the project progressed, Sam became a natural leader and was promoted to manager, leading his part of the effort. He stayed on the project during its duration, and was instrumental in helping the user complete documentation of the system, especially the user interfaces and procedures on the billing modules. At the end of the project, Sam requested and was given a well-deserved one-month vacation.

When personnel in the information systems department found out that CAI planned to keep five people in the systems area and that they would be doing maintenance work on the installed system, most opted to look for more challenging work elsewhere. Because of their experience in the design and installation of some vary advanced systems, they had no problem finding work in the insurance industry. CAI management was hard pressed to find five people who were willing to stay. In 1978, experienced systems people who knew assembler language programming were very valuable in the New York City market and could get any job they wanted. All of the managers who worked on the project left, and management was left with four relatively junior people who were willing to stay and work on maintenance activities. CAI management knew that they had to convince someone experienced on the project to stay as the systems manager. The users suggested that they try to get Sam Levine from the consultants since they really liked him and thought he would make a good manager. Most importantly, Sam was involved with the system from the beginning and knew its more technical aspects, a factor that would be extremely valuable from a maintenance point of view. Sam had been out of college for five years, so he would not be commanding too high a salary for CAI. Management approached the consulting firm for permission to talk to Sam and permission was granted. (It should be noted that most consultants like to have "one of their own" located in the systems department of a client company where they know they would be considered on any future consulting assignment for that company.)

When Sam returned from his vacation, he found two items waiting for him. First, he found that his new assignment would be in the Midwest, working on the design of an on-line system for an electrical utility. The anticipated length of the assignment would be under a year, so he would be expected to commute between his home and his work, returning home every other weekend. This worried Sam because his wife was pregnant with their first child and Sam did not want to be away from home. It also started Sam thinking about his lifestyle working as a consultant, traveling to wherever the work was, and not being able to plan his home life. Sam tended to be a methodical, well-organized person and he was having second thoughts about the life of a consultant, especially the lack of family life.

The second item Sam found was a message to call CAI. Sam decided that before calling CAI, he would call his office first to see if anything happened to the system that he should know about. When he called, he got the message to come in and talk to his manager immediately. When Sam reported into his office, he found that most of his co-workers had left for the new assignment and that they wanted him to go as soon as possible, preferably that evening. This was upsetting to Sam since he had not even unpacked from his vacation trip. There were other things Sam wanted to do before going away for nine months, the main one being telling his wife about the new assignment. Sam had not told her yet because he did not want her upset until she had time to settle back down to a routine after the vacation. He told his manager that he would try to sort out his home life and make the trip as soon as possible but it could not be that evening, he thought that next week would be a more appropriate time. There was an argument over that, and Sam left the office a little upset. Instead of calling CAI, Sam decided to visit them and see if everything was all right.

When Sam arrived at CAI, he found everyone asking about his vacation, whether he had a good time, and how much they missed him. Certainly a different atmosphere than his own office. When he went to see the president, he got a terrific reception, and after a few minutes of talking about his vacation, the president explained his problem, the need for a manager to supervise the systems staff and maintain the system that Sam had helped install. The salary was 20 percent above what Sam was making with other benefits such as stock options and year-end bonuses that were not available working with a consulting firm. Most important to Sam, it would be a nine-to-five job, no travel, and a chance to spend time with his family. He rationalized that once you have seen one system, you have seen them all. The joy of consulting with its variety of assignments and travel did not seem as exciting as it did five years ago. Without hesitating, he told management he would accept.

The first year was not bad at all. Systems errors and abnormal aborts were few and far between. There were a few minor changes and enough work to keep his four people busy, but not overworked. The major changes were in formats for the billing tapes, since these had to be changed whenever the customer changed his accounts payable program. Maintaining this system kept one and a half persons busy full time. Sam found time to plan his evenings and weekends, could buy theater and concert tickets without worrying about missing the performances because he might be out of town. All in all, he thought he had made the right choice. Management was pleased that the system was running so well, and started to apply pressure on Sam to release one more analyst to keep costs at a minimum. Sam resisted these pressures because the older systems: payroll, payables, general ledger, regulatory reporting, all needed changes and enhancements and were demanding more and more maintenance time.

As time progressed, more and more changes were implemented on the system. These were necessitated by changes in the way the company did its business, changes in what the customers wanted, and changes in insurance regulations. Sam had difficulty hanging on to his people. Most of them found maintaining programs boring and not challenging. They soon left for more exciting work. Finding replacements who knew assembly language coding and were willing to work in a maintenance environment was impossible, especially at the pay scales offered by management. As a last alternative, Sam hired inexperienced programmers and trained them in assembly language coding. Understanding someone else's program written in COBOL of FORTRAN is difficult enough; to try to do it in assembler language, especially when the programmer is inexperienced, made it an impossible task. Changes were slow to make and took a long time to test and implement. Where efficiency was not critical to the system, Sam allowed the programmers to recode that part of the system in COBOL. By the end of the third year of production, the system became a mixture of assembly language and COBOL. The documentation was kept reasonably current, but because of the inexperience of the programmers, interface points between assembler coding and COBOL were not well documented. As more code was added to the system, response time started to degradate. It took longer and longer to find out what was wrong and even longer to make the changes and test the system. It had become almost impossible to keep up with changes to the billing tapes as customers changed and upgraded their computer systems. Six of the original fourteen companies participating in the billing tape program had dropped out because CAI could not modify their programs to provide the company with a new format for their system. CAI management was not happy about that but felt that it was not worth the expense of hiring more people to make the necessary changes. Since the billing system had to provide invoices for those companies that had dropped out of the tape system, additional modules had to be coded to produce the invoices for the six companies. Needless to say, all of them wanted their invoices in a unique format. Sam asked management if it would be possible to standardize on a uniform invoice format, and was given a look as if he had lost his senses.

During this period, Sam's patience and persistence saved the day. The workload was mounting, users had to wait longer and longer for "fixes" to be made to their programs, and emergencies were becoming more frequent. As the small staff worked overtime to keep up with the amount of changes, documentation suffered, and not all changes were posted, especially the minor ones made on an emergency basis. Sam worked late alongside his staff, and was extremely helpful with the users in explaining the problems they were having in trying to straighten out any errors or in making changes to the programs. When the users saw how hard they were working and the effort made to accommodate them, they were generally understanding and tried not to apply too much pressure on the small staff.

By 1983, the system had deteriorated to the point where Sam felt that a major revision had to be made, and that it should be made in conjunction with the evaluation of new hardware and software. Since the system was to be amortized over a seven-year period, management was reluctant to make any major changes until 1985, but was willing to let Sam develop a plan for upgrading and enhancing the system. The one request management made to Sam was to "come up with a plan for dealing with maintenance of a system so that after enhancements and upgrades were made, the problems they had had in the last five years would not happen again."

Most computer installations today are engaged in maintaining systems rather than in developing new ones. Yet there is more work done on improving the productivity of development people than on improving techniques for supporting production systems. Maintenance accounts for 65 percent of labor costs and 75 percent of system life. Management has consistently held the misconception that a system that costs millions of dollars to develop should not need maintenance. This is not true even if requirements do not change, users request no new enhancements, and regulatory agencies do not impose new requirements. Programmers do not develop error-free programs. With the most extensive system testing, there still will be latent "bugs" uncovered only through system usage. This fact, together with the inescapable certainty that requirements will change, means that management should be prepared to support a production system from the day it is declared operational until it is replaced.

Since systems will require maintenance and eventually replacement, production systems support encompasses two important tasks: managing system maintenance, and replacement systems planning. Often management has difficulty understanding that information systems have a definite life span. After the system is declared operational, it is maintained until someone (the users or the information systems department) declares that it is functionally or procedurally deficient and that it might be more practical to replace it with a new system rather than to continue operating the old system. How long this life span is depends on the application and the industry. Accounting applications are relatively stable and have a long life span as long as procedures do not change. Marketing systems usually have short life spans because marketing strategies, pricing, and distribution plans change frequently to meet competition.

In nonautomated systems, policies and procedures become outdated and are replaced by new ones. If inconsistencies between the new policies and some old procedures are discovered, changes are made to correct them. Seldom, if ever, are all the policies and procedures changed at the same time. Changes in computer systems follow the same pattern. An automated procedure is implemented in great detail on the computer. A manual procedure relies on the worker understanding what has to be done; an automated procedure requires that the computer program define in infinite detail everything that has to be done so that the computer will function as well as the indivudual worker. Any change in the way the procedure is to be executed means changes to the computer program rather than telling the worker to change his way of working. As changes to procedures occur, the computer system ages. Eventually, there comes a point where one of two things happen: analysts or programmers give up in despair and ask to start over because they cannot incorporate any more changes into the system, or, more cost-effective software and hardware becomes available making it more economically attractive to replace the existing system rather than to continue to make changes to it. In both cases the results are the same, the entire system is reevaluated, reorganized, and a commitment is made to redesign and implement a new system using new software and hardware, a very costly process. The key to prolonging existing systems, in which a heavy investment has been made, is to improve the procedures for maintaining systems and develop an orderly approach to planning for the replacement of those systems.

THE NEED FOR MAINTENANCE

"If the system was designed right, it wouldn't need fixing." This is the reaction of many companies when confronted with budgets for maintenance of systems. In many cases management views maintenance negatively, thinking that maintenance means something is wrong or needs fixing. Sometimes, management is correct; system deficiencies are a cause for maintenance. However, if we look at system maintenance by cause (see Figure 6-1), we see that problem resolution is only 20 percent of the total maintenance effort.

Requirement changes account for 40 percent of the maintenance effort. These changes include enhancements requested by the users, changes in government regulations, or changes in the way business is done, for example a new product line, pricing structure, or distribution system, that requires changing the existing system. Finally, changes in the processing environment account for another 40 percent of the maintenance effort. Environmental changes include activities like installing the latest

FIGURE 6-1 **SYSTEM MAINTENANCE BY CAUSE**

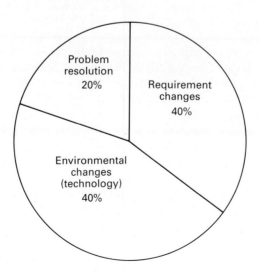

Problem
resolution
20%

Requirement
changes
40%

Environmental
changes
(technology)
40%

version of the operating system, an upgrade to the data management system, installing an integrated data dictionary, hardware changes, and installing system software.

The problems associated with system maintenance are controllable if management anticipates the requirements in maintaining systems. By recognizing that 20 percent of the maintenance effort will be problem solving, this problem area can be controlled by ensuring that systems are well designed and programs are developed on a structured basis. Structured walkthroughs, code reviews, adequate systems testing, and a user-prepared acceptance test should minimize programming problems. Understanding the business environment and the problems the system is to solve before designing a system will eliminate problems arising from poorly designed systems and systems that require significant changes because the do not meet user requirements. Eliminating poorly designed systems and poorly designed programs as the reasons for maintenance will only affect 20 percent of the maintenance effort. To address the remaining 80 percent, maintenance has to be built into the system.

BUILDING MAINTAINABILITY

While system maintenance, or production system support, is the final phase of the system development life cycle, each of the preceding phases (analysis, design, and implementation) affect the maintainability of the system being developed. For a system to be maintainable, features must be designed into the system. During the analysis phase a model must be constructed showing the system flows and computational processes. This model is used during the analysis phase to ensure understanding of the system and to define system scope. During the maintenance phase, it is used to track down sources of errors and identify the impact of changing one portion of the system on other portions. Moreover, the model should be designed to cover a broader functional area than the one being automated. This will help in the integration of additonal functions into the system when they are implemented. The original model should be used as the basis for system changes, and therefore must be updated as procedures in the company change. Without this type of model, the effect of a change and its impact on other functional areas of the system cannot be evaluated. The result could be maintenance efforts that themselves create further maintenance efforts to correct problems created by changes.

Poor analysis usually leads to poor or improper design; in turn, this results in a large volume of change requests immediately after implementation of the project to correct the deficiencies in the analysis and design of the system. To prevent this from occurring, the design phase should follow the model developed in the analysis phase and strive to design a system that is an exact model of the target system. Using the techniques of structured design, the specifications created in the design phase should be modular and allow for integration of functions in the future. In effect, "user exits" should be designed into the system whereby such things as enhancements, new reporting requirements, data extraction routines could be implemented by adding routines at these "user exits." Since most change requests are for additional reports (either hard copy or on terminal screens), the inclusion of a data extraction package and a generalized report formatter package would be helpful to keep maintenance efforts at a minimum after implementation.

Of all the phases in a system life cycle, the implementation phase (programming and testing) probably has the greatest impact on the maintainability of a system. A system that is poorly programmed, documented, and tested will create maintenance headaches for years to come. Programming must be performed according to programming standards that are strictly adhered to. Programmers cannot be treated as craftsmen and they should be no more creative with a design specification than a carpenter should be with an architectural blueprint. Stringent system testing should be performed on each system module and on an integrated system basis. Finally, a user developed acceptance test should be performed with the results evaluated by the user before the system is declared to be in production status and accepted by the user. Too often the user relies on the systems people to declare the system operational, then finds that the system does not perform what it is supposed to do, and starts submitting change requests to correct the system. A user designed acceptance test will identify these shortcomings before the system is accepted and corrections will be made during the development phase rather than in the maintenance phase. Finally, all the test procedures (system tests and user acceptance test) and test data should be available for the maintenance team. These will provide the basis for validating system modifications. The final step after user acceptance is acceptance of the system by the maintenance team. It is their responsibility to ensure that adequate documentation, an accurate system model, and system test procedures and data are available before they accept the system for maintenance (see Figure 6-2).

THE MAINTENANCE PROCESS

Ongoing maintenance includes three categories of projects: (1) Systems errors—abnormal program terminations, inability to execute a job, incorrect outputs. Regardless of the cause of the error, these problems must be dealt with immediately. (2) Changes in business requirements—these changes are caused by changes in business activities such as price changes, new government regulations, a new product line. They can be anticipated and planned for, and usually have a deadline date for completing the change. (3) Enhancements—these are changes that improve the efficiency of the system or provide features not included in the original version of the system. They are usually requested by the users or by information systems personnel and require cost justification as well as project review and approval.

In terms of priorities, system errors have top priority and must be corrected as they occur. If these errors occur frequently, it is a strong indication that the system was poorly designed and inadequately tested. The system department must then evaluate the system and determine why the errors are occurring. In severe cases, the system may have to be withdrawn from production status to retest the entire system and correct the faults. Modifications due to changes in government regulations or in business requirements have the next highest priority. These changes have to be made to meet the new requirements, therefore most businesses do not perform a cost/benefit evaluation or go through project evaluation and approval on these projects. They must be scheduled so that the required modifications are made in sufficient time to be tested and implemented before the new requirements go into effect. Sometimes the changes are of sufficient magnitude that requests are made by businesses to government agencies for more time to implement the change. Examples of these are changes in the postal code, and the proposed conversion to metric measurements.

FIGURE 6-2   **SOFTWARE MAINTENANCE PROCESS**

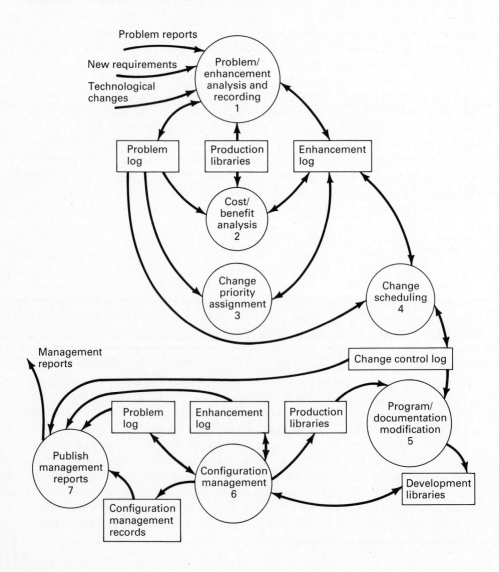

The majority of changes fall into the enhancement category. Procedures for implementing these changes should be consistent with those applied in system development. Each change should be evaluated based on the same criteria used to approve system development projects; a cost/benefit evaluation should be made and intangible benefits identified. The maintenance process would include the following steps:

1. Analyze the Change Request

The maintenance group would review each request for system change and identify the technical problems and changes required. Depending on the type of request, this analysis may only require a review of technical documentation such as the design specifications and/or programming specifications, or may require a more extensive analysis including interviews with user personnel to establish the scope of the change and its effect on existing automated and manual procedures. It is most important to identify the users of the system being modified. In most large business organizations, a system has many users besides those who have requested the change. All the users should be consulted on how the change would affect them and get their imput on the change. Quite often this review process will uncover other proposed changes being planned by other users that would have impact on the change being considered. A review of this type brings all the proposed modifications into the open so that they can be considered as a group prior to making any changes.

In analyzing the request for change, the maintenance group must go back to the model developed in the analysis phase of development showing the proposed system and where it fits into the broader business applications being automated. This review should identify whether other systems planned for implementation would be affected by the change, or whether the change can be better made by including it in a related system rather than as a change to the existing system. This type of review would also identify plans for replacing the existing system. If the proposed change is complex and costly, and the system is planned for replacement in the near future, this should be noted in the evaluation so that a decision can be made to accelerate the replacement date, or delay the proposed change for inclusion in the design of the replacement system.

2. Prepare Economic Evaluation

Enhancements to existing systems quite often are major efforts, for example changing the input processor of an application from batch to on-line. After an analysis of the requirements have been made, the next step is to assess the cost of making the change. This economic analysis is of the same type performed on projects being considered for development. However, because the system exists and is understood in detail by systems personnel, the effort to estimate the cost of the change should be more accurate and easier to make than the effort in initially estimating the cost of implementation. Also the scope of the maintenance effort is better known and understood, therefore the analysis of costs and benefits should require considerably less time and effort. Costs and benefits are time related; that is, an economic evaluation spreads anticipated costs and savings over a predictable period, sometimes over several years. The maintenance group making these estimates should be aware that different time spans may be involved than those used for a systems development project. The normal assumption in a development project is a life span of five to seven years. In a maintenance project, some of this useful life may have already been used, therefore, economic projections must be limited to the system's remaining useful life.

After the economic evaluations have been completed, some projects will be eliminated because they simply do not deliver sufficient return on investment. Others will be dropped because they are inconsistent with plans for the organization or because they duplicate the intended effect of other projects. Information systems managers should always participate in the evaluation of maintenance requests since they know the information plans for the various organizational units within their companies and also pending systems development projects. If a maintenance request is to be superseded by a pending system development project, the information systems manager will be able to assess the projected life of the proposed change realistically. A short life span does not necessarily mean that a project will be dropped. In some cases, the short-term benefits will be great enough to overcome the short life span involved.

3. Establish Priorities

The final task before performing maintenance is to assign priorities to approved maintenance projects. Management can do little to control the mix or scheduling of jobs when it is dealing with maintenance brought about by system errors or normal business needs. In these areas, establishing priorities is limited to meeting schedules while ensuring that the work performed meets quality standards. In the area of enhancements, management has more control. Since there is a fixed cost associated with opening any program and changing it, the more changes that can be implemented when a given program or system is opened for modification, the lower the cost per change. It is normal practice to accumulate small changes and apply them at one time, usually when a major revision is involved. This, of course, does not include changes due to system errors or changes in business requirements which must be made immediately. Enhancement changes are usually assigned a priority and placed in line. When the top priority change comes up for implementation, the line should be reviewed for all other lower priority changes that affect that system or program so that they can all be made at the same time. The setting of priorities could follow the same procedure for setting priorities for development projects, a joint consultation process between users, information systems, and company management.

4. Make the Change

A maintenance group would make the requested changes based on priorities, and the grouping of all changes affecting a program or system. Once these changes have been completed, the entire system must be tested to be sure that the change has been made properly and that the integrity of the system has not been compromised. The system test data and acceptance test data would be used to perform this verification. Too often, maintenance projects fail to test the entire system. This omission can lead to undetected errors that subsequently require emergency maintenance. Any maintenance project that involves file manipulation, input processing, or computational logic requires a new system test. Maintaining test files, test data, procedures, and expected results may appear to be cumbersome and time-consuming. However, it assures that maintenance changes are properly applied and it minimizes the disruption and high costs associated with emergency maintenance. After the change has been applied and tested, the user must approve the results. Once the new system is accepted by the user, the appropriate documentation is updated and placed in the program and systems history files. The entire package is then reviewed by the quality assurance group to ensure proper implementation of the change and most importantly, that all documentation has been correctly updated to reflect the latest status of both the system and programs affected by the change.

PERSONNEL MANAGEMENT

The most obvious personnel problem in information systems is the aversion of programmers and analysts to maintenance work. Contributing to this dislike are poor documentation, junk code, stifled creativity, high pressure, midnight call-outs, and little prestige and recognition. Fixing someone else's problem does not give the same satisfaction as developing your own system and seeing it implemented and working. The poor attitude towards being assigned to the maintenance group, together with the economic necessity to extend system life as long as possible, provides a continuing challenge to management. Unfortunately, many companies succumb to pressures from their top development personnel and assign only the weak analysts and programmers to maintenance, where if they quit, the loss will be minimal. This practice guarantees that maintenance will be poorly performed and systems will be unsatisfactory for their remaining life.

Management must get the point across that maintenance is an important responsibility and that people must be qualified before they can be entrusted with this important task. Some of the things that management can do to improve morale and make maintenance assignment attractive include:

1. Weigh the pay scales between development and maintenance personnel in favor of maintenance. The maintenance team should consist of a more experienced group of analysts and programmers since they will be required to work independently, especially where documentation is inadequate. They have greater responsibilities and the effects of errors are greater than those on a development team. Therefore, there is justification for a higher salary.

2. Provide training to the maintenance group. A major source of dissatisfaction is that once assigned to maintenance, training ceases. The development group gets sent to classes on new software, and programming languages. The main-

tenance group rarely attends these training sessions and seminars. Training is as important as salary in maintaining high morale. It should be seen as an investment for maintenance personnel, who can serve as the source of talent for future development efforts.

3. Rotation in and out of maintenance assignments. In most cases, the maintenance team should be drawn from the original development team. One or two people for each 10 man-years of development effort should be allocated to maintenance. The proper level of technical and application experience should be included on the maintenance team. Junior level positions should be assigned only in addition to the base level of support required. The junior level positions should be used as training to replace the experienced people on the team. Since maintenance activities are highest immediately after implementation, a core of development people are available to make the necessary fixes. There should be little maintenance during the "middle" part of the system life. Maintenance increases again at the end of the life cycle as more and more enhancements are needed to keep up with technology and changing business requirements. Junior analysts can work with the developers during the first two years of the maintenance cycle to learn the system, take over the primary resonsibility for maintenance during the middle life (two years) and train new junior people, and be the project leaders for the replacement-planning projects at the end of system life for the existing system. Thus assignments to the maintenance group are limited to two-year terms for experienced people, and four-year terms for junior people under the assumption of a typical six-year system life.

Good maintenance requires careful planning, skillful management, and a talented staff. Unfortunately, these resources usually are reserved exclusively for development efforts, and maintenance is often entrusted to junior personnel as a training exercise. A large information system is a multimillion dollar investment and should be treated as such. While no single poorly done repair or enhancement will destroy a system, a continually incompetent assault will jeopardize the useful life of any system, no matter how great the original design and implementation effort. A successful maintenance effort depends on the availability of a sufficient level of systems expertise throughout the system life. The level of expertise often increases throughout the development phases, then decreases as personnel are reassigned after implementation. If the level of experience falls too far below the critical level, maintenance can suffer to the point where the system cannot be restored to an acceptable level of operation and will have to be redeveloped.

REPLACEMENT SYSTEMS PLANNING

Eventually, all production systems will have to be replaced. There will come a time when the cost of maintaining and operating an obsolete system is more than the cost of replacing it with a more efficient, current system. Many installations wait until it is physically impossible to maintain the old system before entertaining thoughts of how to replace it. The first thought is to custom develop another one, because the system in use was developed in-house. Today's information system is more likely to be a replacement than a new installation. Moreover, it is likely to be a package rather than a custom-developed system. The risks associated with replacing today's systems increases markedly if a replacement plan does not exist. Although there are many reasons for replacement planning, all are based on the assumption that change will be necessary, that any system will eventually outlive its usefulness. If a plan to replace these systems does not exist, the cost of replacement will be higher because none of the benefits of planning can be realized. There will be a period of deteriorating service to users, perhaps even an interruption of service. Poor or interrupted service will, among its other bad effects, diminish user confidence and raise questions regarding the quality of the replacement. Perhaps the most important reason to develop a replacement plan is the opportunity to examine the range of alternatives for system replacement, that is various software packages, changes in system software, new technology, new hardware, alternative processing concepts, and greater use of microcomputers (see Figure 6-3).

There are also risks in having a replacement plan. The foremost risk is that it may be implemented prematurely. Planners must remember that their work is to prepare for change, not to precipitate change. Another risk is that after all the time and effort put into developing a replacement plan, the planners may be reluctant to change the plan even when faced with new technology and new processing concepts. Finally, there is a tendency for people to equate plans with promises. Because a plan has been prepared does not necessarily mean that it will be implemented. Replacement systems planning is contingency planning; it is a continuous effort to update plans for replacing existing systems based on current technology and current business requirements.

Replacement planning is based on the model of the information-processing environment developed during the strategic planning sessions with top management. The model shows the overall environment, relationships of systems, and the status of systems development. It is similar to a model of a downtown development project, showing models of office buildings, retail stores, parking garages, malls, parks, theaters. Some will already be in existence, others will be torn down and replaced, and still others will be developed. All of this will be done over a period of time. A systems model shows systems in existence, those under development, and those to be replaced as well as those to be developed in the future. By looking at this model (which is constantly updated), one can see at a glance what the overall plans are for information processing in the company and what the current status is in implementing these plans.

Looking at our model, it is easy to see which systems are operational, which are under development and the anticipated completion dates, and which system will be implemented next. What about replacement systems? When do we start planning

FIGURE 6-3   **REPLACEMENT PLANNING CHOICES**

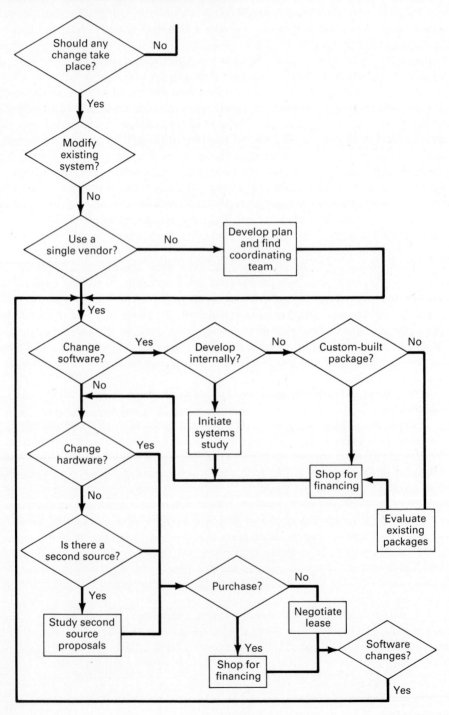

on replacing the existing systems? Because it is so difficult to predict the time needed for advance planning, the best approach might be to view replacement planning as an ongoing activity. This approach is bolstered by the fact that a large number of information systems stay in place no more than three years. Although it is quite realistic to plan a system's period of operational usefulness for seven or eight years, or longer, systems developers have an almost irresistible inclination to take advantage of technological changes through frequent replacement of systems.

Obtaining a package or developing programs, installing the system, testing, user training, and gaining user acceptance of new systems will take a year or longer. Prior to that, detailed analysis and design work is necessary, including evaluation of alternative ways to replace existing systems, evaluation of packages, determining modifications necessary, and cost/benefit analysis. All of these could conceivably take a year's time. First, however, a thorough investigation of users' needs, functional and technical weaknesses in the existing systems, and the impact of replacing one system on the total information systems development strategy has to be performed. This could take up to a year. Added together, the process of replacing a system could take three years. Given that some systems have a productive life of three years, it would be necessary to start planning for the replacement of that system on the date of installation.

Several problems come to mind: management would be shocked to learn that on the day of installation, designers would start to consider replacing the system. Second, there is no motivation to consider a system's replacement so early in its life; considering replacement on the day of installation would reflect poorly on the systems department's confidence in its product. Planning should, however, begin in the early stages of a system's life cycle. There are certain steps that all organizations can take to sustain an ongoing replacement plan:

1. Create and maintain a library of technical applications and vendor data on appropriate products and services. These could be used to support processing functions or to replace existing applications.

2. Keep the maintenance staff current in state-of-the-art technology and the user personnel current in new technologies and their applications to business situations.

3. Conduct annual systems audits, including measurement of system performance against system specifications. Maintain a history of changes to the specifications and evaluate system performance after changes have been made to the system.

4. Conduct monthly system review meetings for users, system developers, and operations management to discuss plans, problems, and changes in requirements.

5. As a result of audits and monthly review meetings, maintain documents on the state of the system, its current life cycle expectations, and a history of products and services that have been evaluated. Update the corporate system model based on these reviews.

REPLACING WITH A PACKAGE

As application packages gain in popularity and acceptance, many installations faced with replacing obsolete systems are turning to them rather than custom developing replacement systems. While replacing with a package is less time-consuming and costly than custom developing, there are pitfalls to avoid and the entire effort must be planned properly if it is to succeed (see Figure 6-4). As in all replacement systems, the place to start is to develop a requirements list of the functions the replacement system is to perform. This would include the functions included in the present system and the list of modifications awaiting implementation. Since there will rarely be a perfect match between the requirements list and the functions performed by the package, priorities will have to be set so that packages can be evaluated on how closely the critical functions are performed. Even then, there may be some top priority requirements which may have to be user coded in order to meet all of the critical

---

FIGURE 6-4   **SELECTING AND EVALUATING PACKAGES**

Steps in Acquiring an Application Package	Pitfalls of Application Packages
1 List present and future requirements of the application in detail.	1 The package does not fully adapt to changes in requirements.
2 Survey all available packages for that application.	2 The data processing department must modify the package when it is installed and subsequent maintenance becomes almost as expensive as in-house application programs are.
3 Examine package documentation and user manuals.	
4 Check whether the packages is sufficiently parameterized.	3 Expensive maintenance becomes necessary later when the hardware, operating system, terminals, network, or user requirements are changed.
5 Check whether the package has adequate aids to maintenance.	
6 Draw up a short list of suitable packages.	4 The package is hard to maintain due to poor documentation, lack of hooks for user-created code, poor structure, absence of source code, excessive complexity, low-level languages, or poor quality coding.
7 Try out each package with corporate data if possible.	
8 Determine whether the package can link into the corporate data base plans.	5 The package has been made difficult to maintain because it has been tinkered with in-house and modifications have been made that are ill-documented and difficult for others to understand.
9 Conduct benchmarks if performance is critical.	
10 Allow end users to implement them on a temporary basis if the end user interface is critical.	6 The package does not fit with the corporate data base implementation and strategy.
11 Negotiate and write an appropriate contract.	7 The software house that owns the package ceases operations.

Source: Reprinted by permission of *Harvard Business Review.* An exhibit from "Buying Software Off the Rack" by James Martin and Carma McClure (Nov./Dec. 1983.) Copyright © 1983 by the President and Fellows of Harvard College; all rights reserved.

requirements. Another factor to consider is that the way the business is done presently is dictated to some extent by the present automated system. Converting to a package may mean changes in present procedures and policies. It is easier to change manual procedures and modify some policies than it is to make extensive changes to an application package. As long as the end result is what the business wants, they should not be bound to the way things are done presently when converting to a package.

In addition to the requirements list, a list of questions for the vendors should be prepared. What support do they give? What training is provided? Will they modify the software to meet user specifications? What are the hardware and software requirements? How many installations are there in our industry and finally, can they provide user references? The answers will be used to evaluate alternatives.

Once a package has been selected, a project leader can be assigned and a team created to do the actual conversion. What design work has to be done? What open issues have to be resolved? What conversion programs have to be written? How is the conversion to be phased in? What testing has to be done? The project leader has to develop a work program and assign the tasks to team members. There should be a special conversion team dedicated to installing the system. Trying to do the conversion while doing one's regular assignments will not work. Not only is a conversion team needed, top management and executive support is needed. They must realize that there could be some changes that they will have to approve or disapprove and that they will have to meet the deadlines for these decisions.

In the planning stage the project team has to decide whether to install the package in phases. With a package, more of the system can be operational earlier than in custom development. This can put a strain on the user departments involved if they cannot handle the workload. A phased installation means installing individual pieces (modules) of the system so that users can understand and digest them before going on to other pieces. The phased approach also eliminates the problem that all users may not be ready for implementation at the same time. Since large systems will affect many areas of the company, the phased approach allows those departments ready for installation to proceed, and those requiring more time for training and preparation to wait for implementation. In deciding what the phases will be, the conversion team can review the rankings assigned by the users to functional requirements of the package. Then the installation plan can be divided into phases, based on priority rankings, by function, by warehouse, or by product line. This will get the important things done first.

In a custom development project, after planning the next step is design. The same is true when installing a package. Since there are no programs to design, unless major modifications are being considered, the two major design issues are forms and manual procedures. There has to be a trade-off between the procedures necessary to use the package and the procedures currently in place. When possible, the procedures associated with the package should be used. The analyst has to discuss these procedures with the users and help them adapt their present procedures to the new ones. During the design process, the analyst will finalize what parts of the package will be used "as is", what parts need modifications, and the portions that will not be used at all, or delayed for later implementation. How much should the package be changed to meet user needs?—as little as possible. If additional reports are required, extract data from the package and use a report writer to generate the reports. Cosmetic changes can be implemented using pre- and post-processors. A well-designed package will provide user exits to custom programs. It is not wise to meddle with the package's basic design. The more changes that are made, the harder it will be to support the product. When changes are made, the vendor will not support the package. The installation will have to support its changes, and also make changes when the vendor supplies them with a new release, which could be significantly different from the version in use. The usual result is that several versions of the software become catalogued into the library: the original purchased version, the modified version, user changes made to the modified version, and new releases from the vendor. As can be seen, this will eventually lead to a situation where the software becomes unmaintainable. If logic changes must be made, the best way to do it is to have the vendor provide a user exit in the software (if none are available where needed) and "hook" custom coding into the exit point. By having the vendor develop the exit, subsequent releases of the software will maintain the integrity of the exit and the user will not have to go through lengthy analysis to determine whether the custom coding has to be changed.

After design, procedures for data conversion have to be developed. The users will expect the information systems department to do the conversion this time since the data is already captured in existing computer files. Moreover, only the conversion team knows what the application package requires in terms of files and data. One issue which usually arises is when the package keeps more detailed information than the old system. Should information systems go to history tapes or manual records to collect the historical detail needed to compare this year's activity with historical activity? What if a new chart of accounts or a new sales structure invalidates any comparisons. These issues have to be resolved with the user before data conversion can take place.

The data conversion should be automated as much as possible and the user should check the data at each stage. Conversion programs should translate data from existing files into transactions that can be processed through the new system, rather than go directly file to file. The conversion program can include automatic defaults to build new information or can produce worksheets for the user to complete and enter into the system. By going through the package's input processing module, the old data will be subject to the normal data entry edits. The package will provide a listing showing errors which can be used as the audit trail for the conversion. By going directly from old file to new file through a translation program, the new system data will be no better than the old system it came from.

The final steps are user training and testing. In replacing a system with a package, it is difficult to get the user interested in learning about the new package, once they know that the functions they want will be provided. It is difficult to get users' full attention when they are busy keeping the old system going. If training is not performed adequately, problems will arise in the post-installation period: the clerk does not know how to code a form, does not understand the documentation, and decides to throw it into a batch and see what happens. Later, the maintenance team will spend hours trying to find out what went wrong. Proper training includes sending key user personnel to the vendor's school, then developing a user procedures manual from the material supplied by the vendor. Many installations give the users the vendor's manual. Usually this is not successful. The vendor's manual is written to provide a general description of how the software works. What is needed is the specific procedures for how the software will work at your particular installation, on your particular application. It has to be tailored specifically to the user, showing what is done now, and how it has to be done for the new system. It would also include changes made to the software, even though these changes are transparent to the users. The vendor's manuals have to be tailored to the installation taking into the account the level of competence of user personnel. It should contain real life examples and step-by-step instructions. Classes should be provided first to introduce all user personnel to the new system, then to train those that will be involved in preparing inputs to the system and handling its outputs. The aim is to provide clear, confident training to educate and inspire the clerical staff, not a low-key, unprepared ramble that will cause confusion and apprehension. This means that the system must be working well enough to be demonstrated during these classroom training sessions.

Testing the system should be done in two steps. First, the conversion team has to develop test data to system test the package. The test data from the old system may not be useable depending on the number of new functions added and the degree of changes to processing logic. Some vendors provide test data files and job streams that will test the standard package. These can provide the initial test of the system. However, the only adequate test is for the user to define the test criteria, run the test, and reconcile the reports. These tests should be modular and have predetermined results upon which to match computer-generated results. They should be comprehensive enough to test all aspects of the system. The reason that a comprehensive test is needed is to avoid running the new system in parallel with the old. In the past, conversion to a new system always meant a period of parallel operations. This created unreasonable demands on user personnel, meant keeping all input transactions, processing them twice, and reconciling the differences. The extra time involved was tremendous and very costly. Furthermore, the results were always different since the new system was never identical to the old. Without data constructed to provide anticipated results, it became impossible to reconcile the differences. This led the user to suspect the new system immediately, even though they were trying to compare apples and oranges. By developing user tests and analyzing outputs with predetermined results, the new system can be tested and accepted on a module-by-module basis.

After acceptance of the new system, the conversion team should be monitoring the system's performance. Testing may have been done on small test files, and a 10-minute report may have grown into an eight-hour job. Many packages include a report generator that allows users to specify the reports they want. This flexibility has a price: report generators can be inefficient. Frequently produced reports may be candidates for reprogramming. Once the package has been installed and the team has watched over it for a while, the conversion project team can complete the documentation, update the information system model, and move on to other projects. This approach permits the vendor to provide software support, the system department to write an occasional report program or develop some custom code and install new releases from the vendor.

The benefits of packages over in-house development are becoming more apparent. There are some additional tasks and problems that do not occur in custom developed projects. Once these are identified and handled, replacing obsolete systems with packages can save a company time and money. In the final analysis, the rules for success are still, know what the requirements are, get management support, put together a team of users and development personnel, and plan well.

PROFESSIONAL APPLICATION COMMENT: THE CAI REPLACEMENT PLAN

Sam Levine understood that the amortization period for the existing system would be over in two years. Management would be more receptive to investing in new systems after the present one had been fully amortized. He also recognized that he had to present a plan for replacing the existing system and maintaining the new systems in a more satisfactory fashion than practised in the past five years. With the help of his old consulting firm, Sam developed the following approach:

1. He developed an information schematic showing all the systems at CAI, the dates they were designed and the dates they became operational. It showed how all the systems were interrelated, the volume of transactions processed or the number of inquiries responded to, and the number of modifications made since the system was operational. Sam worked with the users to get this chart completed. Even the users were surprised at the number of interrelated systems and the workload processed by these programs.

2. Next, Sam asked the users to rank all the systems shown in the information schematic by their importance to the business. He then ranked the systems by ease of maintenance, ranging from those which could not be maintained much longer to those with few maintenance problems. An overlay was prepared to place over the information schematic which showed the ease of maintenance and importance of each system. The result was that one could see all the very critical systems and the probability of them failing due to "non-maintainability." This analysis really shocked some of the user departments when they saw that their system was a critical one to the business and that it appeared that it could not be maintained for much longer. "Why?" they asked. Sam showed them the date the requirements were defined, the date the system became operational, and the system life including the number of modifications made during the system life. It then became very apparent that the systems were all

about 7–10 years old or older, had had significant changes made reflecting changes in the insurance industry over the past decade, and had provided them with what they wanted reasonably well during the life of the system. The users were impressed, especially since they knew that Sam had very little resources to work with in maintaining the systems over the past five years.

3. Knowing the priorities for replacing systems, Sam started to look for application packages which could be used to replace existing systems. A small team was formed to evaluate packages. The team always included the manager of the user department most affected by the system. For example, when accounts receivable packages were evaluated, the accounts receivable manager participated in the review. Sam found that while none of the packages met all the requirements, user personnel were the ones that suggested how existing procedures could be changed to make use of the package with minimum modifications. They were motivated by fear that the existing system might collapse at any moment and by fear that if they insisted on doing everything the way it was presently done, the new system would never be ready. The users were the ones urging Sam to hurry up and select a replacement system before more changes had to be made to the existing programs.

4. Systematically, Sam evaluated all alternatives, identified and costed out new hardware and software, made estimates of the cost of replacing with packages versus custom development, and developed a preliminary schedule for phasing in new systems over a three-year period. Working with the users, he developed cost/benefit analysis showing that the average cost per transaction or average cost per inquiry would be lower using new software and hardware than with the present system, that there would be more information available for analysis, and that future maintenance of the system would be reduced because the vendor would maintain the application software.

5. Sam then asked each user to present the plans for their functional area to the management committee at one of their monthly meetings. They took the lead in presenting a history of the system, the status today, the changes required, and the proposed approach to improve the system. Sam presented the overall information system plan showing all systems and the replacement plan. A detailed budget was then presented to show the costs of the proposed changes and the resulting benefits. Finally, a maintenance plan was presented that showed how the new systems would be maintained including the planning for their eventual replacement.

The management committee was impressed with the enthusiasm of the users for the proposed changes, their sense of urgency, and their complete confidence in the information systems department's ability to do the job. Sam had the foresight to alert IBM to the plan and they were ready when top management asked them for a hardware proposal and their approach to helping the company convert to new hardware and system software. The economics were right, and the company approved Sam's plan in total.

Perhaps the biggest lesson learned by Sam in developing his replacement strategy was the importance of user support and enthusiasm. By involving the user departments in each step of the planning process, they sold the concept and approach to top management. Sam had done his homework well, was prepared, and could handle any questions from the management committee. The fact that Sam built outstanding relationships between the information systems department and the users over the life of the old systems paid off in having users support and fight for the systems department plans before management. If only more information systems managers could learn that lesson.

CHAPTER 6   DISCUSSION QUESTIONS

1. What do you think about the approach of minimizing information systems costs by hiring consultants to do the design and implementation work and keeping a small staff to maintain systems? Is this cost effective in the long run?

2. Maintenance accounts for 65 percent of labor costs in the life of a system. Since some management feel that "if it were done right, it wouldn't need fixing" what can be done to reduce maintenance costs and efforts?

3. Since 80 percent of all maintenance arises because of changes to user requirement or changes due to technology, can we reduce the maintenance effort by having users develop and maintain their own systems? Is this practical?

4. How would you motivate programmers so that maintenance assignments are not shunned?

5. What do you think about assigning "junior" (less experienced) programmers to look after maintenance?

6. Eventually systems become obsolete and need to be replaced. How does one determine when that point occurs? If the system has no errors and few changes are requested, could it run "forever" and not need replacing?

7. What alternatives should be considered in replacing systems? Why is a replacement plan necessary? What risks are involved?

8. Is it realistic to ask users to change the way they do business so that an application package can be used without major modification? How would you make such an evaluation?

9. After making modifications to an application package, what problems can be anticipated in maintaining that package?

10. What is the best way for making logic changes to an application package? Who should do it?

11. What do you think about the concept of running parallel before converting to a new system? What are the advantages and disadvantages? Would you recommend it as a standard procedure?

7

COMPUTER OPERATIONS MANAGEMENT

ISSUES

- As hardware prices fall, replacing existing equipment may be cost effective; how can management be convinced of this?

- Does the increased use of on-line systems mean that future systems will be fully duplexed to prevent down time?

- Adding additional memory and other hardware resources is becoming less costly. Is capacity planning still necessary when it is so inexpensive to add more resources?

- Is performance analysis on the mainframe critical today when so much processing is distributed to the end users on microcomputers or small distributed minicomputer systems?

- What is the role of the operations manager?

MIDWEST PUBLIC SERVICE COMPANY

Grace Norman was the senior vice-president of planning, for the Midwest Public Service Company, a large electrical utility serving over 1.5 million customers in a midwestern state. At the most recent management committee meeting, the request to upgrade computer hardware was not received as well as similar requests in the past. Since information services reported to Grace, she had to make her recommendations to the board of directors at the next quarterly meeting, two months hence. Before that, Grace and the CEO had to reach agreement on what should be done with the request to upgrade the existing IBM 370/168 to the IBM 3083 system. (See Appendix B for description of major IBM systems.)

Grace had been with Midwest PSC since graduation from engineering school in 1955. With the exception of two years to get her MBA at Harvard (funded by the company), Grace had spent her career in various departments with the company including engineering, plant, finance, field operations, and now planning. She was one of the candidates to succeed the present CEO when he reached mandatory retirement age in two years. The information services department used to report to the controller, but in 1972, when construction started on its nuclear-generating facilities and the computer was used for network analysis and scheduling as well as for project control, the department was moved to the planning directorate.

The first computer application at Midwest PSC was a punched card system installed in 1955. In 1960, the IBM 305 RAMAC system was installed, then came the 1401, 1410, 360/50, 370/155, and 370/168. In 1983, IBM proposed that the 168 be replaced by the 3083 to gain more capacity and a better price performance. In the past, upgrading of computer hardware was pretty much routine. The big change was in going from the 1410 to the 360 since everything had to be redesigned and recoded from autocoder to COBOL. Since then, the major systems only had changes made caused by new regulations from the regulatory commission, or changes due to new rate structures. The reason for upgrading hardware had always been reaching capacity on the old equipment and better price performance on the new equipment. In addition, there were always new software programs or systems that could be used on the new hardware that were not available on the old. The information systems manager was very active in professional societies and had presented several papers to the

Edison Electric Institute describing the advanced technologies used in the computer applications at Midwest PSC. This reputation for technical excellence made it easy to convince management that upgrading hardware was necessary every three to four years. "Leader in Technology" had been the theme of several advertising campaigns showing the computer room and its project management system for construction of the new nuclear generators. Both management and the board liked the way computers had enhanced the reputation of Midwest PSC.

Even before Three Mile Island, things started to go sour at PSC. A lengthy strike by construction workers had delayed the completion target date badly. There were problems with the design of the reactors that were tricky and difficult to work out. Interest rates were going out of sight and the capital cost of construction was skyrocketing. Farm income was starting to decline, and new businesses were not coming into the state as projected. The demand for power started to fall, and some had predicted that the output of the reactors could not be sold at a profit. All of a sudden, everything seemed to be going wrong with the plans to switch from fossil fuels to nuclear energy. As earnings declined and costs mounted, management was under significant pressures to contain costs and reduce them where possible. Was the upgrade to the IBM 3083 computer system really necessary? While there was a price performance advantage, there was also the capital outlay to consider. Was the company really at capacity or could it live with the existing configuration for a few more years?

In discussing these questions with the information services people, Grace was surprised at how adamant they were that the new computer was an absolute necessity. They would lose their leading edge advantage over other companies in the industry. There were things that they had planned to do with the new software that they could not do with the existing system. The present system was fully loaded, and significant overtime work would have to be undertaken just to keep up with the existing workload. Changing the system was essential if the company wanted to continue to operate efficiently.

The other vice-presidents were urging Grace to do her part in the cost-cutting program. "Computers has always had what they want. Now that the company is in a financial crisis, they should live with what they have and not behave like spoiled children when refused a new toy. After all, the existing system is less than five years old, how can it possibly be obsolete when IBM is still selling the hardware to other users?" They urged Grace to stand firm and refuse the request for hardware upgrade.

Grace had decided that the issue had become too emotional to be resolved internally. What had started out as excellent relationships between information services and the other operating departments had turned ugly. The major departments had taken personnel cuts and had their budgets reduced significantly. The information services department had a freeze on hiring but had not taken any personnel or budget cuts. Now, they were asking for new computers. This was just too much for the other departments to take. When a threat was phoned in that there was a bomb placed in the computer center, Grace decided that she had to take action.

Grace called in a consulting firm to do a thorough review of the existing systems and facilities. She wanted to know if there was spare capacity on the present equipment, whether the equipment could be better utilized, and whether a change was necessary now. She also asked for a review of the facilities and how secure they were from unauthorized access. Finally, she asked the consulting firm to recommend ways to reduce the cost of providing information services to the company. The initial meeting between the consulting firm and the company was to take place the following day. Grace was wondering what the consulting firm would do, how they would approach the problem of determining capacity without disrupting the daily workload. She knew that the people in information services were not happy about calling in a consulting firm and she wondered if the consultants could get anything done without their complete and willing support. Well, thought Grace, at least she had got everyone to agree to let the recommendations of the consultant be the guide as to whether to replace the existing hardware.

As more of our daily lives are affected by computers, perhaps the most frustrating statement we can hear is: "The computer is down." Picture a long line of shoppers at the checkout counters of a supermarket. The computer is down and the clerks cannot scan the prices on the items nor operate the cash registers. Even if the cash registers were working, they could not check out the customers because prices are no longer marked on the product but kept on computer files and recalled when the product is scanned. The same thing can happen at a bank, an airport ticket counter or check-in counter, a theater box office, a department store. If the computer is not down, you may have to wait a few minutes to get the information you want because the computer is loaded and calls are being handled on a delayed basis. We hear of the New York Stock Exchange ticker tape running 15 minutes behind actual trades because of heavy volume. We hear of brokerage houses unable to cope with back-office volume when the New York exchange volume hits 200 million shares in daily trading. All of these occurrences are becoming more and more frequent as our society automates and computers become a greater part of our daily lives. The problems are caused by lack of capacity, reliability, or availability; or, in other words, poor computer operations management and resource planning.

With the growth of on-line systems for everything ranging from word processing to at-home banking, resource planning for computer operations is becoming more complex. In the past, resource planning consisted of looking at the capacity provided by the computer system today, estimating what would be needed in three years, and making the appropriate hardware and software plan. In those days the workload consisted of batch applications and increased according to the growth rate of the business. Scheduling of the workload was done by the data-processing department. They did the development work and could estimate accurately the resources needed for program development as well as the additional capacity needed when new systems became operational. Since scheduling for daily work as well as future work was done completely by the data-processing department, there were few surprises. Moreover, since the installation of new hardware and software occurred rather infrequently, there was ample time for installation planning. In this batch environment, if the computer was down for a short period, the users probably would not even realize that the system had been down.

Today's environment is much different. Users drive the system through terminals. Demand cannot be anticipated and the system must be available almost on a 24-hour basis. Files are updated on-line, and inquiry requires instant responses. Users will not accept responses that take longer than three seconds. The system has to be more reliable since even short disruptions cannot be tolerated. Today's computers are much more reliable than those of 10 or 20 years ago. However, technology itself is creating reliability problems. The very large integrated circuits have proven very reliable; but it has been found that a chip with 100,000 circuits is much more prone to fail than one with 10,000 circuits. Steps are now being taken to increase the reliability of the "ultra" large integrated circuits.

Adequate capacity means more than having sufficient CPU power. Most on-line systems require very few CPU cycles to process and respond to a request for information. What is always underestimated is the requirement for direct access storage devices and for on-line storage. When the problems of estimating resource requirements for linking microprocessors to the mainframes, and for integrating word processing with data processing are considered, the topics of computer operations management and resource planning become very important.

RESOURCE ASSESSMENT

Computer operations management starts with determining the resources needed to satisfy user requirements. This determination is based on: demand, availability, and contingency requirements.

Demand

Demand systems allow the user to access the system at will. They include the typical customer inquiry system as well as office systems such as word processing and text retrieval, and multiuse systems such as financial models, spreadsheets, and other time-sharing systems. In the 1970s, demand systems accounted for 20 to 30 percent of all processing in a typical installation. In 1985, they accounted for over 60 percent of total processing. The growth in demand systems has created a new set of problems in resource planning because of the complexities of networking, communication requirements, and the need for higher reliability and security. The demand on the system as a whole is difficult to project and schedule. These systems are most heavily used during the typical working hours of 8:00 A.M. to 6:00 P.M., forming a peak load which the system has to handle.

Availability

Availability is the ability of the system to satisfy the demands placed on it by the user. Included in the availability component is reliability or the percentage of time any single component is available (known as uptime). To have a system available for demand processing during the peak period may mean shifting other work to off-peak hours in order to balance the workload. A redundant configuration would provide for both availability and reliability but could result in considerable unused capacity during off-peak periods. Computer resource planning addresses these problems.

Contingency

Contingency planning is preparing for the unexpected. Most installations treat contingency planning as what happens when disaster (such as fire or vandalism) strikes. In operations management, contingency planning is establishing reserve margins so that resources are available to handle unanticipated demands. These resources could be expressed as percentages of known need such as expressing CPU capacity as known load plus 15 percent, or as actual contingency equipment such as four extra disk drives to handle contingencies. Sufficient resources should be reserved for handling contingencies.

CAPACITY PLANNING AND LOAD ANALYSIS

The first step in capacity planning is performing a load analysis on the computer center to determine the processing characteristics for that center. The load analysis is a chart of CPU hours available and how these hours are allocated to processing streams. Figure 7-1 presents a typical load analysis chart.

The load is usually measured in CPU hours. For example, a CPU scheduled to be available 24 hours a day, six days a week would have 576 available hours. How these hours are utilized is presented along the horizontal axis. It is usually convenient to show usage by work shift and weekend work. By plotting the load on the CPU, reserve capacity can be planned to meet contingency needs. For example, instead of planning for use of the CPU at 100 percent of capacity, allow for a 15 percent reserve and plan to use the CPU at 85 percent capacity. When actual usage reaches the 85 percent capacity level on a consistent basis, it should trigger a signal to management that the CPU may be operating at maximum capacity and that replacement planning should look at alternatives for handling additional workload. This same type of analysis can be used on other devices such as tapes, disks, and channel utilization. Load analysis can help in establishing reasonable operating levels for various hardware components, especially the CPU; forecasting needed increments of processing power; determining the point where capacity reaches the reserve level and service levels could deteriorate; and demonstrating to top management the need for a reserve margin.

Once the load analysis is completed, it will be apparent that there are peak periods during the processing day where all resources are heavily used. A separate chart can be drawn to show the daily peak demand by hour (see Figure 7-2).

If the load analysis combined with the peak load analysis shows that there is ample capacity for processing other than during the peak hours, management will have to weigh the alternatives for peak load management. Some of the more common techniques to "shave the peak" include load shifting, peak shaving, time-of-day pricing, and port closure.

Load shifting is probably the most convenient way to shift processing load from peak hours. It involves the use of outside resources to temporarily delay the installation of more processing power. If the peak load is temporary, a period of system testing before conversion of a major system, for example, then buying outside computer time on a temporary basis is feasible. However, if the peak load is a result of growing volume, then load shifting only buys time before installing more capacity. In installations where applications are integrated or where a data base is involved, load shifting to outside sources may not be practical.

Peak shaving involves identifying those requirements that make up the peak and "shaving" them off. For example, if there is a low-priority application that uses a lot of resources, financial modeling for example, this application can be shifted to non-peak hours. Whether this can be done practically will depend on the application and the users involved. Program compilation and testing can be shifted to other than prime shift, but financial modeling may have to be done when the financial analysts need access to resources during prime shift hours. Another approach is to change employees' working hours, installing "flex-time" where employees can work any eight-hour period between 7:00 A.M. and 7:00 P.M. Flexible working hours usually result in a lowered peak load.

FIGURE 7-1   **LOAD ANALYSIS CHART**

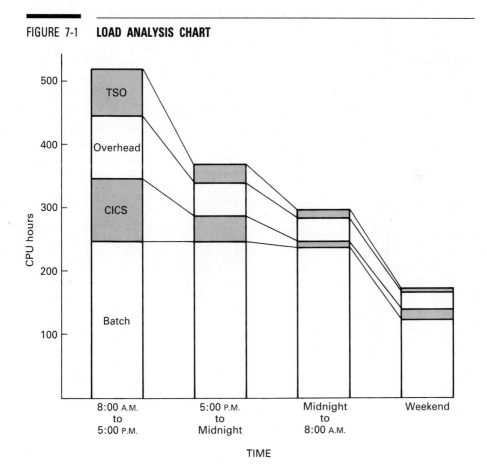

If users are charged for use of the computing resources, then time-of-day pricing, charging more for processing performed during prime shift, can result in users voluntarily shifting their workload to off-peak processing. However, the difference between peak rates and off-peak rates must be substantial in order to entice users to take advantage of the lower costs of information processing. If prime shift rates are $500 per hour and there is a "discount" of $400 per hour if processing is done in other than prime time, users will think carefully before requiring that their processing be done in prime time. Unfortunately those users whose processing must be done during prime hours will complain loudly about the unfairness of this type of pricing.

Finally, since most peak loads are caused by demands for on-line processing, one way of reducing peak loads is to restrict the number of terminals with access to the CPU. This is called port closure and while it will reduce the peak load, it usually negatively affects productivity and results in irate users.

All of these techniques to reduce peak loads indicate that the existing equipment is approaching capacity or that the company needs to reassess the way it is providing computing resources. Perhaps a single CPU environment should be changed to a multiprocessing environment, or what is now done centrally should be decentralized. Load analysis and capacity planning alerts management to potential

FIGURE 7-2   **PEAK DEMAND BY HOUR**

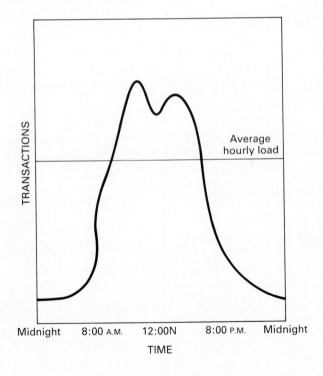

problems in resources and allows them sufficient time to evaluate alternative courses of action.

PROJECTING NEEDS

While load analysis shows the current capacity of the system, future needs must be projected to plan for total system needs in the future. Projecting needs for processing resources is a critical part of the information-planning process. If the company permits information systems management to participate in the corporate planning process so that the strategic direction of the company is known and the information needs can be built into corporate plans, then planning for computing resources is made easier. Even without this type of participation, resource planning can be performed by maintaining assumptions about the growth of the business, expansion in product lines, and increases in transaction volumes. Assuming that the business will grow by six percent a year compounded over the next five years, and that new businesses will be purchased in 1988 and 1990, adding an additional 300,000 customers to the existing customer base, will help the information systems manager in projecting future workload.

Within the information systems department itself, an application development plan together with the plan for replacing systems will provide the basis for projecting the need for resources generated by growth in applications and replacement of existing systems. A seasoned information systems manager will also recognize that as usage approaches capacity, a latent demand for resources is created. Latent demand is the workload that would be processed if there were enough resources. It is created by two fundamental laws in information processing: "Workload expands to fill existing capacity," and "There is never enough disk space." Latent demand builds up during periods when processing resources are saturated while processing needs continue to grow. When new capacity becomes available, this demand is quickly imposed on the system and may absorb up to 50 percent of the new capacity. Information system managers who fail to take latent demand into consideration when increasing capacity are often embarrassed to find that the newly installed additional resources are quickly used up.

COMPUTER PERFORMANCE MEASUREMENT

When capacity appears to be reaching the saturation point, the first reaction is to purchase more capacity. Whether this is necessary depends on how efficiently the existing capacity is being used. Could additional capacity be found through fine-tuning the system or readjusting the processing schedule? While ordering more equipment is the line of least resistance, before doing that there are numerous ways that machine performance can be evaluated using accounting and operations data, soft-

ware monitoring, hardware monitoring, and simulation. These techniques may uncover unexpected computer availability or may indicate equipment modification that
will produce more efficient utilization.

The need for measuring the performance of systems is directly proportional to
the complexity of the system environment. A small business system, able to execute
only one program at a time can be adequately measured by means of simple observation. Observation of an on-line, transaction driven, multiuser system to collect
performance information would be useless. Today's computer systems with their increasing amount of resource sharing and parallel processing are becoming more complex, making the collection of pertinent data and its effective analysis and interpretation more difficult. Fortunately the tools of computer performance measurement
have also been evolving. They include hardware monitors, data collection capabilities
in vendor-supplied operating systems, special software monitors, simulation and
other data collection and analysis techniques. By using these tools effectively, the
cost of the computer center could be reduced by as much as several hundred thousand
dollars per year. There could be an increase in processing throughput (the number of
jobs processed per day) or in job turnaround time. Most importantly, suggested upgrading of hardware and software could be rationally appraised using these techniques. Most of the benefits have been obtained by identifying bottlenecks and removing them by making changes indicated by the performance measurement data.
The cost reductions have resulted from removing equipment that the computer performance measurement data indicated was unnecessary.

The performance of the computer operations department is measured by four
factors: availability, throughput, elapsed time, and resources used. Collectively these
performance attributes affect how the users view the services provided by the operations center: How quickly can the center process my job? Do they have the capability
and capacity to handle my job? What will it cost? and Do they have problems running my job?

Availability is the percentage of time available to process user jobs. This is
always less than 100 percent due to scheduled and unscheduled maintenance, reruns
due to problems, and other unanticipated requirements.

Throughput is the number of jobs processed during a period of time. Of and
by itself, it has no meaning; when measured over time and a trend is apparent,
throughput provides an indication of increasing levels of service. When throughput
is decreasing, it is an indication that there is some blockage in the system or that the
job mix has been changed to degrade system performance.

Elapsed time is the amount of time each job spends within the computer system. This would also include the procedures involved in job preparation and output
distribution outside of computer operations. Elapsed time is an important factor in
how users judge response time. Increasing elapsed time could indicate that there are
problems running the application programs or that the manual procedures associated
with the application need examination.

Resources used identifies all the resources used in processing a job. They
would include CPU time, main storage, disk and tape storage, channel usage, and
printers.

Collectively, these performance attributes affect the user's service with respect to response, capability and problems. While the attributes define the production of a computer system, they do not indicate how to increase the throughput, reduce elapsed time, or reduce the occurrence of problems. This requires an examination of how a computer system processes jobs and an analysis of how work flows through the system. The workflow may be very complex in a large on-line multiprogramming environment. Several processes are active concurrently, and in a multiprocessor environment, they are active simultaneously. The various resources of the system are shared among the jobs in process. Bottlenecks may occur at any point in the system, slowing down the workflow with the resultant lowering of throughput and impairment of response. The measurement and analysis of the details of workflow within a computer system is the essence of performance measurement.

Computer performance can be measured in several ways:

- Analysis of data collected for job accounting and control
- Software monitors—programs to collect and analyse specific data
- Hardware monitors—special hardware devices that are connected to the computer to collect and analyse performance data.
- Simulation of the operation of the computer system.

The data needed for analysis includes data on job events and device events. Once information is collected to indicate what is happening on each job and on the devices used on the job, any aspect of computer performance can be computed from the event data. As jobs are submitted for processing, they go through a series of events, for example entering a job line, start of loading into main storage, end of loading, start of execution, issuing an I/O request, or interruption of processing for I/O servicing. Data describing each of these events consists of three data elements: the job identifier, event identifier, and the time of occurrence of the event.

In addition to job events, operating system event data may also be collected. Here the data also involves three elements: operating system module identifier, event identifier, and the time of occurrence of the event. Each device in a computer system, such as the CPU, main storage, channels, disk units, tape units, printer, also undergoes a series of events such as start/stop operations, and data transfer. Data describing these events include: device identifier, event identifier, and time. Some devices such as main storage need to include the amount of storage involved in the event to fully describe the event. By accumulating data on job events, device events, and operating system events, an analyst can calculate the usage of system resources in a period of time. In theory, all of the event data can be obtained from the operating system through analysing system data on CPU time, storage utilization, and disk accesses. However, not all operating systems make this data available to the user and those that do, provide data in a way that is not easy to use or that is incomplete. Some of the data needed for performance analysis have to be collected by additional routines, software monitors, or hardware monitors, each of which has a cost associated with its use.

Job Accounting and Control Data

Operating systems collect data that is used for job accounting and operations control use. The data that is provided will vary from one operating system to another. Some provide a listing of event data, although it may not be quite complete. Others provide only the minimum necessary for elementary accounting functions. The system management facility (SMF) of IBM's operating systems provides a more comprehensive set of accounting data for control and job-billing purposes. In the larger computer centers, SMF data may be supplemented by internal accounting routines to obtain more detailed data for their control and accounting needs. This data would include such information as elapsed time for each job, reruns, and abnormal job terminations. By itself, job accounting data are usually not sufficient for detailed performance measurement and must be supplemented with data from software or hardware monitors.

Software Monitors

A software monitor is a computer program that collects data on computer performance. It operates as a user program which observes the operation of the operating system and other user programs by interrupting normal processing at periodic intervals, examining control blocks, machine registers, and other operating system control information, and recording appropriate data to indicate the usage of CPU and storage devices associated with each job. Software monitors can be of two types: intercept and sampling. Intercept monitors insert additional coding at key points in the application program or the operating system. When execution hits these key points, event data is accumulated. Sampling monitors stop the program at periodic intervals and note the time and status of events. Most software monitors in use today are sampling monitors.

Software monitors are particularly useful because of their ability to distinguish between user program activities and operating system activities or system overhead. This facility is important in establishing criteria for charging for computer services. When jobs are run one at a time, service charges can be based on elapsed clock time, total I/O activity, and resource utilization. In a multiuser system, however, the elapsed time and I/O activity will vary from run to run depending on the priority of the job and the job mix during processing. Because the software monitor distinguishes CPU time for program activity from CPU time for system overhead, the data center manager can develop a billing algorithm that is repeatable, that is, charges that will be consistent from run to run.

Compilation of data for all jobs during a time period will provide the user with information on how efficiently the entire system is operating. For example, by analysing the usage on different I/O channels, improved throughput can be obtained by balancing the usage of each channel. Similarly, throughput in a multiprogramming environment can be improved by analysing device usage and CPU usage to balance high compute programs with I/O bound programs. Since software monitors create their own overhead, truly accurate measurement of performance can only be obtained through the use of both software and hardware monitors.

Hardware Monitors

Hardware monitors are electronic counters, in most cases microprocessors, that can measure time or count events. The results are stored on magnetic devices for later analysis and display. Hardware monitors measure the duration of events or the number of events by recording in electronic counters, pulses from specific computer circuits. This requires attaching probes at specific points on the circuits to be monitored. These probe points are usually supplied by the vendor to help identify the function to be measured. As the system operates, every time the circuit being monitored is used, it is recorded on tape. By counting the number of times the circuit is used and the duration of the use, accurate data can be obtained without system overhead.

Why use a hardware monitor instead of a software monitor? The reasons are as follows:

1. General system tuning can be achieved with a hardware monitor since all data needed to tune a system can be acquired with hardware monitors.

2. Certain computers do not have software monitors available. Hardware monitors are device independent and will work on all computer makes and models as long as the user understands where to attach the probes to measure specific circuitry functions. Hopefully, the manufacturer will supply this information.

3. In a multiple CPU environment, the only way to tune the multiprocessing environment is through a hardware monitor. There is no method of running a software monitor on multiple CPUs. Probes can be attached to a number of CPUs and their associated I/O devices to record processing activities.

4. Hardware monitors can tune subsystems like disks, channels, printers, and terminals. Most I/O subsystems have critical time relationships which cannot be seen by software monitors. Moreover, there is often critical activity within the I/O controllers that is invisible to the CPU programs.

5. Hardware monitors can measure events that software monitors cannot record. Seek time on disks occurs faster than the smallest time increment that can be measured with software monitors operating on 60Hz equipment. Hardware monitors can generally measure times as short as 50 nanoseconds and, therefore, have no problems measuring disk or drum seeks. Asynchronous activities is another example of events that cannot be measured by software monitors but can be through the hardware monitor.

6. Hardware monitors can be used to verify software monitors. With the increasing number of software monitors on the market, one needs to make sure that the software monitor is really measuring what it claims to measure. Verification should be obtained with a hardware monitor either by the vendor, and made

available by the vendor to the user, or owned by the user if the vendor cannot supply the information. There have been cases of serious programming errors in software monitors that give distorted data leading to wrong conclusions. Before acquiring a software monitor, the vendor should supply hardware monitor verification of its programs and results.

A comparison of hardware and software monitors is as follows:

- HM: Attached electrically to equipment.
  SM: Runs as a problem program.
- HM: Can be attached to any computer device.
  SM: Can run only on a machine for which it is programmed.
- HM: Takes no main storage.
  SM: Takes 6–15 bytes of main storage.
- HM: Probes can be attached to wrong points giving misleading information.
  SM: Consistent measures always possible once program is debugged.
- HM: Probe attachment takes some time and skill for each new major measurement.
  SM: Loading of program is generally trivial.
- HM: No overhead or interference with computer operations
  SM: Overhead can run from 1 percent to 40 percent. Typically, overhead is 1 to 5 percent.
- HM: Any and all activity can be measured.
  SM: Can measure only information available through machine commands.
- HM: Difficult to measure file activity
  SM: Easy to measure file activity
- HM: Some cannot determine core location usage.
  SM: Easy to determine activity by core location
- HM: Sampling rate can be controlled independently of computer or tied to computer cycles.
  SM: Sampling rate dependent on computer cycles
- HM: Simultaneous multiple measure normal
  SM: Simultaneous measure not possible; approach by frequent sampling
- HM: Purchase price from $1000 to $200,000
  SM: Purchase price from $300 to $25,000
- HM: Can easily measure IBM and non-IBM equipment.
  SM: Most software monitors are available only for IBM equipment.
- HM: Attaching probes makes maintenance men (customer engineers) nervous.
  SM: Running program is no problem.
- HM: Makes mainframe sales representatives very nervous.
  SM: Ditto.

Simulation of Computer Systems

The performance of a computer system can also be analysed by simulating the system through a model. While this method is rarely used to measure the performance of ongoing systems, it is used to estimate the resources required by a system under development. For example, if an on-line order entry system is being developed and the systems department wants to confirm estimates of response time, storage requirements, and transaction processing time, a model of the system can be constructed to anticipate the behavior of the proposed system. In the simulation model, elements of the proposed system are represented by logical rules, tables, and mathematical algorithms. The type of processing, that is, I/O, compute, and update, and the software overhead is estimated for each transaction. Total processing time can be computed from the model. The result will be an estimate since it is based on assumptions concerning the average processing time, average number of seeks, and the type of processing performed on each transaction. Nevertheless, simulation of systems will quite often reveal problems, unacceptable response time for example, that are not anticipated by the designers and afford time to consider alternative processing modes prior to freezing the design.

Choice of Performance Analysis Method

The choice of the data collection method will depend on the costs and benefits anticipated as well as the complexity of the system environment being evaluated. Hardware monitors are the most costly, but they perform the most detailed and accurate data collection. The main drawback to the use of hardware monitors is the natural reluctance to insert probes into electronic circuitry for fear of damaging a multimillion dollar piece of equipment. Actually, the risk of damage is minimal with the manufacturer supplying detailed instructions on probe points. Hardware monitors almost have to be used in measuring total system performance if the system is a comprehensive on-line multiprocessing environment. For simpler systems, software monitors can suffice, providing the results of the software monitor have been verified by a hardware monitor by the vendor. If performance measurements has not been used before, then the best approach is first to use the accounting data provided by the operating system. Careful analysis of this data can often result in significant improvements in system performance. Analysis of performance measurement data can result in improved performance if one or more of the following problems are found:

- Devices have excess idle time.
- Jobs have excess wait time.
- Main storage is underutilized.
- There is excessive lost time due to operating systems problems.
- Operating system overhead is excessive.
- There is significant thrashing during paging operations.

- There is substantial queuing of jobs.
- Channel usage is imbalanced.

Attaining optimum performance depends on identifying and eliminating individual bottlenecks and having a system configuration that is balanced so that the work flows smoothly through it. A balanced configuration has a CPU or CPUs with adequate processing power to handle the workload, a sufficient number of I/O channels to provide enough data paths to keep the CPUs busy, enough disks and tapes, and main storage to allow a high level of multiprogramming activity, and the I/O devices should have sufficient speed to prevent I/O waits. The entire exercise of performance measurement is to assess how balanced the configuration is and the changes necessary to achieve optimum performance within a given system environment.

FACILITIES PLANNING

The performance of a computer center can also be affected by the facility itself. An inefficient, poorly designed facility can reduce the efficiency and effectiveness of the people working at the data center. Computer centers today range from the "fishbowl" types built in the 1960s to showcase a company's computer to facilities buried below ground level with restricted access and heavy security. The "fishbowl" facilities have a computer room encased in glass next to a main traffic thoroughfare to show passers-by the beauty of the company's new electronic marvel. During the late 1960s and 1970s when computer centers were bombed and targets for vandals, most companies removed the plate glass windows and hid the hardware from view. As more hardware is planned for installation, almost every business today is reevaluating its data center philosophy and trying to decide whether to maintain its central facility or provide several smaller computer centers to serve users in the local area. As equipment is upgraded, at the very least upgrading a computer facility means making some adjustments in the existing computer room to accommodate new equipment, and in some cases, building a new facility from the ground up.

The trend today is away from the central facility and towards distributing hardware into user areas. This is especially applicable to minicomputers and microprocessors, neither of which require environmental controls other than the normal office air-conditioning. Whether considering adding mainframes or smaller pieces of equipment, selecting new equipment and upgrading facilities should be done concurrently. The two functions are interdependent. The type of equipment selected directly influences a number of design considerations: room layout and environment, mechanical and electrical support systems, human elements, and space for growth. In turn, the design of the room will directly affect the reliability and efficiency of the computer equipment located in the room.

While the size of computers is getting smaller and the power requirements are less, computer rooms seem to be expanding, simply because everyone is finding more uses for computers. Where at one time, the computer may have had 10–12 user departments, today hundreds of terminals are spread throughout an office. Changes to equipment occur frequently and systems themselves have a life span of only five to seven years. It is a fact of life that for the foreseeable future, computer centers will be changing equipment on a regular basis. This mandates a flexible floor plan with ample room for expansion and reconfiguration. Besides the actual computer floor space, a number of other factors must be considered in planning for an efficient and cost effective computer center:

- Comfortable offices and workstations for data preparation and programming
- Temperature control and secure storage areas
- Maintenance and support function areas where spare parts and testing equipment are kept
- Electrical and mechanical systems, located in discrete areas and acoustically isolated
- Lounges and conference/training facilities
- Delivery docks and warehouse areas, conveniently located and secure.

All of these areas must be near the computer center with good traffic flow between them and the computer room. Some computer facilities are simply stuck into an existing room with little regard for people, creating unpleasant and inefficient working conditions. Over the long run, this can be most detrimental to system efficiency. Good design can help. Movable wall panels, for example, give a sense of privacy without isolating a worker completely. Adjustable tabletops, chairs, and the position of the terminals themselves can reduce fatigue and eye strain. Workstations should have shelves for manuals and storage for personal belongings. Carpets can help absorb noise; if the area is still noisy, background music or "white noise" units may be in order, with frequency and volume controlled by individual areas. A recent study by the National Institute for Occupational Safety and Health recommends that people working on terminals be given 15-minute rest periods every one or two hours. Lounges should be provided at conveniently located areas.

Usually, considerable thought goes into the planning for a new computer room. Unfortunately, little thought is given to storage areas. Just where do you put all those disk packs, microfilm or microfiche cassettes, tape reels, cartridges, printouts, and manuals? Providing an optimum amount of good storage space near the computer room is essential to a smooth flow of work. Moreover, like the computer itself, the storage areas must be temperature and humidity controlled. The Midwest Public Service Company's 10,000 square foot computer center required an entire warehouse to store computer paper. The warehouse was climatized to keep too dry or too wet paper from clogging sensitive equipment. In addition, a staging area was included inside the computer room where paper could be further climatized before it ever reached the machines.

Consider also that disk storage racks have what is called "library load"; that is, they can weigh in at 150 to 250 pounds a square foot as opposed to the 70 pounds a square foot most office floors support. The tape and disk storage facility may require extra underfloor reinforcement. A major new skyscraper in New York was designed as an office building with 70 pounds a square foot load. None of the tenants could construct a computer center because of this load factor and the building remains mostly unoccupied. Other factors to consider in designing the physical facility is the need for raised access or plenum flooring. Power lines, air source, and fire suppression systems are located in the plenum to be out of everyone's way and still be easily accessible for maintenance or moving. Assessing the electrical load and bringing in enough lines to handle it are essential. Many computer manufacturers will not honor warranties if equipment malfunction is traced to power line irregularities. Moreover, in the event of a power failure, the system could lose its entire data bank or the equipment itself could be damaged. The most basic protection is redundant power lines. There should be at least two dedicated power lines into the computer room, independent of the rest of the building's power lines and of each other. The lines should come from two different substations. If computer processing is critical as in banks, airline reservations systems, and brokerage houses, the greatest degree of power protection is an uninterruptible power source (UPS).

Finally, planning for a new computer center should always consider the latest in environmental controls: heating, ventilation, and air conditioning (HVAC). The cost of an HVAC system in a computer facility often comes to 10 percent or more of the total construction costs. Computer rooms should be kept at 72 degrees with 50 percent humidity. Like any mechanical system, air conditioning systems can fail so the AC system should be redundant and completely separate from the building's air-conditioning system. Since redundancy is expensive some organizations have tried to cut expenses by installing undersized air-conditioning systems, supplemented with air from the central building system. The problem is that this leads to filtration and humidity problems and frequently ends up costing more than it would have cost to install the right equipment in the first place. To put the cost in the proper perspective, the environmental controls are to protect an investment of several millions of dollars in equipment and supplies; it does not make economic sense to spend $10 to $12 million on multiprocessors and skimp on providing the proper operating environment for this equipment.

Finally, the computer center should have adequate protection against fire. The optimum fire protection system is a microprocessor controlled system that, when activated by underfloor detectors, performs decision-making logic, releases extinguishing agents, takes sequential emergency shutdown actions, controls HVAC and other systems, and reports status on a regular basis. Some of these systems even produce a hardcopy printout of events and locations, a plus for insurance collection. They require floor space for only a small cabinet and a monitor panel. Most large centers use a halon gas fire suppression system. Held in pressurized bottles beneath the floor, the halon is discharged in half a second under hazardous smoke or fire conditions. The gas does not adversely affect humans nor does it affect computer hardware. A shutoff mechanism for HVAC systems will prevent fans from helping to spread fire. Further protection includes barriers at walls, floors, and doors, and smoke vents and smoke shafts. At the very least, the computer room should be equipped with Class A and Class C fire extinguishers, light enough for women to handle.

OPERATIONS MANAGEMENT

The people responsible for managing computer centers are operations managers. What do operations managers do? When the job is done well, they appear to do nothing. In order for centers to operate smoothly, operations managers have to make all the plans and execute them efficiently. First, they have to provide places to house the computers. This could be anywhere, on the top floor of an office tower, in a specially built facility, in a warehouse. They have to provide the proper environment. If water is needed, it must be provided at the right temperature; sufficient power must be provided, and the computer must be protected from fire as well as from unauthorized usage. So operations managers are plumbers, and air-conditioning experts, floor designers, electricians, and security specialists. They are also the schedulers. They schedule vendors who provide maintenance, users who want access to computer resources, programmers who want test time, systems personnel who want to install new system software, top executives who want tours of the facilities, salespeople who want to sell centers anything and everything from office supplies to an uninterruptible power source. When things do not work out right, the operations manager becomes a Henry Kissinger. They handle meetings where everyone is pointing the finger at someone else. "Not my job" or "Not my fault" are the phrases heard most frequently by operations managers. In addition to caring for the computer, operations managers must coddle users. To deal effectively with users, operations managers must have user-friendly people. They are the ones who can answer the users' questions in the same language the questions were posed, and solve problems in a friendly manner. Operations managers make sure that there are enough machine cycles to satisfy everyone's needs. When it appears that machines are reaching capacity, they juggle schedules, reconfigure I/O channels, and change the application mix to squeeze the last bit of capacity out of the machines. While they are doing this, they are doing replacement system planning and working with the applications developers to anticipate their resource requirements. In sum, they keep everyone happy and centers running smoothly. An operations manager, like the head of a family keeps all parts together and running smoothly. Just as the head of the family receives no praise when things go right, but when the family runs out of milk, or when family members cannot get what they want, the head of the family will get flack; so the operations manager receives no praise when things run smoothly but gets all the abuse when things are not perfect. When data centers are running efficiently and effectively, we know that there is an operations manager who is doing a good job, managing an important company resource.

PROFESSIONAL APPLICATION COMMENT:
THE RESULTS AT MIDWEST PUBLIC
SERVICE COMPANY

Grace Norman's meeting with the consultants went smoothly. She expressed her concerns about ordering new equipment without an outside, independent assessment of the present usage of existing equipment. "Are we really at the saturation point and must we replace the equipment with more capacity? What are my options?" Grace asked. Also, the consultants were told that they would not be working in a friendly environment. Most of the operations people were convinced that the present system had to be replaced so they would not volunteer any information that would lead to any other conclusion. The consultants told Grace that this was not new to them, usually in projects of this type, they were in a hostile environment. However, the technique they would use was to measure the system using a hardware monitor. All aspects of the system would be measured and the effort would take at least 8 to 12 weeks to get sufficient measurement covering a monthly cycle, and allow for sufficient time to analyse the results and make recommendations for improvement. If the results were challenged, additional time might be needed to verify the results. Grace told them that the results would most likely be challenged and that they should prepare for that eventuality now. Upon hearing this, the consultants decided to supplement their hardware monitor with a software monitor to measure file activity and usage of main storage, the two areas where a hardware monitor was weak in measuring.

The decision to use a hardware monitor was challenged by the operations manager who did not want anyone putting probes into the hardware. He solicited the help of the marketing representatives who urged Grace not to allow anyone to attach foreign objects to the CPU and warned that the warranty might be voided by these attachments. However, the consultants showed Grace and the IBM salespeople the library of probe points provided by IBM to help in measuring the proper circuit functions, and a list of companies using hardware monitors on similar equipment. Reluctantly, the operations manager gave them permission to use the probes, and also gave them the computer center schedule, showing what applications were scheduled for what time of the day. However, since this was a multiprogramming environment, all the consultants got was a listing of the jobs scheduled to be run in a particular job stream. Using both the software and hardware monitor, the consultants were able to measure, for each job, the CPU usage, channel usage, number of I/O access, number of I/O waits, and the elapsed time of each job. Analysis of the data showed that the entire system was operating at 45-percent efficiency. In fact, the statistics showed that 90 percent of CPU activity was occurring in "system space" and 10 percent in "application program space," meaning that most of the time the CPU was busy with operating system requests. Several I/O channels were utilized 22 percent while others were at the 98-percent level. There were significant thrashing problems as well as contention problems causing excessive rolling in and out of programs.

The initial reaction by the operations manager was one of complete disbelief.

There was no way the system could be operating that inefficiently. The consultants had to go through each test and show the operations manager that it was reasonable. For example, nothing totaled to more than 100 percent of elapsed time; CPU wait, plus CPU busy should equal elapsed time. In addition, the operations manager was shown how the data correlated to visual counters of CPU and channel activities. Since the data showed that the problems were mainly scheduling of job mix, and imbalance in channel usage, the consultant took a small job stream, reconfigured it to optimize the use of the CPU and channels, and reran the job stream to compare results. The reconfigured run took half the time of the original run. The operations manager was convinced.

Fine tuning could now be started by analyzing the results of the software monitor with the results of the hardware monitor. Where there were areas of questions, the hardware monitor was used again to focus on a specific problem. After reconfiguring the job streams and assigning lesser active channels to I/O devices, elapsed time for processing was reduced 42 percent, freeing up significant excess capacity. This was done without shifting any work out of the prime shift into off-shift processing. The consultants provided Grace with additional techniques to get more processing capacity. Since PSC was planning to shift some of the work done on the mainframes to personal computers, for example word processing, the consultants recommended that the company look at its long-term hardware strategy to see if it was still valid. The increased use of personal computers would reduce the load on the mainframes and perhaps the next hardware upgrade should be to mainframes that could link the microprocessors together into a network-processing environment. In any case, sufficient capacity had been found through more effective scheduling and allocation of resources to eliminate the need for an immediate hardware upgrade. The additional time gained could be used to reevaluate the overall processing strategy and new hardware plans could be developed to meet the new processing requirements. Perhaps the only party not too happy with the results of the study was the IBM salespeople who lost a replacement sale.

CHAPTER 7   DISCUSSION QUESTIONS

1. During periods of cost cutting in a company, should information systems be required to take its share of the cost-cutting measures? Justify your answer.

2. Should equipment always be upgraded if the present equipment is at capacity and new equipment would offer a better price/performance advantage?

3. Comment on Grace Norman's decision to bring in a consulting firm to solve her problem. What alternatives did she have, what would you have done?

4. If analysis shows that existing equipment is approaching capacity, what alternatives should management consider in evaluating new hardware?

5. From a user's viewpoint, comment on the various ways the computer center can shift workload away from peak hours.

6. How does one project future processing needs in planning for total system needs?

7. How can system performance be measured and why should one measure it?

8. Discuss the pros and cons of charging users for computer processing. What would you recommend?

9. How can the performance of the computer operations department be measured? How do the users assess their performance?

8

INFORMATION AND SYSTEMS SECURITY

ISSUES

- How serious is the problem of computer security? One hears of "hackers" getting into data files, but nothing important or valuable seems to have been lost.

- What method is best for assessing the likelihood of unauthorized access to a computer system and evaluating the exposure created by such a threat?

- How can management evaluate internal and external threats to system security?

- Are public communications networks more vulnerable to breaches of security than internal or private networks?

- Could installing safeguards cost more than the assets being protected?

PROFESSIONAL APPLICATION

BANK SECURITY

Bill Davenport, the president and CEO of one of Canada's largest chartered banks, was reading an article in the morning newspaper about a multimillion loss at a large San Francisco bank. One of their assistant branch managers had gone to his branch on a Saturday morning. It was one of the branches that did not open on Saturdays although some of the management people normally came in to do some catch-up work. The guard recognized him and admitted him to the branch. Luckily, there was no-one else present that particular Saturday morning. He went to a terminal set aside for management use and logged on. Periodically the bank scanned accounts that had been inactive for six months and sent letters to these accounts reminding them of the services offered but actually hoping that the letter would remind them of the account and get the customer to either close the account or start using it. The list was quite lengthy and some of the outstanding balances were very large since interest at over nine percent was paid on balances over $3000. The assistant bank manager pulled a list of these accounts from the files and systematically started transferring large balances into 20 different accounts he had previously opened in different branches in the city. He then created electronic funds transfer transactions on the terminal to close each of the accounts he had opened and sent the balance to a numbered Swiss bank account which he had established when he visited the Swiss bank on business. These transactions were created so that they would be processed on different work days making them look like they were normal instructions from depositors for transfer of funds. Knowing that the internal controls of the bank scanned all accounts for large transfers of funds in or out of the account every two weeks, he made sure that each transfer was for less than $100,000, the cut-off point, and that there was only one transfer from any single account every two weeks. He managed to do all of this at one time working with the customer instruction program at his terminal and creating post-dated transactions. He also knew that at the end of each quarter, a more comprehensive internal control review was made on fund transfers, and at the end of every six months, the inactive account check was made. When this happened, the bank would see that the total dollars in the inactive accounts had dropped sharply and start looking into why. By then, he would be in Switzerland with $2.5 million dollars in his Swiss numbered account.

While the newspaper article described how it happened, it did not describe how the manager was caught and what he did wrong. Bill was very interested and called the president of the San Francisco bank, whom he had met several times at bankers' conferences. The manager was caught because he had used the initials of a teller on the customer instruction form who had gone on maternity leave a week earlier. The branch manager had been checking large transfers of funds from his branch as a routine check and noticed that the instruction was signed by the girl he had just given maternity leave to the week before. Had he not known this, the transfer form would have gone through unquestioned since the amount was under $100,000 and it was approved by the assistant branch manager. The president of the San Francisco bank told Bill that this was at least the third time in the past year that some inside employee had used the bank's computer system to "rob" the bank. Most were covered up and never reached the press because of the bad publicity. This was one case that had slipped through and managed to get out of the bank. He asked Bill: "What do you do at your bank to prevent this type of crime from happening?" "How often does it happen at your bank?" Bill could honestly say that he did not know. He had not heard of a case where this had happened, but that did not mean that it had not happened, just that he had not heard about any instances. After the customary small talk about the family, banking, and the weather, they said goodbye.

Bill's bank was one of the five largest in Canada. As in all Canadian banks, it had a sophisticated computer network linking its 1200 branches across the country. The system had over 6000 terminals with customer files centrally located in Toronto. A customer whose home was in Vancouver would have no problem cashing a check in Halifax on vacation because the branch bank in Halifax would have access to the customer's file and be able to verify account balances as well as debit the account when a check was cashed. This meant that anyone from any terminal anywhere in the country had access to every account in the bank. This worried Bill. His systems people had assured him that all the required safeguards controlling unauthorized use of the system were in place and working. However, they could not assure him that what happened in San Francisco could not happen in their bank too. The system kept out unauthorized users, but in San Francisco, the perpetrator was an officer of the bank, authorized to use the terminal. The same would be true here, Bill was told. However, the safeguard was that the system could not initiate an international money transfer. It was a domestic branch network system so while money could be transferred from one account to another within the country, it could not move money overseas without manual approval. Bill was not satisfied with the answers and decided to call in outside help to review the security of the computer system and make suggestions for improvement. Because he wanted no publicity on this study, he asked the chartered accounting firms to submit a proposal on how they would conduct such a study. All but one used the security checklist approach, namely going through a comprehensive checklist in evaluating the levels of security and reliability in the system. They stressed that: ". . . the use of a checklist does not guarantee the security levels achieved, or even indicate what the level of security is; but the checklist is useful to point out the major areas of investigation, and while not appropriate in its entirety to every situation, it can be a valuable asset in planning and engaging in a security review." Bill thought that this approach could be done by anyone, including his own security department. He was not impressed with the questions on the checklist, for example:

- Is entry to the operating area restricted to authorized personnel?
- Is a list of authorized personnel maintained and kept current?
- Is there a password procedure to log on the terminals?
- Is the password changed frequently?
- Can accounting or other programs be altered by computer operators?
- Are there batch control totals to control the integrity of inputs?

These questions were so basic that Bill could not see hiring a consultant to get the answers from his own people. Surely the security department had similar checklists.

Upon checking, he found that they did. One of the accounting firms submitting a proposal had an entirely different approach. They suggested that a security review be initiated by first identifying the assets that the bank wanted protected, what they were and what they were worth. Next, how could any person, authorized or unauthorized gain access to these assets; what were the risks? If someone got into the asset, what was the exposure or loss? Finally, how did you control access to the assets so that only authorized personnel had access to them and even then, how did you institute procedures to minimize the exposure should the authorized person prove to be untrustworthy? Through the risk/exposure analysis, the effort could concentrate on those high risk/high exposure situations where the loss would be great. It would eliminate spending thousands of dollars to prevent a $500 exposure. This proposal was the most costly of all because it involved a detailed study of every possible path of access to an asset, for example, through a terminal, through the operating system, through telephone lines, through programmer workstations, through normal program maintenance, through access by the vendor's customer or systems engineers doing hardware or software maintenance. It was a comprehensive review and the firm suggested that it be done only for the assets with the highest exposure. Bill was impressed with the proposal and wanted to do it for all assets. After discussions with the firm, it was agreed to use the customer files in the domestic branch network application as the pilot, with the consulting firm leading the effort and documenting the procedures for conducting such a review in great detail so that subsequent reviews could be conducted by personnel in the security department.

The consultants flowcharted all the procedures for accessing the customer files starting with transactions initiated at teller terminals, then branch manager terminals, terminals at regional offices, at the central computer facilities, and at the vendor for remote diagnostics. Every possible transaction that reached the customer file was charted. Once this was completed, paths to the assets were identified and control points plotted at the most critical places. The charts were reviewed to see if control points were in fact present at these places. If they were not, a risk scenario was created to show what could happen, how probable the event was, the degree of difficulty in detection, and when detection could occur, before or after the asset had been reached. The bank has specifically asked the consulting firm to identify the risks and exposures, not to provide solutions. They wanted bank personnel to design the solution and keep it unknown to anyone outside the bank. This approach created a problem for the consultants. How could they demonstrate what they found was in fact a risk? Short of actually doing it, it would be difficult to demonstrate what the weakness was in the system that needed correction. The solution was to develop a series of possible scenarios of how a crime could be committed. Every time a control weakness was found or an area was not controlled which should have been, the consultants developed scenarios of how these weakness could be taken advantage of by someone who knew about them. In fact they were scripts for "breaking the bank". All told, over 150 scenarios were created for management. Some resulted in significant losses, others in small losses. Nevertheless, they identified all the ways someone knowledgeable about the system could take advantage of its weaknesses.

Bill was very impressed with the results of the study and immediately formed a task force to evaluate all 150 exposure scenarios and rank them in priority for action. The ones with the highest risk and greatest exposure would be taken care of first. It would take about two years to correct all of the exposures given the staffing of the security department and the systems staff. In the final meeting between the consultants and the bank security group, the consultants had a word of warning: the domestic customer file and its access was important because of the number of people who had access to the file and the fact that the access could come from any one of over 6000 terminals spread across Canada. However, the dollar amount of exposure was relatively small. The far bigger risk was the international money transfer system which routinely handled transactions whose average dollar value was in the millions. It would not take many of these transactions for the bank to suffer a huge loss. They urged the bank to look into this area as soon as possible. Their words became prophetic; a year after the study was completed the bank lost three and a half million dollars in a computer fraud in the international money transfer department. They had not had time to start the review of the international activities and were still engaged in improving the domestic branch-banking network.

As computers replace the typewriter and the calculator for much of our daily work, concern is growing over the unauthorized access to information and facilities. Within the past few years a group of teenagers called the "414 Gang" (named after the area code of Milwaukee, the city from which they operated) managed to break into computer systems at the Los Alamos National Laboratory, Security Pacific Bank, the Sloan Kettering Cancer Center in New York, a Dallas consulting firm, and a Canadian cement company. According to the FBI, these "hackers" used an Apple II computer to gain access to the system over Telenet, a nationwide computer data-link network, and then cracked the computer center's password security system.

A student from the California Institute of Technology, as a class project, rigged the computerized scoreboard at the Rose Bowl so that it showed bogus scores in place of the real game score. His "achievements" were hailed on the cover of the CalTech alumni news. Although Rose Bowl officials estimated that $30,000 would be needed to repair the damage, the student received an "A" for the course.

A group of high school students in a private school in New York City using a personal computer programmed a random search of telephone exchanges looking for unpublished computer telephone numbers. Using this technique, they managed to access a time-sharing network and a data network and the customers' files on these networks. Once they discovered the telephone numbers and access passwords, they were traded among other hackers, similar to the trading of bubble gum baseball cards in the 1940s and 1950s.

These incidents serve as warnings to businesses: there is a growing computer crime wave accompanying the explosion in personal computers and computer literacy. If this is what kids can do on a lark, imagine what can be done by people who seriously want to perpetrate a computer crime. Unfortunately most on-line systems are vulnerable to break-ins; companies are finally realizing that if they keep their assets on computer files, they had better use something better than a password to protect those files. High-security military computer systems use sophisticated encryption and elaborate physical security precautions. Most commercial computer data traffic is not encrypted. Every day more than $400 billion is transferred, unencoded, over the banks' financial networks—SWIFT, CHIPS, FEDWIRE. Commercial data centers consider themselves secure if they have a cipher lock on the computer room door. Experts have said that it is only a matter of time before the financial community faces a catastrophic computer crime—a Three-Mile-Island type of financial disaster. When that happens, business will drop its "it can't happen here" attitude and seriously attack the problem of information and system security.

DEFINITION OF SECURITY TERMS

Before describing procedures for information and system security, the terminology used in this area should be defined:

- *Threats* The dangers to which an organization and/or system can be exposed.
- *Vulnerabilities* Given a threat (danger), a vulnerability is a lack of protection against that threat. It is the susceptibility of the organization or system to harm from that threat.
- *Risks* The risk is the likelihood (chance) that the danger will come to pass. It is based on subjective judgment using statistics based on the experiences of others.
- *Exposure* If a threat does actually happen, the exposure is the harm or loss that can result—the consequences. The bad consequences are what the security measures are designed to prevent.
- *Vulnerability analysis* Given a specific threat, a vulnerability analysis seeks to determine the degree of protection that exists against that threat and the consequences that can result if the threat materializes.
- *Risk analysis* Given a list of specific threats, what are the likelihoods that the dangers will actually come to pass? For example, an earthquake can conceivably occur anywhere on earth, but the risk of an earthquake is higher in California than in Florida.
- *Vulnerability/risk analysis* The result of this analysis is the "bottom line" for security planning. For each specific danger, it indicates the likelihood of that danger happening and the harm or loss that will result from it happening. In the worst case, the organization may be forced out of business. In many other instances of danger, the harm will be more of an annoyance or temporary disruption of business. The vulnerability/risk analysis attempts to rank the dangers in terms of how likely they are to occur and what can happen if they do occur.

INTERNAL AND EXTERNAL THREATS

In the early days of computers, security was primarily concerned with computer sites and their protection from disasters such as fire, floods, and power outages. With the exception of installations that stored classified material, physical security was the main concern of business. The introduction of sophisticated software increased the need for security over programs. For example, in a multiprogramming environment, programs running concurrently must be secure from each other. As mini- and microprocessors were introduced, security expanded to protect communication links and terminal access to processing power and data. Finally, the use of computers in engineering and manufacturing introduced another dimension in security—the protection of automated manufacturing processes from disgruntled employees displaced by computers. To assess the seriousness of a computer breakdown or loss of data to a company, each business has to evaluate the potential threats and the seriousness of the consequences. The security for a computer at a bank or brokerage house would be significantly different than that for a food-processing company with the same size of computer system. Therefore the degree of security to be designed into a computer installation would depend on management's assessment of the threats to the company, the potential losses if the threats were to happen, and the time and cost to recover from the breach in security.

Studies of detected computer misuse show that 61 percent of the cases are fraud and embezzlement cases and the amount of money involved is generally higher than has been true in manual systems. There has been some theft of data, perhaps for the purpose of selling to a third party. The remainder of the cases has been involved with the destruction of data or equipment, or the denial of computer services to legitimate users. In a study of 33 cases of detected misuse,[1] it was found that members of the computer staff itself (programmers, analysts, operators) were the perpetrators 42 percent of the time, outsiders to the company were the offenders 33 percent of the time, and users (within the company) constituted the remaining 25 percent of the cases.

The point of attack of these perpetrators was: manipulation of input (45 percent of the cases), hands-on use or damage of the computer itself (27 percent), modification of computer programs (24 percent), and other (4 percent). The manipulation of input was used by all three groups of perpetrators, the hands-on use or damage of the equipment was performed mainly by outsiders, and the modification of computer programs was done almost entirely by the computer staff. Most experts agree that the vast majority of computer crimes go unreported and are not published. The organizations involved tend to keep quiet about them so they never show up in the statistics. Only in the spectacularly big ones, such as Equity Funding, is the public made aware of the magnitude of the crime and the amount of loss. From these statisitcs, it is apparent that the place to start in evaluating threats is with company employees, especially those in the computer department and those having the opportunity to manipulate inputs.

Internal Threats

Internal threats come primarily from employees who are unhappy with the company and seek revenge by damaging the computer or its critical files, and by employees who seek to defraud the company by stealing its assets or stealing computer resources to use for their own purposes. Just as employees use company photocopiers for personal business, they may increasingly use company computers for their own ends. Most employees working with computers have used them to play computer games or

1. *Eleventh Annual Computer Security Conference,* Nov. 12-14, 1984, Chicago.

to draw fancy graphic displays (the most popular being the Santa Claus sleigh and reindeers during the Christmas season). However, there have been instances of employees caught using the company's computer to run their own service bureau or to run an illegal gambling operation.

Protecting information against internal threats becomes even more difficult as computers proliferate in organizations. Where companies once maintained a single data center, there are now hundreds of minicomputers and microprocessors scattered throughout the organization. While many of the microprocessors are stand-alone computers, it is inevitable that they soon will be linked into networks with the ability to access information stored in the mainframe computers. Determining which of these personal computers should have top security because they are critical to daily operations or contain highly confidential data will be an enormous task. Moreover, word processing has compounded the problem with many word processors holding quantities of sensitive and confidential information. On the plus side, security protection against internal threats can focus on the employee, especially those working in data processing. The procedures for selecting, screening, and training employees will be the topic for the next chapter. Here, it is important to note that disgruntled employees cause most of the damage when it comes to stealing or destroying computer information. To prevent this, employees must be screened and continuously monitored. A programmer was driving a new Mercedes Benz convertible for months and parking it in the employee parking lot before it was discovered that he had stolen several hundred thousand dollars from a company's bank accounts. Employees whose life styles all of a sudden exceed what can be expected from people at their income level should be suspect. Access to terminals must be controlled and even when authorized personnel use a terminal, there should be definite procedures to screen whether they are authorized to access specific types of information in the system. Specific procedures to check for authorized access to terminals will be presented later in this chapter.

A strike by a small group of data-processing employees could have a disastrous effect on an entire company. Organized labor recognized the strategic importance of data-processing installations in the 1970s and have made inroads into unionizing computer analysts and programmers in several European countries. While most analysts and programmers in the United States are considered professionals and are not members of a union, the union employees of European subsidiaries of U.S. multinational firms may inspire the unionization of the parent company. The risk is present and management should recognize that organized data-processing labor is gaining leverage outside the U.S. If a company starts programs to encourage end user programming, replaces custom coded systems with application packages, and converts to user-friendly data management systems, programmers and analysts may feel threatened by these moves. As the control and use of computers moves out of the data-processing center and into user departments, they may feel more insecure and threatened. These conditions may lead to unionization and management must take positive action to ensure that their information system personnel understand what management plans to do in managing its information resources and that they should not be concerned about job security or opportunities for advancement within the company. Management should anticipate possible problems and do what it can to defuse situations before they get out of hand.

External Threats

External threats used to be limited to protection against people breaking into the computer center and destroying it, as happened in many universities in the late 1960s. Today, the threat exist whenever anyone with a terminal and a telephone can access data stored in a company's data center or on the files of a computer utility used by the business. Personal computers are already in millions of households and more people are becoming computer literate and qualified to use computer systems to serve their own ends. Data communications now link together computer networks of a single company or networks of service bureaus such as Telenet and Tymshare. These networks are used by government and private industry, with much of the data being of a sensitive nature (financial forecasts, planning models, pricing algorithms). It was through Telenet that the teenage computer hackers entered the Los Alamos computer.

There is also a trend to use networks shared by a multiple number of users, for example the money transfer networks run by the Federal Reserve or the money center banks, airline reservation systems developed by one airline and used by many smaller airlines. Food distributors use a network that links them with manufacturers so that their orders can be placed electronically. The transportation industry links senders, truckers, and freight terminals together in an integrated system. Interdependence offers many advantages from a business viewpoint, but in many cases it means using a system over which the company has no control and one where security may be minimal. If this system fails, the result can be just as devastating as a strike or an act of sabotage. Meeting internal and external threats demands management awareness of the potential threat and the analysis required to determine how to react and meet this threat. This means an organization devoted to providing information and system security.

ORGANIZING FOR SECURITY

Ensuring that both information and systems are secure is becoming a full-time job for specially trained people, especially in large organizations with on-line systems. An effective security program is based on organizational and administrative controls. Before establishing a security program, management must develop a description of potential exposures and the adverse effects each exposure might have on the company. This list of exposures can be used in developing the security plan. The plan should identify and put in place administrative, physical, and technical safeguards to counter the threats identified in the security evaluation scenario. Figure 8-1 portrays how a security department may be organized to install and manage the security program.

Administrative Safeguards

Administrative safeguards include the security program and the policies, procedures and standards to execute the program. Management control must be established in the areas of:

- Identification of threats
- Assessment of risks and exposures
- Preparation of a vulnerability/risk analysis
- Detection methods that can minimize loss when accidents, disasters, or security violations occur.
- Recovery methods and steps that can prevent future losses.

Control procedures vary from one organization to another depending on the scope of the security program and the associated vulnerability/risk analysis. Typical control procedures include:

- Establishing formal security procedures and periodic reviews of compliance
- Establishing progress reviews and analyses (for example security walkthroughs during system development phases, and scenario development showing what threats could happen).

FIGURE 8-1   **COMPUTER SECURITY ORGANIZATION FUNCTIONS**

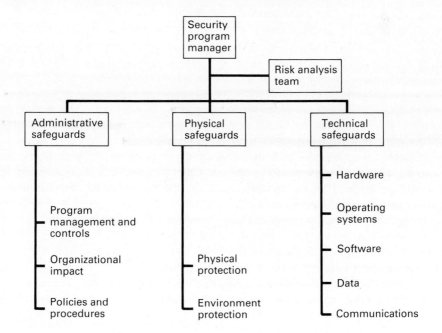

■ Establishing formal communication channels for monitoring adherence to security procedures

■ Periodically evaluating the entire security program.

These control procedures are crucial to an effective security program, especially in a quickly changing or high-risk environment.

Since the implementation of a security program affects the entire organization, three areas that will impact the organization should be reviewed and monitored: awareness and education, attitude, personnel selection and assignment. Of the three, personnel selection and assignment is regarded as the most critical area. Such factors as background checks and separation of duties are important, however, even with proper personnel selection and assignment, a security program can fail if employees are unaware of or uneducated about the need to maintain security. An ongoing awareness and education program must be instituted and updated frequently to reflect the latest changes in the processing environment. Employee attitude is another important security consideration. Dissatisfied or disgruntled employees are the ones most prone to sabotage or to do malicious damage to computer installations. Moreover, employee dissatisfaction often results in shoddy work habits that can destroy the effectiveness of even the best security measure.

To ensure that everyone in the organization understands the security program and their part in it, security policies and procedures should be published in a security manual and employees given a copy. To quote an old army saying: "Security is everybody's business." The need for security and the specific policies and procedures in effect must be understood by the entire organization, not just the security officer or the information system manager. A well-prepared policies and procedures manual can act as an effective control in itself and facilitate development of a structured, coordinated security program.

Physical Security

Physical security measures are intended to reduce or prevent disruption of service, loss of assets, or unauthorized access to equipment. In most businesses today, the computer is an integral part of the company's operations. Disruption of computer processing would be as devastating as any natural disaster. Unauthorized access could mean loss of assets or malicious destruction of equipment and files. Unless the computer equipment is physically secure, any attempt to protect the system and its data will be futile. Physical security should be the first thing to consider in any security program.

Threats to physical security can arise from two sources: environmental hazards and human destruction. Environmental hazards include: fire, earthquake, severe storms, flooding, power failures or brownouts, and air-conditioning failure. Protection against environmental hazards requires that there are detection devices in the computer center to warn of an environmental failure and automatic correction systems. For example, there should be heat and smoke sensors to warn of fire and a halon fire-fighting system, or thermostats to record temperature and humidity with automatic shutoff of equipment when critical limits are exceeded. An uninterruptable power source can protect against power outages. For those natural disasters which cannot be protected against by alarm systems, for example storms, earthquakes, or explosions, disruption of service can be kept to a minimum through the use of backup centers. Some companies have made arrangements with other companies to use their data center for processing in case of disruption to their own center. This approach has limited value. Few data-processing centers have sufficient excess capacity to process another company's processing load for any period of time. Even if only the critical applications were processed, there would be conflicts in scheduling, problems with communication lines, and reallocation of disk and storage space. It gives false comfort to management to think that if their computer goes down for whatever reason, processing can be maintained by using someone else's computer for any length of time. What can be done is to participate in groups that establish data centers just for the purpose of disaster recovery. For example, a group of insurance companies in New York have created a service bureau and equipped it with systems capable of handling the total workload of any single company should a disaster occur. Until that happens, the equipment is used to sell time to any outside party. If a disaster should occur, the service bureau will be immediately available to the affected company to handle its complete workload. It is interesting to note that in the 11 years the backup center has been in operation, it has never been used by a member company as an alternative processing center because of a disaster at the main center. It has been used by member companies to handle peak load processing and special requirements so as not to disrupt normal processing at the main center. The fact that it has not been used should be good news to the companies; after all, it is an insurance policy— no one who takes out fire insurance on his home expects it to burn down, yet all homeowners have fire insurance.

Protection of data and equipment against human destruction is much more difficult. The first line of security is always restricting access to authorized personnel only, and hoping that those authorized will not take advantage of their unique opportunity to cripple the business. Restricting access means access to the computer center as well as access via remote terminals and microprocessors. Restricting access to the data center does not mean issuing authorized personnel a key or even a code to enter on a cipher lock. Anyone neatly dressed in a business suit and looking important can easily follow someone with a key to a computer room without challenge. Large data centers today use a "man-trap" to screen authorized personnel. To enter the center, you identify yourself to the sentry outside the center. If you are a visitor, you say who you want to see and this person is called to come down to identify you, and accompany you into the center. Once you have been cleared, you leave your briefcase, purse, or any packages with the sentry and enter a glass-enclosed booth. While you are inside the booth, your belongings are inspected and returned to you through a glass opening in the booth. When you are cleared, the door admitting you into the center is opened and you can enter. This door cannot be opened when the door into the booth is open, thereby preventing anyone from forcing a way in. All personnel entering the center have to be identified with a picture ID, a palm print, or a voice print. Being admitted through this first entry level does not get you into the computer room or sensitive areas of the data center, it just admits you into the center. Additional security restricts entry in the computer areas, terminal areas, storage vaults, and other sensitive areas.

People build computers, and some people will always be able to find a way to break into them if they try hard enough. Unfortunately, often it is human nature—being too friendly or too casual—that compromises computer security. For example, the weakness of IDs and passwords is that people often share them with co-workers, paste them on terminals, or post them on bulletin boards. Moreover, the passwords are easily guessed, the name of a child, wife, or even the company. It is rumored that the password at Pepsico Inc. at one time was "Pepsi". This is a critical personnel problem for managers who must recognize that a successful security program depends to a large extent on the individual user protecting his ID and password.

The question of employees losing or stealing data is another problem. People who work with information during the day may want to take the information home to continue working at night. If this information is on a diskette, can you rely on these individuals? Many managers take the approach that if the individuals could take papers home in their briefcases, why restrict them from taking diskettes home. This issue has to be resolved by the manager's personal judgment.

Over the past ten years, the focus of computer security has moved from protecting data to identifying the user. Software systems used to require an individual to supply a special password each time they wished to get certain information. Now, once a user has been identified to the system, he may request any information within a particular field. Sooner or later, somebody will market a computer system so "user-friendly" that anyone who can flip the on-off switch on the machine will be coached by the software in how to gain access to the information they want. While that scenario may frighten some managers, it really raises the central security question: who shall have access, and how much shall they have? This question places a heavy burden on management—one which it has not fully recognized as yet—to develop better security consciousness among its personnel. Management must assume the corporate responsibility for security.

Software Security

If security is to be a major consideration in developing application software, security features must be designed into the system and implemented in each phase of the system development life cycle. The complexity of interaction among various parts of any application software system makes retrofitting security control features a time-consuming and expensive task. Therefore, control features and security considerations should be built into the software as part of the initial design.

Project initiation phase. This phase identifies the requirements and use of a proposed system. As data is gathered to prepare preliminary functional specifications, analysts should also identify control features and security requirements. For example, when developing a human resource information system, analysts should identify potentially private information and possible access control features. They should identify potential threats, and exposures, and formulate security measures to minimize the threats.

Cost/benefit analysis. During this phase, the vulnerability/risk analysis should be performed to quantify overall security requirements, threats, and countermeasures. The cost/benefit analysis must include the results of the vulnerability/risk analysis to identify the costs of protecting the system. For example, a cost/benefit analysis for an electronic funds transfer system (EFTS) that did not include considerations of security and control features would overlook a very expensive segment of the system.

Preliminary system design. Overall software requirements are determined and functional specifications are developed during this phase. Security control features should be included as part of the preliminary design. For example, in designing an accounts payable system, controls to prevent unauthorized checks from being prepared should be designed into the system. This could be accomplished through hash controls and batch totals.

System design. All security features such as password protection of data, authorization lists, key number verification, and data encryption, are identified and included in the development of programming specifications in this phase. This should be done by having security analysts working side by side with the system designers to develop the most efficient way of including security features into the technical design.

Programming. The security features developed in the preceding phase are coded in this phase. On sensitive applications, the modules containing the security feature are programmed by someone from the security staff rather than by the application programmer. For example, banks find that fraud through accessing computer files and modifying programs to siphon funds into illegal accounts is usually done by programmers who are familiar with the application programs. By including security modules in the programs coded by someone else, it would be more difficult to change the program without being detected.

System test and conversion. As the system is being tested, separate tests should be made of the security and control features. Scenarios should be prepared to test different ways of breaking the security of the system. These scenarios could be prepared by the designers of the system who are familiar with the logic of the program flow and the functions the application performs. If the controls are found inadequate, they must be tightened up before the system is turned over to the user for operation. The conversion plan is also tested for adequacy and effectiveness of the controls to be used during the conversion phase.

System installation. As the system is installed in a full operating mode, the security features are given a system test to ensure that they function properly. All testing of security features should be done by the security group with no involvement from the information systems department analysts and programmers. This separation of functions is critical to maintaining the integrity of the security system.

Post-installation reviews. As the system changes through use, security features should be reviewed to ensure that they encompass the changes being implemented. Moreover, the change procedures themselves should be monitored to make sure that the change is authorized and that the new code performs only the processing that the changed specifications indicate.

As the trend to user-friendly systems continues, the difficult problem of keeping sensitive business information confidential is compounded. Whether the software is developed in-house or purchased, software security should be multilevel security that allows a manager to determine how information will be distributed. Terminal codes, operator IDs and passwords have always been the first level of security for computer software systems. Certain terminals may be authorized to enter the company's personnel system, while others may not. The same goes for operator IDs. If the operator ID does not match an authorization list, he does not get in. In addition to an operator ID, a user must supply the right password which should be changed regularly. Since operators' IDs and passwords can be stolen, in some instances the operator may have to answer a question to verify identity, for example, his or her mother's maiden name. The question can be taken from the personnel file and should be of a type that only the real operator would know the answer.

Another level of security is application security. With integrated software systems, each individual application within the system should have its own security. Thus, an individual authorized to work on the general ledger may not be able to enter into the payroll system. Also, a user may be restricted to a certain division rather than have access to the entire company.

Some employees may be allowed only to look at screens. Some may be permitted to enter data onto those screens, but not to change the existing information. Others will have the authority to make changes and generate reports. Finally, a manager may want to allow an individual in the personnel office access to information about a certain field, such as education, training, and skills, but not salary.

Audit trails are another critical part of any software systems's security functions, although they are after-the-fact. They allow a manager to review precisely which employee entered or looked at a specific piece of information. The trail typically identifies the employee, the terminal that was used, the date, time of day, and finally the screen that the employee was using. To be of any value, these audit trails should produce exception reports which the manager has to review daily. For example, instead of a report listing all employees accessing files through terminals, a report should be presented showing those employees who made changes to the payroll file. The manager should review this to make sure that the person and the change was authorized. Unless this is done daily, the value of the security feature is lost.

This layering of security features makes it possible for a manager to maintain detailed control over access to the information stored within a computer system. Such software features are not infallible, but they go a long way toward keeping business information in the right hands.

Hardware Security

The phone lines, hardwired terminals, and microcomputers used to gain access to software systems can be viewed as the "hard" or physical aspect of security. A call-in phone system may include automatic dial-back programs that make certain a user calling into the mainframe is at an authorized telephone. Other systems may terminate a call if a user is unable to give the proper password within a certain period of time. Any computer system that can be reached through the public telephone system is potentially vulnerable to break-ins. Hackers, as well as more serious computer criminals, can use inexpensive, hobbyist-type computer equipment to discover unpublished computer telephone numbers by programming a random search of telephone exchanges. From there, they can detect the type of computer being accessed and use well-known techniques to attempt entry.

There are three primary requirements for an effective computer log-on system. The first requirement, as mentioned in a previous section, is to select and properly administer a set of user identification codes and passwords that have a very large number of possible combinations. This reduces the chances for success of an outsider who either guesses the codes or uses a computer to make repetitive "brute force" attempts to break the code. The passwords should consist of randomly selected groups of at least four alphanumeric digits. It is useful for passwords to contain pronounceable combinations of characters so users can easily remember them and avoid writing them down. It is seldom a good practice to permit users to assign their own passwords. A review of password files in systems using this approach often shows that people use names, dates, and other readily guessed information. That type of password system is very easy to break. A five-digit alphanumeric password would have 36 to the fifth power (60,466,176) possible combinations. In security jargon, the number of possible combinations is called the "keyspace." This keyspace size sounds very large, but it may not be large enough if two further security considerations are not met.

The second requirement for effective log-on security is automatic disconnection of the incoming terminal line after a small number of invalid password attempts have been made. The usual limit is three attempts. This disconnection, which requires the perpetrator to hang up and redial after every three tries, can increase the time required to perform a brute force penetration by a year or more, depending on password characteristics. A related and very valuable feature is automatic deactivation of a user identification code if it is used in multiple, invalid log-on attempts.

The third requirement for log-on security is an operating system module that logs and reports invalid sign-on attempts and other events with security implications. These could include such things as an unauthorized person attempting to run sensitive applications programs such as the payroll or personnel programs, or using high-powered system utility programs to copy or modify files. This feature will reveal whether attempts at computer vandalism are taking place, so that further, more positive means can be used to report and apprehend the hackers. Security reports can also be used as evidence in police or FBI investigations and trials.

If the computer system effectively uses all three of the security procedures described above, then it can be considered reasonably resistant to penetration via telephone by unauthorized persons using random or computer assisted search patterns. Of course the most important additional ingredient is careful security administration that focuses on procedures for the distribution and changing of passwords. If these procedures are either missing or poorly administered, then the security problem increases greatly. Users should be reminded of the need to protect their passwords from disclosure.

Within the past year, a new device called the port protection device (PPD) can reinforce the protective measures described above. This device can be viewed as a black box placed between an incoming telephone set and the computer to screen out unauthorized callers (see Figure 8-2). It is completely external to the computer's dial-up access ports, does not communicate with the computer host in any way, and is completely transparent to it. All PPDs have on-board microprocessors or intelligence, which are used to add a layer of external password protection to any communication

FIGURE 8-2   TYPICAL CONFIGURATION PORT PROTECTION DEVICES

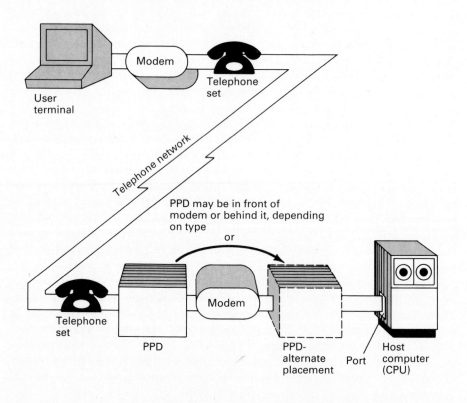

line. The PPD will require a potential dial-up terminal user to enter some form of password as a first step toward connecting with the host computer. The PPD then matches this password code with a table of valid user codes stored in its own memory. If the match is correct, the user is connected with the host and permitted to go through the routine log-on sequence. If the code provided by the user is invalid, the user cannot access the host and the call is terminated. The important thing here is that this password checking is completely external and independent of the host computer system. The potential user cannot even contact the host unless the initial password code is correct. These devices are resistant to the brute force computer-based attacks described earlier. Once users pass the obstacle of the PPD, they will still be required to log-on and deal with any security measures for identification, authentication, and authorization that are in use by the host operating system and application programs.

More and more companies are using special devices and programs to encrypt information sent over the telephone so that it is unintelligible without a decrypting device. Moreover, voice recognition devices make it possible for the computer to positively identify users before they enter the system. The fact that certain terminals, such as those authorized to get into a company's payroll records, can be physically isolated makes keeping watch over who is using those terminals easier for managers. Some terminals require a key to turn them on, and microprocessors can have security built into the system. The degree of protection and number of levels of security to use in log-on procedures will depend on the asset being protected. This protection is based on risk assessment and exposure evaluation.

VULNERABILITY AND RISK ANALYSIS

It probably is not possible to give complete protection against even one type of threat, and it is not practical to try to give some protection against every conceivable type of threat. So the design of a security system involves setting priorities, to indicate where attention is to be directed. As suggested in the bank security professional application, this initial step should be an assessment of the assets to be protected and an assignment of priorities based on the exposure should loss occur. Once the assets (information) to be protected are identified, a list of threats to the information can be made. These threats would include the deliberate or accidental modification, destruction, or disclosure of information. The next step would be to give rough appraisal of the current protection against each type of threat. This may require that all access paths to the asset be identified and the controls along this access path evaluated for adequacy and timeliness. A group consisting of representatives from the users, information systems, and security should make this assessment. This group should try to identify some of the consequences of those threats coming to pass. The exposures can include direct losses, indirect losses, and loss of prestige if a penetration becomes publicly known. The threats, the weaknesses in protection against those threats, and the consequences if those threats come to pass, constitute the vulnerability analysis.

The next step is to perform a risk analysis, or assessing the likelihood of those threats ever happening. This step is subjective, although statistics are available on reported security violations. Risk is measured as a probability, the likelihood of an event occurring within some specified time period. In the final analysis, it will be a guess. "I think that there is about one chance in ten that someone will try to gain unauthorized access to such a file within the year," might be an example of such an assessment. Combining the risk factor with the vulnerability analysis can provide the basis for setting priorities in security systems to indicate where controls are most needed. It brings together the following types of information:

- The threats to which the organization seems to be vulnerable.
- The exposure for each threat, the harm or loss that the threat could bring should it come to pass.
- The risk of that threat actually occurring
- The expected loss from that threat
- The possible controls to bolster the protection against that threat.

The term "expected loss" needs more explanation. Suppose that the likelihood of a threat actually occurring in a one-year period is one in ten (10 percent). If it does occur, the maximum loss would be $100,000. Within a ten-year span, it is almost certain that the threat will occur and the $100,000 loss will be realized. Thus, the loss will be $100,000 in the year that the threat occurs and zero in the other nine years of the period. The expected loss is then $10,000 each year for the ten years. The concept is valid over the long run, and provides an estimate of the average loss per year. In any one year, one or more threats may actually materialize and the losses for that year can be substantially greater than the expected loss.

Another approach is to ignore risk analysis and the expected loss concept. It uses a very pragmatic point of view: if an exposure is large enough, it should be guarded against, almost regardless of the likelihood of the threat occurring. Maybe the likelihood is only one chance in one hundred that the threat will occur within the next year, but it has just as great a likelihood of occurring next year as it has of occurring in the 50th year. Exposure is very important, but an organization simply cannot afford to protect against every eventuality. Risk must be considered also and the concept of expected loss is important too. It says, in effect, with the set of controls that we are using today, here is the average loss that we should expect a year for this set of threats. This type of analysis should be very helpful in setting security requirements for management information.

INFORMATION OWNERSHIP

Ask today's information-processing professionals to describe the changes which have most strongly influenced their current work environment and they would probably answer in terms of the growth of personal computers and the strong reemergence of the end user in taking control of application processing. As more users have access to information and want to look at it, change it, reformat it, and present it in different sequences on different reports, the questions raised are: Who owns this information and what is an "information owner?" Probably the most useful definition in the security context is: the individual who sets the rules for information usage. Who may have access to specific information and processes, and under what circumstances? Thousands of managers in finance, manufacturing, development, traffic, personnel, and other functional units are now getting their information ownership rights back, rights which they earlier turned over to the data-processing department. Each new personal computer and intelligent workstation under their direct management control reaffirms this transition. However, with the return of those rights has also come corresponding difficulties and a certain degree of discomfort. Sometimes users and managers are not adequately prepared to take on or reassume these ownership responsibilities. In some situations, ownership can be a very powerful managerial prerogative and the source of some conflict. But identifying and clearly establishing ownership rights and responsibilities is absolutely essential today for an effective security plan. From it comes the process of information classification and personal authorization. Both classification and authorization are more usefully expressed in terms of information and application, not in terms of specific pieces of hardware or specific operating environments such as on-line or batch.

What is important to the business? With increasing frequency, the cost of the system is significantly less than the value of the information it is processing. Do we really know what it is we want to protect? Answering this does not necessarily require determining the information value in the traditional return-on-investment sense so much as it calls for setting priorities. This is nothing more than determining what information you can least afford to lose or reveal.

Who should be involved in this process? Certainly audit and security specialists, information systems personnel, even users, and above all else, general management needs to be involved, to direct, motivate, and inspect. Because of the pervasive nature of this new processing power through the organization, general management in this case means top-level management.

Given all these varied people, the application orientation to security now becomes even more valuable. A general manager may not be an expert in computers, but almost all general managers know how their business works and how information moves through the organization. Good general managers can get a tremendous amount of mileage out of simply asking the right questions about controls and usage by function. And they insist on answers in the same terms. It is not necessary to know the mechanics of encryption to understand its value. How an access control system handles profiles and passwords is not important if the manager knows what it can do; if it can determine who can access data and resources, and whether that is adequate to control the information.

The key to security is a clear statement that information security and audit are now more important to the organization than ever before and that a workable, sensible information security plan needs to be developed and implemented. In today's information environment, security should not be a single project, it should be a way of life.

CHAPTER 8   DISCUSSION QUESTIONS

1. Banks do not release information about computer crimes occuring inside their organization. Do you think that this would lead potential criminals into thinking that they could get away with it? Would publicizing the fact that a crime has occurred and the perpetrator caught discourage others from trying?

2. What is wrong with the checklist approach to security reviews? How would you improve this approach?

3. Critique present terminal access procedures, identify their strengths and weaknesses and recommend improvements.

4. As factories become automated, should there be concern over security for industrial computers? How should they be protected?

5. Most companies "overlook" the use of photocopiers by employees for personal use (making a copy of one's income tax return or printing an invitation to a party, for example). What attitude should the company adopt towards using terminals or microprocessors for personal use—personal correspondence using word-processing software, for example?

6. Is unionization of the information systems department a threat to the company? What should management do, if anything, to avoid unionization?

7. What is a practical way to test a security program/procedures to determine if they work?

8. What do you think of the arrangement to process your data at another company's computer in case of a disaster at your company, and allowing the other company reciprocal privileges?

9. People take work home in briefcases. Should they be allowed to take diskettes with important company information home with them?

10. How can one prevent programmers from coding illegal code into an application?—code to transfer funds into one's payroll account, for example.

9

HUMAN RESOURCE
DEVELOPMENT

ISSUES

- End users are becoming computer literate through the use of personal computers and application development software. How has this affected the role of the information systems manager?

- Does the shift towards distributed systems and microcomputers mean less demand for systems analysts and programmers?

- Will managers from the information systems department ever be appointed CEOs of major business corporations?

- What is the threat to computer security from a disgruntled employee?

- How important is training in the information systems area?

BLACK ELECTRICAL WHOLESALERS, INC.

Black Electrical Wholesalers, Inc., commonly referred to in the industry as Black Electric, was one of the largest wholesalers of electrical equipment in the United States. Its 148 stores reported through 12 regional headquarters to corporate head-quarters in New York City. Sales exceeded one billion dollars annually with major construction projects accounting for over half of the sales revenues. Black Electric worked with construction contractors to "stage" delivery of electrical components going into a building based on the construction schedule. For example, a large office tower in New York would require thousands of fluorescent light fixtures. Black would stage the deliveries so that they were available when needed on each floor. In rural locations, Black worked with the smaller home builders and local contractors through home improvement centers. Each store carried a large inventory replenished from a central warehouse in each region. Shipments to the stores and warehouses were made directly from the large electrical manufacturers such as General Electric, Westinghouse, Square D. Inventory was maintained based on the manufacturer's part number, cross referenced to show substitute parts from another manufacturer if the specified part was out of stock. All of this was done manually from central purchasing in Chicago.

While Black Electric had a computer located in the Chicago regionl head-quarters, it was primarily used for billing, accounts receivable, and accounts payable. Part numbers were listed on punched cards and sorted to produce a price list. The applications were those first implemented on tabulating equipment in the 1950s. As most businesses converted from card equipment to electronic computers, IBM attempted to convert Black Electric. In doing so, it annoyed the chairman of Black Electric so much, that he promised never to have IBM equipment in the company as long as he was chairman. He converted his card equipment to a Honeywell computer, using card inputs and 80 character records. No-one seems to know what IBM did to anger the chairman, but to this day, Black Electric does not even have an IBM typewriter in its offices.

When the chairman was five years from retirement, he decided that he would spend the last five years automating the company. Black Electric was probably the last major corporation to have manual systems in their most important business functions: order entry and inventory control. Management was very happy with the manual system. The average age of the executive team was over 60. Retirement was mandatory at age 70. The company was an employee owned company and all of top management had come through the ranks and had been with the company for over 25 years. None of them had a college education and they were reluctant to try anything new and untested. The management philosophy at the company was centralized control, decentralized operations. Corporate headquarters set policies on pricing, stocking levels, and store profitability criteria. They purchased inventory items centrally and gained volume discounts from the manufacturers. A computer center was located in Chicago to handle all payables and receivables for the company. Regional offices were major stocking points and consolidated sales information from the stores in their region. They provided administrative assistance to the local store managers by performing functions such as credit checking for customers, advertising, construction planning, purchasing, and direct shipment to major customers. Local stores performed the sales and inventory control functions. If they were out of an item, they could order from the regional warehouse, or if the region was also out, the store would phone the nearest stores and ask them if any were available. Each day, the store manager would send the region sales data for the day. The data would be used for inventory control and sales analysis. All information was consolidated manually in New York on a monthly basis.

The chairman of Black Electric recognized that he did not have the resources to plan, design, and build a computer based information system for the company, so he asked his accounting firm for help. The management advisory services group of the accounting firm provided a team of people to go through the system life cycle in designing an automated system. When these consultants asked the chairman to provide someone from the company to lead the project and also people to work with the study team, the chairman appointed Bill McPhee, a former director of operations, to act as Black Electric's project manager. Bill had been with the company for over 30 years, spending most of those years in marketing. Because of his drinking problem, he had been "retired" into the position of director of operations which carried no significant operational responsibilities. Bill was directed by the chairman to provide the consultants with anything they wanted to know about how Black Electric operated. Since both Bill and the chairman felt that morale would be adversely affected if employees found out that a consulting team was conducting a study to automate the company, the project was to be kept confidential at least until the implementation phase. Instead of talking to the users to learn their requirements, the study team would interview top management to ascertain requirements and how various functions were performed. "We know how it should be done" was Bill's answer when his permission was asked to talk to regional and branch personnel. In order to keep the project confidential, no-one from the systems area would participate until the programming phase started. Moreover, the feasibility phase and requirements determination phase would be performed at corporate headquarters in New York to minimize exposure of the study team to the working level.

The consultants argued strongly for visiting users and learning requirements by observing their work in an operating environment. They were told by Bill that top management had over 250 man-years of experience and could tell them all they needed to know. The system was designed with inputs solely from the top management team. After the requirements were determined, two alternative processing methods were presented by the consultants for consideration by management. One was a centralized processing concept with a large mainframe in Chicago linked to terminals in the regional offices. In turn, the regional offices would be linked to the local offices for data entry and report generation. All of the terminals would be on-line to the mainframe for order entry processing and stock status reporting. The alternative processing concept was to locate superminis in the regional offices with small minis in the local office. Each region would perform order entry processing and stock status reporting for all the stores in its region. After the close of business, each regional minicomputer would be polled by the Chicago computer to collect data for consolidation and management reporting. After discussing the merits of centralized versus decentralized processing, and the fit of the alternatives to the way Black Electric did business, the chairman made his decision. The least expensive system would be implemented. The decentralized system was selected since the communication costs and the large mainframe required for a centralized system made it significantly more expensive than that of 12 minicomputers located at the regions. Hardware vendors (with the exception of IBM) were asked to submit bids. The low-bid vendor came in with a price of $8.5 million for hardware and was selected. The range of bids were from $8.5 million to $31 million. Most bids were in the $18 to $24 million range. The consultants recommended several systems in the $18–$20 million area, but when the chairman asked if the $8.5 million bid could work, they had to answer yes.

The low-bid vendor proposed hardware only. No software was available except for a programming language, basic FORTRAN, and a rudimentary operating system under development. When this was pointed out to the chairman, his response was that the consultant would design all the necessary programs and that his programming department would provide the programmers necessary to code the system. Since this would cost considerably less than $10 million, he saw no reason not to accept the low bid. The consultants had estimated a fee of $2.5 million to do the programming design and supervise the coding effort, as well as making some modifications to the operating system to provide some required functions not included in the operating system. The hardware price and consultants' fee together was less than the next higher hardware bid from the vendors.

As program design started, it became apparent that the existing programming staff in Chicago did not have the time or the technical ability to program an on-line system. They were used to a batch, punched card environment and in the opinion of the consultants, would not be able to code and test a sophisticated design. Black Electric decided to hire programmers to do the coding. They went to the programming institutes in the Chicago area, the ones that advertise inside match book covers and guarantee you a job if you complete their programming course, and hired 15 people at salaries of $12,000 to $14,000. It was company policy to give all potential employees polygraph tests to ascertain their honesty and integrity. They also passed a programming aptitude test supplied by the programming institute from which they had graduated. When the validity of this procedure was questioned by the consultants, Bill McPhee told them that the hiring procedures at Black Electric had proven superior over the years and produced outstanding, loyal employees. He was sure that the same procedures used in hiring programmers would work equally well. Subsequent firing of five of the programmers for smoking pot at work and being "stoned" did not change his opinion of the hiring procedures one iota.

The programming effort was planned for 18 months and turned into a disaster. The new programmers were glad to have found work but could not adjust to working under strict programming standards and coding conventions. They had been taught that programming was a creative, innovative effort, requiring individual imagination and creativity. They found that they had to observe structured programming rules and conventions with no innovation or creativity allowed. Moreover, these were the first programs they had written outside of the classroom, and they had no idea of the business requirements for the program. When none of the programs worked during initial tests, they were at a loss to understand why. The older people in the department resented these newcomers and did very little to help them. The situation was not helped any by differences in life style and dress, since the new programmers were called "hippies" and "punks" by the more conservative older group. After the first year, career progression became a problem. The new people found that there was no formal career progression program. Advancement depended on senior people leaving and creating vacancies. With the loyal group of people in the department, they saw few vacancies coming up in the future. Bored with the rigid programming environment, and unhappy with the lack of promotion and the attitude of senior people in the department, they quit. Turnover was high and whatever experience that was gained by the original group was lost to the company. The consultants took over more and more of the programming effort. In addition, they had to test the operating system since the version supplied by the manufacturer had design problems. While the operating system was to have required only 12K of core, it actually required over 30K, leaving very little room for application programs on the 32K minicomputers going into the local offices. The consultants had to recode parts of the operating system to reduce core usage.

When the system was finally ready for a pilot test, a region in the south was selected and the people involved notified of the project and the benefits to be gained. Initially, the local people were happy finally to have the use of computers, although many of the more than 30 people in the order entry function at regional headquarters were worried about their jobs. The first surprise in the pilot test was the changes required in procedures in order for the system to work. It seemed that the procedures described by top management had not been used for years at the local level. They had put in their own procedures to improve efficiency. Response time was unacceptable since the system was designed to handle a certain number of transactions per day. The designers did not realize that 69 percent of those transactions occurred during the first two hours of processing during the business day. Local personnel rebelled at the security procedures for logging on to terminals or to gain access to the computer via phone modems. They felt that since all of them had taken polygraph tests as a condition of employment, the log-on procedures were "an insult to their honesty.'' Training was poorly planned and performed. It consisted of speeches from head office personnel telling of the benefits of automation, and a demonstration of the system using contrived data designed by the top management team. It was so far from the way things were actually done that many of the employees laughed during the demonstration.

The pilot test lasted six months, after which the region rejected the system as not meeting their requirements. They preferred to have their own manual system, and some of the local store managers suggested doing parts of the system themselves on their personal computers. Since this was an employee-owned company, the chairman decided not to press the issue and canceled the project. After discussions with Bill McPhee, he also decided that the entire blame was to be laid at the feet of the consultants. They should have known that the approach would not work and warned the company earlier. He asked for a refund of the $2.5 million in consulting fees or else Black Electric would select new auditors. The fact that over $4 million had been spent by the consultant to make up for work not done by Black Electric personnel or by the hardware vendor was not relevant to the chairman, who called the cost overrun poor judgment on the part of the consultants. To protect annual audit fees of over $250,000 the entire amount of the consulting fee was refunded.

At the retirement party, the chairman pointed out the lesson learned in his attempt to automate Black Electric, namely a business built on people does not need to be automated. ''Success is attributable to hard work, good customer relationships, and providing good products and services at a fair and equitable price. These are factors that cannot be automated and to impose computers into this successful envi- ronment could only harm, not help the company.'' The audit partner, listening to this speech, only nodded in complete agreement. From the consultants' viewpoint, the episode ended on a happy note: Bill McPhee, who had high hopes of being selected the new chairman of the board, was asked to retire early, at age 66.

John F. Rockart, director of the Center for Information and System Research (CISR) at M.I.T. did a study of nine major companies whose top information systems executives held an excellent reputation in their field. The purpose of the study[1] was to identify the key critical success factors which enabled the information system function to perform well in their organizations. The companies studied were selected at random from a list of twenty companies that were ranked outstanding by academic colleagues or by industry contacts. Results showed that four critical success factors were cited by a majority of the companies studied: good people, high-quality service, top management communication, and leadership role with users. All of these critical success factors imply effective human resource management, starting with the top people in the information systems function down to the newest programmer trainee. Human resource development addresses the problems faced by today's information system executive as well as the environment in which people are recruited into the information systems organization, their selection and training and the career paths for advancement.

THE CHANGING ROLE OF THE INFORMATION SYSTEM EXECUTIVE

Information processing is now reaching a critical stage in its development. Many information systems departments are saddled with outdated systems and support organizations based on the architecture of the 1960s and 1970. During the 1960s, focus was on the technical aspects of data processing. Hardware was centralized and easy to manage. Concern was over capacity, application development, operating efficiency, and technical upgrades of equipment. The manager of the information-processing function was a line executive, responsible for running his department. Interface with user departments was at a minimum since the applications being developed were primarily accounting applications with very rigid rules and procedures. All the designers and coders had to do was translate these rules and procedures into program code and get the program running. User interface consisted of showing the accountants the final results, testing the system and proving that it worked in accordance with accounting policies and procedures.

In the 1970s, this relatively simple environment was shaken by the concept of

1. Rockart, John, "The Changing Role of the Information Executive: A Critical Success Factors Perspective," *Sloan Management Review*, Fall 1982.

distributed processing. Now information systems management had to be concerned with communications, terminals, on-line access to data files, and security over the hardware and the data. Since some processing power was given to the users at their location, user interest in computers started to rise. Top management still relied on the information system manager to direct and guide the company's information-processing efforts.

This all changed in the 1980s. Users became computer literate. Vendors showed them how easy it was to have access to their own computer power through personal computers. The processing environment became an integrated one, merging word processing with data processing. Software became user-friendly, and all of a sudden, nontechnical personnel found that they did not need the people from information systems to provide them with processing power or training, they could buy user-friendly software and hardware and learn to use a computer by themselves. Information systems management found themselves switching from a line department supervising hardware and system development people to a functional staff-oriented department offering low-cost processing and a central switching function for mini- and microcomputers. The people in the department changed. No longer were coders and programmers needed to interpret rules and procedures and produce operating programs. Generalists were now needed to help users develop and use data bases of their own. The new information systems manager had to be technically literate and managerially competent—a switch away from the image of technicians with limited business knowledge. Most important, managers now had to cope with a new environment: users, supported by increased computer awareness and the power of personal computing, were demanding, and in many cases assuming, direct control of their information-processing requirements. Perhaps an information-processing manager described it best by saying: "In the 1960s, we called them dumb users, in the 1970s, they were unwilling customers, today, they are our valued clients."

A New Information-Processing Environment

How well have the information systems managers adjusted to their new environment? If the number of information systems managers appointed to high corporate positions is an indicator, they have not adjusted well. There is still the perception by top management that these people are competent technicians, but not movers and shakers. They do not communicate well with users, they tend to guard their own territory jealously, and appear to want to create the impression that they are different, perhaps better, smarter, than the people in the rest of the company. One industry analyst says that the problem is: ". . . . computer people want to stay with their machines, their empires. Machines are easier; adjusting a dial, debugging a code, interpreting numbers—that's what makes many of these guys tick. Their own technical orientation and excessive specialization is doing them in. They shun people problems."

Rapid technological change and improved hardware and software capabilities have bailed out systems managers and made their jobs easier. They have benefited from externally initiated breakthroughs. While they guided their companies in the purchase of equipment, development of application software, and maintenance of programs, unit costs in even the most poorly managed operations have come down substantially over the years. Thus, for years users did not know about the inefficiencies in data processing; did not know that the industry was plagued with excess people and poorly used equipment. No one knew about or understood what was going on in the computer department. Equipment was often purchased because it was the latest technological goodie, something nice to have and something that could be justified based on projected increased business needs. Today, alternative methods of providing processing power means that the users can choose different alternatives to achieve the same ends, and often prefer to bypass the central department altogether. As long as information systems personnel think of their field as unique, and that because of its complex theories and applications, rapid change, and technically oriented personnel they should be treated differently from the rest of the company with respect to budgeting, salary levels, and planning and reporting, their managers will never be accepted as part of the corporate executive team. Yet there is nothing unique about information systems. Their management should be an integral part of every business, along with the management of the other operating divisions in the company. All the issues confronting information systems are merely basic business management issues. Problems are speeded up by a rapidly changing technology but every aspect of the field can be handled by generally sound management tools.

Top management is now demanding that the information systems department operate under the same philosophy and rules as the rest of the company. Lacking people with a management perspective within the organization, top management has had to look elsewhere for candidates to run the information systems department. Corporate management does not want technicians to head information systems. Their role in the company's overall well being is too vital to entrust to someone not part of the company's management team. The search is for people who are profit/balance sheet oriented, people who have a general management orientation and experience. The emerging role of the information executive is becoming increasingly clear. From an earlier position as manager of a huge technical empire furnishing processed data to the end user, the new manager is moving toward a position that is primarily one of consultation and institutional support. It will be the responsibility of information systems to set the policies on how the company postures itself with regard to information. This role will link the information executive to every aspect of the business.

Corporate management and departmental users of information services have overcome the mystique of data processing. They are now computer literate and no longer in awe of the computer and its people. Information systems professionals must face the fact that they are now expected not only to manage their own environment but also to be familiar with all aspects of the company's business. While no-one expects them to be expert in all areas of the business, it is expected that they become generalists on the business and specialists in the information-processing function. The growth of distributed processing and personal computers is now exposing the deficiencies in business and communication skills of some information systems personnel. Doing business with other managers in the company may be almost as foreign to many systems managers as COBOL is to the head of customer relations. The establishment of an effective interface with senior management may provoke real feelings of inadequacy. Many of the current problems may result from a lack of self confidence on the part of information systems managers. They think they have to keep what they do a mystery to hang on to what they have got. They do not realize that they are in an ideal position to learn how to run the business because their projects involve all aspects of their companies.

Gaining Control Over the New Environment

The first step in gaining control of the new user environment is to learn to communicate in business terms. Dramatically increased amounts of time working with middle and top management will be routine in any manager's job. Today's college graduates are increasingly comfortable with computers as an integral part of day-to-day operations. They expect to use this tool in business to assist them in their work and to aid in decision making, but their knowledge of hardware and systems specifics is limited. Information systems managers must simplify the computer so that users will continue to call on them and be able to understand them. Nuts and bolts technicians will not get anywhere and will stifle their own growth because they do not use analogies that business feels comfortable with.

The second step is to recognize that users ''own'' the applications and data processed by information systems. In the past, many data-processing people felt that they owned the systems and could make changes and enhancements just to keep current with the latest technology. The idea that information and projects should be ''owned'' by the user department is a new concept to them and one they must adopt if they are to understand the needs of the user departments better. The new role of information systems is to help their clients work in a smarter way. They should deliver a set of tools and services to support the clients as they do their jobs. By giving users the ownership of systems and data, users will be made an integral part of the planning and development of information systems and services. If users participate in the planning and design of systems, when projects are completed they will already have broad support. If knowledgeable people work on and set priorities on projects, the completed product will be more responsive and better received. It will not be systems that reach beyond the capabilities of the users to absorb and use the systems. By working with users, and at times, letting the user take the lead on design decisions, systems will be developed that do not get ahead of what users understand but ones that can be modified as users mature with regard to existing technology and create advanced needs. One approach to improving user understanding and fostering innovation is to provide users with direct access to computing facilities, whether central or distributed, and with high-level, user oriented utilities that allow them to develop and modify their own small systems and reports. By acting as the consultant to the user, helping them when they are stuck on a technical or system problem, information systems professionals can build the rapport with both user and top management that leads to management confidence in their technical ability as well as their ability to work as part of the executive team. When this happens, the information system executive will have an open door to top executive positions in the organization.

CAREERS AND CAREER PATHS

If the role of the information systems manager can change from a technical one to one that is more management oriented, then there is hope for expanding the career paths of systems professionals. Until that happens, most people view the career path for information systems personnel as being a dead end. The career path model used by most firms is a variation of entry level programmer to analyst to project leader to manager. Sometimes the adjectives junior and senior are used, along with combinations of the above three titles, linked by slashes. A typical organization chart is shown in Figure 9-1. A more progressive approach is to separate the technical and application functions offering parallel career paths with equivalent structure. The bind for most individuals is that they attain the level of senior systems analyst in four to ten years, often because of turnover and demand rather than ability. Those indi-

FIGURE 9-1   **POSSIBLE SYSTEMS PROFESSIONAL CAREER PATH**

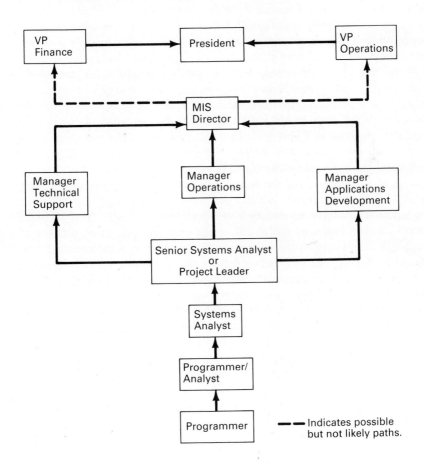

viduals that want a continuing challenge see few formal routes that provide motivation. The head of the information systems department is faced with a similar dilemma, since it is almost impossible to move from information systems to top management. As companies recognize the value of information as a corporate resource, this may change, but for now most feel that career paths in information systems are dead ends, stopped up or isolated.

The growth of user involvement in computers may change the career path situation. There appears to be a trend toward computer people joining user staffs, and user personnel working on programming assignments. The use of matrix organization to assign user and systems personnel to a specific project has accelerated this trend. The migration of systems personnel into user areas may be a direct result of the lack of data-processing career paths and the high growth needs of systems professionals. Today, most management people will stress the importance of having a systems staff that understands the business environment. At the same time users' computer literacy is growing with the infusion of micros into the home and the office. The heightened user interest in computers, and the desire of systems personnel to learn more about the business will result in a new group of people called "systems related professionals", a blend of user and technical people working in the information systems area. Where will these people come from? A bachelor's degree is still the main ticket into programming and systems work, but a large number of companies have expressed frustration with the computer science graduates they have hired and look with interest to liberal arts or business students. The main complaints about computer science graduates are their narrow span of interest and their inability to communicate in a business environment. Many information systems managers have indicated that if given the choice, they would hire from within the company, giving perference to those with demonstrated ability to work well with users and colleagues. Retraining for clerical workers and other people with experience in the company is becoming more common in the information systems area.

A likely scenario for the future information resource department is a small technical staff with a core of trainers that users can call on to help solve problems. The department will be headed by a vice-president of planning and information resources. Some companies are already promoting this type of department with the concept of information centers. There are information systems managers who complain about losing their best people to user departments when these people are assigned to the information centers to assist users. Instead of complaining, the manager should make it a policy to place his best people in user organizations where they have a chance to train user personnel to be systems proficient. This would enable user departments to develop their own systems, reduce the applications backlog in the information systems area, and build a user base of people who recognize the value of information as a corporate resource. The migration of personnel from systems to user areas and vice versa should enhance, not diminish the information systems department power base, and should be something that is to be encouraged.

If the career paths of people in information systems appear to be dead ends, careers for people going into this area are still growing. The U.S. Department of Labor estimates that the number of programmer positions will increase 5.9 percent annually between 1985 and 1995. Annual increase in the number of system analyst positions for the same period is projected at 6.5 percent. At the most optimistic end of the spectrum, Forecasting International Ltd. predicts that the number of computer software developers will grow at a rate of 87 percent annually. They also predict that the growth rate of analyst/programmer will be 51 percent a year.

Forecasts of *Decreasing* Need for Computer Professionals

Most forecasters also believe that the user knowledge growth rate shoud slow before 1990, but the level of their knowledge should continue to expand. They see the information systems professional doing the most sophisticated work while users use the computer for simpler tasks such as information retrieval and report generation. Both users and systems professionals will continue to increase their levels of sophistication. By 1995, some users will reach the 1980 level of technical knowledge held by computer professionals. Will this growth in users' computer capabilities reduce the need for programmers, analysts, data base designers, data communication designers, system programmers? Those who think that it will give the following reasons:

- The applications backlog is diminishing; the increased sophistication of computer users will enable them to develop many of their own applications, thereby reducing the need for computer professionals.
- There is a decreasing need for technical assistance. The new computer knowledgeable user community will reduce the need for technical assistance and therefore the need for computer personnel.
- Simplified development tools will require fewer professionals. With the advent of higher-level languages and improved system development tools for computer professionals, fewer technical personnel will be needed.
- Career paths for computer professionals will become attenuated. Increased computer user sophistication will narrow the career paths for computer personnel.
- Low data-processing stature limits advancements. Because the systems organization reports at a low level, there are fewer opportunities for advancement.
- The information systems managerial path is dead ended. The top information systems executive will never become the executive vice-president much less the CEO or chairman.

Forecasts of *Increasing* Need for Computer Professionals

However, there is a large group of people who believe that these reasons are just misconceptions. They think that computer career paths are expanding and give the following reasons:

■ The applications backlog is *not* diminishing. If the applications backlog is diminishing because users are developing their own applications, those applications have had low priority in the information systems department. As they are taken off the backlog, they are immediately replaced by other applications awaiting development. Moreover, the applications that users can develop themselves using user-friendly tools are usually the easier applications. Tough technical projects will still require computer professionals, and there appear to be more tough technical projects on the horizon than there are easy ones. Finally, as users start develping their own applications, they will soon realize that they do not have the time or the resources to develop large-scale applications. They will confine their efforts to small information retrieval-type projects leaving the transaction-processing-type systems, the data management systems, and the communication systems to the professionals.

■ There is an *increasing* need for technical assistance. As users start to learn about computers and start to develop their own applications, they will want to do more sophisticated things. This will require more, not less, technical assistance. As users get interested in computers, they will want more training, this also will require more technical personnel to provide the training. Once first-time users are trained, some will want advanced training, others will enjoy the technical aspect so much they will want a transfer into the systems department where additional software training can be obtained. All of these factors point to an increasing need for technical personnel rather than a decreasing one.

■ Simplified development tools for users will require *more* systems personnel. This may not be true for the simpler types of development projects but as users take over the simpler applications, highly technical personnel will be required to develop the advanced, sophisticated applications such as artificial intelligence systems, expert systems, decision support systems using relational data bases, integration of office automation and data processing, and advanced communication systems. Since systems professionals are motivated by sophisticated challenging work, these state-of-the-art applications should encourage people to move into this career path rather than avoid it.

■ Career paths for computer professionals will *not* become attenuated. Because of the expansion of computer activities throughout the organization, career paths should become wider, not narrower. Examples supporting this would be the growing use of information centers staffed by computer professionals, the use of consultants to help users do prototyping and modeling, and the use of specialists in building decision support systems and in working on integrating office automation projects with traditional data-processing work. Greater use of dual career paths with the systems department, one for the technical specialist and one for the business systems generalist, would expand career opportunities rather than restrict them.

■ The low stature of the information systems department *does not* limit advancements. While it is true that a few years ago, most systems departments reported to the comptroller, or a low level vice-president, today more and more departments are reporting to the executive vice-president or the president. This trend will continue to grow as more business enterprises recognize that information is a valuable corporate resource and must command top management attention. As the head of the information systems department moves up a notch in the organizational structure, experience indicates that another complete layer of management will be added to the information systems department. This will expand the career path of everyone in the department, not just the top executive.

■ The information systems managerial path will be dead ended as long as information systems executives are technical specialists and not management oriented. *However,* the trend is away from the technical specialist to a manager who is technically competent but also has broad business knowledge and can communicate with management. The manager with a bachelor's degree in Computer Science and an MBA will move right to the top of the executive ranks. Moreover, as the present management reach retirement age, they will be replaced by younger managers who are computer literate and are not afraid of technology. This new atmosphere will make it easier for the qualified top executive in information systems to have an equal chance for making it to the CEO position in the company.

Only time will tell who is right, those who believe that fewer systems professionals will be needed or those who think that careers in the industry have never been better. The conclusion that can be drawn is that more and more nontechnical people in the business enterprise will be computer literate. Information handling will be a way of life in the company and more and more people will be comfortable handling this information through a computer terminal and using application programs to help them in their daily work. The computer terminal will replace the desk top calculator, adding machine, and typewriter, in most companies by the year 1990. This certainly will increase the number of people involved in information handling. Whether they are in the information systems department or in the users' department really does not matter, there are careers for them.

PERSONNEL SECURITY

As employees in most business organizations become computer literate and start using terminals to access information for their work, the potential for computer fraud, embezzlement, unauthorized disclosure, and other abuses becomes a critical problem for management. During the past decade, considerable advances have taken place in areas such as encryption, access control, and physical security. However, the weakest link in any security system is still the people who use and manage the system. Management has taken steps to safeguard the physical storage and processing of data. It has made significant investments in protecting access to data through terminals. It has made little effort in the area of personnel security in the information systems environment. Many managers think that threats to the system are made by outsiders and therefore can be reasonably controlled by physical security and access control procedures. The threat from insiders is often ignored because the high level of education and technical competence required of information systems professionals seems to place them above suspicion. After all, who can conceive of someone with a graduate degree stealing from the company. These managers do not subject the information systems people to the personnel security requirements (such as bonding) with which other individuals in the organization must comply. Statistics compiled over the past 20 years indicate that approximately 70 percent of computer crimes are committed by insiders, and about half of those by the ''educated'' people in the computer department. Management must start to develop a program for personnel security if they are to have a sound overall security program in the company.

Development of a Security Program

The first step in developing a security program is to outline the organization's philosophy on the conduct of business as well as developing a detailed set of rules outlining expected ethical and legal conduct for all employees. These rules should give clear guidance in such areas as:

- What organizational data and processors are proprietary or sensitive and who can have access to them?
- The extent to which employee use of organizational resources is acceptable, for example permitting access to computers, copiers, and other office equipment for personal use.
- Ownership rights of programs and systems developed using company resources or developed while an employee of the company
- Responsibility of each employee for reporting any misuse, fraud, embezzlement, or disclosure of proprietary and sensitive information.

Unless these and other ethical and legal responsibilities are clearly defined and explained to each employee, it is impossible to enforce organizational standards of conduct.

After establishing an organizational code of conduct, the next step is to identify those positions that handle data considered sensitive or critical to the company's business. In a bank, this may be data such as account balances, money transfer procedures, or standing orders for payments. Individuals involved in daily handling of such data or in the design of systems and procedures for handling the data should have special security checks prior to being assigned to work in this area. The level of personnel security required in these positions would depend on the level of sensitivity, the potential risk, and the magnitude of the loss that the individual could cause. Even after individuals have been screened and given permission to handle sensitive data, they should have access to such data only on a need-to-know basis. Bank officers may have access to account balance information, but access should be limited to their "need to know", for example reviewing a specific customer account, rather than allowing them to "browse" through all the accounts. Sensitive data is thus compartmentalized according to the function of the job. It is axiomatic in security that the probability of compromising an activity increases as the number of individuals with access to that activity increases. The levels of sensitivity and the compartmentalization of sensitive data should then be incorporated into a formal set of job specifications that define the scope, content, and specific duties of each position. This provides employees with a clear and unambiguous statement of their duties and responsibilities as well as providing the company with a standard against which performance can be measured.

After sensitive positions have been identified, there should be established procedures for checking the background of persons being considered for these positions. These background checks are usually done by outside organizations under the administration of the personnel department. The personnel department would evaluate the information obtained through the background check, looking for things such as criminal records, missing gaps in employment history, and any security clearances held while in military service. Educational degrees obtained, previous employment, and all references should be verified preferably by telephoning the previous employer or the reference, and getting written confirmation from the university. Because regular credit checks have been proven successful in identifying individuals who might be prone to illegal activity, candidates for sensitive positions should give the company permission to perform credit checks. For extremely sensitive positions, it may be necessary to have the applicant undergo psychological screening by competent medical personnel. Some companies go so far as having the applicant undergo polygraphic and stress analysis for extremely sensitive positions. This can be done only in those states that do not prohibit polygraph tests as a condition for employment.

After passing the screening, the employee is hired and should be given an indoctrination which fully explains the duties and responsibilities of the position. It is good policy to have employees sign affidavits indicating that they are aware of the personnel policies and security regulations and that they agree to abide by these policies and regulations. The affidavit should stipulate that failure to abide by established policies will result in dismissal and legal action against the employee. This will emphasize to the employee the importance of personnel and security policies and that management is very security conscious.

Execution of a Security Policy

No matter how comprehensive an organization's security procedures, they have to be executed by the company's employees. A training program is necessary to ensure that all employees know what they have to do in safeguarding the information and assets of the company. This training should include areas such as:

■ Access and badge procedures. The types of access to the physical facilities and the various levels of security in accessing data. Who is allowed to access various security levels and the concept of the "need-to-know" basis for sensitive information. Secure areas of the building, entrance control, and the company's escort policy would be included in this training. All employees, regardless of their position in the company should be given this training.

■ Security incident reporting. All employees should know what to do in the event of a bomb threat, riots and disturbances, fire alarm, unauthorized personnel in a controlled area, and other emergency procedures.

■ Specific training for those in security organization or handling sensitive data. Those who grant security clearance and handle other security matters should be trained on procedures used to apply for a security clearance and understand the levels of clearances within the organization. They should know the organizational policies in the areas of risk analysis, security testing and evaluation, and maintaining continuity of operations in the event of disasters. Also, they would need to be trained in the day-to-day procedures for handling sensitive data, conducting daily security checks and maintaining the security and the integrity of facilities and systems.

Since many breaches of security are caused by unhappy employees wanting to get even with the company or some manager in the company, it is important to monitor employee attitudes towards the company and to maintain a loyal and stable work force. Management should address a number of motivational and moral issues such as maintaining a pleasant work environment, establishing an equitable wage and benefits program, providing opportunities for advancement and professional growth, performing frequent performance evaluations to let employees know where and how they stand, providing a fair grievance procedure, and being constantly aware of employee morale and problems. Managers should be alert to major changes in the personal and work habits of employees because these changes sometimes signal an increased potential for fraud, embezzlement, or other security compromises. Significant changes in attendance patterns, evidence of excessive alcohol use, an inordinately high standard of living in relation to salary, evidence of severe indebtedness, and similar changes are all indications of serious personnel problems. Managers should not adopt the attitude that what their employees do outside of the office is not their problem. Quite often they give signals of security compromises to come and management should establish mechanisms for providing effective and timely assistance to employees with these symptoms.

Perhaps the biggest threat to the security of any computer installation is the termination of employees. When notified that employees are being terminated, either through resignation or involuntary termination, the manager should pay employees their severance pay, if any, and terminate them immediately. To keep employees for the last two to four weeks after their notifying the company of their intention to resign causes morale problems for the other employees and affords disgruntled employees an opportunity to perform some mischievous act on the company, or in the worst case, destroy or steal company assets. If employees are transferred to noncritical duties pending termination, they should be removed from all need-to-know access listings, required to turn in any keys or special identification cards, and deleted from computer controlled authorization tables. It is good practice to change passwords and other access codes when an employee leaves for whatever reason. At the time of termination, the employee should be required to turn in all sensitive information, including operator manuals, program documentation, and all work in progress. In addition, all terminating employees should sign a nondisclosure statement reaffirming their understanding of their legal and ethical responsibilities regarding sensitive information. A copy of this statement should be forwarded to the individual's new employer.

Threats to Security

Finally, in order to effectively deal with the problems of personnel security, management must recognize the threat that personnel pose to their information systems, and the threats to which their systems personnel are themselves exposed. Threats to systems and information resources of the firm from personnel fall into four basic categories:

- Destruction. This incudes the loss of data and system resources due to malicious intent (deliberate erasure of files by a disgruntled employee) and by accidental loss.
- Unauthorized modification. This category includes modifications to the system for the purposes of fraud, embezzlement, or concealing other unauthorized actions.
- Unauthorized access. This would include access to restricted data (browsing through a restricted file) or stealing computer time for personal purposes, for example a service bureau on the side, using the company's computer during off-hours.
- Unauthorized disclosure. This ranges from telling co-workers of your password and ID to stealing company confidential information and passing it on to a competitor.

Threats to which company personnel are exposed include bribery, where personnel with access to sensitive information are paid to steal and pass on company data. On a grand scale, this is called industrial espionage. However, it usually is found in situations where relatively low-paid workers have access to sensitive information and are paid to steal this information. To prevent this from happening, employees should be paid commensurate with their level of security and the information handled. All employees should be trained on what action to take when approached by someone offering a bribe.

Individuals in sensitive positions are subject to coercion or blackmail. Coercion may take the form of threats against the employees' families if they do not compromise their position. As in bribes, all employees should be warned that such threats may occur and if this should happen, the procedures that they should follow.

Finally, a common threat to employees is the danger posed by the incompetence or negligence of other employees in such areas as fire safety, physical security, and other operational procedures. In addition, malice and vindictiveness of some employees may lead to the sabotage of work or to other acts designed to injure or embarrass another employee.

In dealing with personnel security, it is important to recognize the two classes of potential perpetrators: those from the outside, and company employees.

Threats from the outside come from:

- Vandals, hackers, and street criminals. Mindless destruction and vandalism have become a fact of life. Computer facilities and systems present a tempting target for such violence because of their high value and high visibility. Their destruction almost certainly leads to publicity and notoriety for the perpetrator. Adequate physical access controls and terminal access controls can minimize damage from vandals and hackers. Of equal concern to management is the threat posed to personnel by street criminals. Since systems personnel frequently work shifts, special efforts must be made to protect all personnel from criminal assaults in such areas as corridors, parking lots, and other isolated areas.

- Terrorists. Unlike vandals, terrorists have clear goals, usually political or ideological, for destruction of facilities and attacks on personnel. Terrorists choose targets such as government facilities or banks that will give them maximum political advantage and exposure and often execute their operation with military precision. If a terrorist threat exists, the company should work with authorities qualified to plan for such attacks.

- Former employees. By far the largest outside threat comes from disgruntled former employees. They know organizational procedures and frequently having friends still working inside the company. They can use this knowledge and inside contacts to gain access to facilities and systems to do damage. This stresses the importance of changing all passwords, identity codes, locks, and authorization lists after employees working in sensitive locations are terminated.

- Building services personnel. Custodial and maintenance personnel frequently have access to many parts of the computer facility during off-hours. They should not be permitted into critical areas without escort. If they are treated under the assumption that they are too unsophisticated to present a threat, the company may be exposed to severe loss. Technically competent individuals may masquerade as custodial personnel to gain access to systems or data, or maintenance personnel may be in collusion with other staff members who do have technical expertise. In addition, a maintenance employee who is emotionally unstable and capable of violent episodes can cause great damage to a computer facility.

In addition to the threats from outsiders, it is equally important to protect an installation and its resources from its own employees. Insiders who present a significant threat to an organization's computer resources include various members of the following four key groups:

- Managers. Management personnel are often in a particular advantageous position to commit fraud, embezzlement, or other unauthorized acts. Security controls therefore must not ignore managers, no matter how high their position within the organization. The biggest computer fraud to date, the Equity Funding scandal was committed by the information systems manager for senior officers of the company.
- Programmers and analysts. Because programmers and analysts have the technical knowledge and the opportunity to access programs and data, these positions have the highest potential for unauthorized actions. Security procedures must provide for monitoring the actions of these individuals such as comparing programs before and after changes to ensure that the change only does what it is supposed to. Monitoring the activities of this group poses the most difficult problem in personnel security.
- Operators and data handlers. Since these people have access to computer facilities, they are susceptible to bribes from outsiders or to do damage on their own. These positions are low-paid positions and usually unsupervised during shift work. It is important to screen candidates for these positions carefully and provide a career path offering them advancement opportunities so that they do not become disgruntled employees.
- Users. With more users accessing the computer through user terminals and becoming computer literate, security measures must be instituted to ensure that only authorized individuals access key data and resources. Various security levels must be designed into each application to limit the damage that could be done by authorized users setting dummy accounts, creating deliberate overpayments, or disclosing data to which they have legitimate access.

Finally, personnel security will depend on the attitude of management and employees towards security. This attitude in turn, is dependent on the morale of the employees and how they view management and the company. A company that is well thought of by its employees and has a reputation for being a well-managed company will find that its security procedures are willingly observed by its employees. Those that face personnel problems will find increasing breaches of security and loss of company assets.

TRAINING FOR INFORMATION SYSTEMS PERSONNEL

One of the key issues in today's system department is training. With the introduction of new technology replacing much of the mainframe concepts that systems personnel are familiar with, training is necessary to keep pace with technology and with user desire to make greater use of computing facilities. Several large companies are shifting away from a standard mainframe-based computer configuration to a processing environment built on applications running locally on superminis and local area networks. Systems personnel at these companies are faced with the choice of mastering LANS and personal computers or looking for another line of work. A recent international survey[2] of large computer departments funded by the British Economic Social Research Council, showed that most college graduates hired must be given basic training because their college training was too theoretical. It seems that the computer science courses stressed independent research on abstract theories. The companies had to provide them with real-world, company-specific training so that they could be productive in the workplace. At the top of the information systems pyramid, top executives need training to update their technical knowledge as well to keep informed of developments in marketing, finance, manufacturing and other functional areas where they are often asked for advice in automation techniques.

All too often, training is done on an individual basis. Those analysts who see a seminar they would like to attend request permission to attend. Based on their past performance and perceived value to the company, they are either granted permission or denied. Since these seminars are held in the major population centers, they usually turn into company-paid vacation for those attending. No wonder the sponsors of these seminars hold them in San Francisco, New Orleans, Boston, New York, Chicago. You do not see too many held in Omaha, Pittsburgh, Cleveland or Detroit. The value of these seminars depends directly on the quality of the instructors. Yet few companies spend the time to investigate the instructor before spending thousands of dollars to send their employees on their company-paid holiday.

Training is a problem-solving activity. Used correctly, it can solve a number of the personnel and workload problems that most systems departments face. It provides basic orientation to company standards and development methodologies for the new hire, and skills upgrading for the experienced professional. When training is coordinated with career development, employees will see a real future with the company and turnover is reduced. Finally, training in improving productivity can reduce workloads, logjams, and stress. Unfortunately, training today in many companies is ineffective. The first thing to go in a cost reduction program is training. The training departments are staffed with people who could not make it in line activities; they are not respected and their activities are largely ignored.

Training should not be a reaction to a request to attend a seminar. It is not scheduling classes and checking to see if everyone attends. It is more than asking a programmer what he would like to learn next year. Training should be part of the planning and development process for the entire department. New employees need orientation and on-the-job training; younger staff members need career path development and information; established personnel need to keep up with the latest developments in information technology; staff members at all levels need training on new equipment and software. To be aware of and respond to these

2. Friedman, Andrew, *Industry and Labour,* University of Bristol Press, 1983.

needs, the director of training must be involved from the very beginning in planning the department's activities. For example, if management decides to buy a major piece of software, such as a data base management system, the training requirements can be substantial and costly, and must be considered in making any purchasing decision.

Managing training is resource management, and the training director must have a departmental perspective to accomplish this. First, a needs analysis has to be performed of the entire department—a complete look at the current skills level of everyone in the department, the types of projects coming up in the next 12 to 18 months, and the skills needed for those projects. Next, the skills of the people proposed for those projects are evaluated to determine the additonal training required by a specific individual and how that training would fit into the individual's career path. The training director should assist the manager in determining the skills individuals need for their current jobs and the skills they need for their next jobs. Once the training needs have been established, the training director must develop a budget and determine the best way to fill those needs.

Where should the training function report and who should be appointed training director? Training directors should report to the highest possible management level in their departments, directors of information systems. If they are to be effectively involved in the planning and budgeting process, they cannot report to system development managers or programming managers. Reporting to the top demonstrates management's commitment to training and forces the selection of more qualified people. Training directors should be highly respected by top management so they really can play the role of consultant to top management and be their training advisors. A major accounting firm spent millions of dollars developing a center for professional education to train all their employees. They staffed it with partners who had failed in the field but had made enough significant contributions in the past that the firm could not fire them. These people knew nothing about training and were too proud to admit it; consequently the center developed a reputation as a ''home for rejects'' and the opportunity for a truly outstanding training facility was lost. Training directors should be managerially oriented and technically competent. They should be able to work with senior-level management as well as the department rank and file. They need to be experienced in planning, budgeting, and management. A 1983 data-processing training survey conducted by the Brandon Systems Institute in Bethesda, Maryland, showed that in the 336 organizations queried, the average data-processing training budget was $305,000. Company budgets varied widely, but this sizeable amount of money and the man-hours spent in training should be handled by a capable, experienced manager who has access to top management in the information systems department. This is particularly important as computer training spreads throughout an organization because of the need for user training. The training director must command the respect of user departments and be able to work with nontechnical personnel at various levels in the company.

Should systems training be part of the corporate training department? Several years ago, one of the big three auto companies attempted to consolidate all its training activities into one corporate training department. The data-processing training director gradually lost touch with the systems department, was no longer considered a member of the systems group, became progressively more ineffectual, and in less than a year, was back, along with the training function, in the systems department. While the specialized nature of information systems training probably could best be met by its own training department, the corporate training department does offer a wealth of experience that the systems training director should make use of, such as expertise in planning and managing educational resources. The training director with a limited background in training can benefit significantly from working with other company trainers.

Many companies today are including an assignment as training director for those people identified as on the fast track to top management positions in the department. Ideally, the training director should not be a career position, but a position through which people rotate. It should be the normal career path to go through positions that focus on the development of people, and the training directorship certainly meets that criterion.

People with education backgrounds are easy to find and many of them are selected for training directorships solely on the basis of this background. An understanding of educational design, curriculum development, and the learning process is very valuable, but it does not necessarily make good managers or even good instructors or trainers. Educators with only two or three years experience in data processing may find it difficult to gain the respect of the more experienced systems staff members. They may never have managed a large budget or a program that has impact on the entire department, if not the entire company. Also they may find the transition from academic to career training difficult. Some educators are used to taking a textbook and teaching from it. That is not data-processing training. The purpose of training is to help people to do their jobs. It is more important that the trainer knows what the job is, than to know how to educate someone. So, a systems background makes more sense than an education background.

Regardless of the background, it is essential that whoever heads up the training function believes in training. Even if top management supports training, others in the department will not, and a strong conviction in the value of training is necessary to overcome that opposition.

One of the problems for training directors is training themselves. Because they are not working in applications development and not attending training programs, training directors may lose contact with new developments in the field. After a few years, their skills may be totally obsolete, and their ability to judge the value of the course materials may be seriously diminished. This is another reason to rotate top people into the training directorship every few years. Few companies allow their training departments enough time to keep abreast of the information systems field. They load training managers and trainers with work the way they load programmers or analysts. They forget that for training to be effective, it must reflect the latest developments. Training directors should have enough time in their schedules to audit the courses bought from outside vendors; they should attend courses specifically for trainers; they should be actively involved in data-processing associations and data-processing training groups; and they should attend conferences and conventions. The more knowledgeable training directors are about trends in information processing, the more productive their training programs will be.

The position of training director is potentially one of the most demanding, complex, and rewarding functions in today's rapidly changing, high-technology environment. The training director must be aware of changes in hardware, software, processing concepts, end user development tools, know their applications, have the skills to direct personnel, and have sufficient business acumen to interact with top corporate management. Since these qualities are also those needed for the top position in the information systems development, it would appear that rotating candidates for the top positions through the training directorship could enhance the knowledge of the person finally chosen to lead the department.

SKILLS OF THE INFORMATION SYSTEMS MANAGER

This chapter started with a description of the changing role of the information systems manager and how the position is perceived in the corporate organization. It will conclude with the skills and training needed to succeed in today's business environment. A recent survey[3] of top business executives who had previously held the position of "data-processing manager" asked what job skills were needed to rise to the top of the corporate organization, specifically the skills they acquired while managing the information systems function which helped most in their advancement to top management positions. Their responses can be summarized as follows:

- Knowledge of the total organization. A comprehensive understanding of organizational operations, objectives, problems, personnel, and management philosophy. Providing systems services to other operating departments meant understanding their needs and problems; this helped the information executive gain better knowledge of the total organization.

- Line and staff experience. A demonstrated ability to manage a line function as well as performing in a high-level staff position. The information systems function was uniquely qualified to provide both types of experience since the manager was a line manager to the information systems department and a staff function to the other departments of the company.

- Ability to deal with complex issues. In addition to the complex technical issues that all information manager must deal with, they also have had experience with EEO/affirmative action issues, privacy of data, business ethics, Occupational Safety and Health Administration standards, union requirements, modi-

---

3. Survey conducted by Fred Held, vice-president of planning and purchasing, Mattel Toys, Hawthorne, California.

fication of mandatory retirement policies, environmental concerns, consumerism, and other issues.

■ Multiple-site experience. Working experience with a multinational or multilocation company and an understanding of the communications and logistic problems of a multisite enterprise. The information systems experience probably helped more in this area since distributed processing concepts and computer communications provided valuable experience in dealing with multilocation problems.

■ Planning experience. Operating experience in developing and executing short-, mid-, and long-range plans; the ability to integrate information systems plans with all other functions of the business; and experience in dealing with top management during this planning process. It is interesting to note that almost all former "data-processing" executives who reached top management positions had had the opportunity to work with top management in developing corporate plans and had their information resource plans incorporated into the overall corporate strategic plans.

■ Large-scale budget experience. Managing a large information systems department afforded ample opportunity to assign priorities to proposed projects, allocate discretionary funds, and to understand budgeting concepts.

■ Project management experience. The ability to conform to predefined budget, schedule, and end-product specifications. Developing systems on time and on budget contributed greatly to this experience.

■ Middle management experience. Demonstrated experience as a productive and cooperative member of a middle management team, the ability to communicate with, and work harmoniously with each other was necessary.

■ Technological experience. Demonstrated ability in dealing with a high-technology organization and in directing the resources of that technology to solve problems to benefit the organization as a whole was considered important.

■ Personnel development experience. Demonstrated ability in developing subordinates and in training a replacement to manage the information systems department would provide this.

If these are the job skills that top management looks for when selecting a chief executive, then the information systems manager should be more qualified than most in fulfilling these requirements. We have already discussed the shortcomings of most incumbents in the position, their lack of general business knowledge, lack of communication skills, and their overly technical solutions to all problems. What education and training should a manager have to rise to the top level of management?

The Importance of Education

The importance of formal education in the information systems professional has been debated for years. The environment in which an information systems manager must operate is quite complex. To prepare to compete in this environment, the manager must be exposed to two formal bodies of knowledge: technology and business.

Technical education is a matter of keeping up with technological advances without trying to learn all the technical details on each new hardware or software announcement. New concepts and the hardware/software supporting these concepts can be learned through seminars provided by vendors and professional associations. Similarly, keeping up to date with trends in technology and in the industry can be accomplished through a program of reading literature and attending seminars. The information systems manager should relegate the bits and bytes to subordinates and concentrate on becoming familiar with the general aspects of technology and managerial techniques.

As for managerial education, some people advocate an MBA for all who aspire to executive ranks. While there is a certain value in the knowledge and discipline gained while working toward the degree, it is not by itself critical for success. The modern information systems manager requires the training provided by courses in finance, business law, governmental regulation, time management, human relations, business modeling and business ethics. If one were available, a course on survival in corporate politics would be indispensable for an aspiring manager. Programs containing most of these subjects are available as "executive programs" at many colleges and universities. They generally last four to eight weeks and are full-time, live-in study programs where participants meet managers from other organizations as well as faculty, sometimes from different colleges and universities. These programs are generally of high quality and are usually expensive. It is the information systems manager's responsibility to seek out such a program and convince management that the investment would be worthwhile.

The Importance of Experience

Knowledge of the total organization ranks high in the job skills of the information systems manager. Obtaining varied experience with all areas of the organization cannot happen by accident. This aspect of the manager's executive development requires planning and commitment. While it may not be practical to work in all functional areas of the business, it is possible to become generally acquainted with them. The most common method of accomplishing this is by participation in corporate level committees or task forces, or doing the staff work for these committees. Being a member of these committees may require nothing more than volunteering or indicating your interest and commitment in working on the committee. Most people shun committee work as a waste of time and a frustrating experience. However, to the manager who wants to know what goes on in other departments and to understand their problems, the committee route is very educational.

Too frequently there are reports that information systems departments are not coordinated with their parent organizations. They are building application systems that are of greater technical interest than real value to the business. When these criticisms occur, they indicate an absence of perspective on top management needs. To avoid this, the systems manager must look for opportunities to become involved in corporate level planning and decision making. Without this important information, the department will only be able to react to rather than to anticipate and participate in corporate development.

If we were to describe successful information systems managers, those who would be likely candidates for advancement, they would, first, help to develop corporate policy on information resource management. That policy should contain a statement of their organizations' approach to information management and a concise description of how information resources would be managed in their companies. This policy would form the basis for the information systems departments' operating policies and plans. Successful information systems managers would be prepared to direct and lead the implementation of these plans by acquiring both the experience and education needed. They would demonstrate perserverance in implementing the plans while recognizing that the operating environment was constantly changing and that the plans must change to meet new corporate needs and strategies.

They would be flexible enough to overcome short-term failures in order to achieve more important long-range goals. They would be generally inquisitive, well read, and capable of speaking intelligently on subjects other than the speed of a mainframe. They would have carefully built and protected their reputations for getting things done through others and for being able to look beyond the confines of their own departments in order to contribute to the growth of their organizations. They would be an asset rather than a drain to their organizations. They would abstain from playing corporate politics and remember that the information systems function operated in a fish bowl for all the organization to see.

Although promotion of the information systems manager to a top corporate position is not directly guaranteed by outstanding leadership of the systems department, it is certainly more likely to occur as a result of such success. In order to be free for promotion, the information systems manager must have selected and trained a replacement. Persons likely to be promoted from systems manager to a high level corporate position must recognize that if guiding the department is difficult, the next step will probably be even more demanding. They must assure themselves that they both want and can handle the responsibilities. Wise managers will not accept appointments in which success is not probable. While the rewards of advancement are great, so too are the responsibilities. Not everyone is destined to captain the team.

CHAPTER 9   DISCUSSION QUESTIONS

1. Can an on-line order entry system be designed with top-level involvement but no inputs from the working level? What are the risks? Why would a company adopt such an approach?
2. Do you think that a company (other than in high-tech industries) will ever select a CEO from the information systems department? Why or why not?
3. What are the ways a "technician" can learn about business and be viewed by management as being business oriented?
4. What is the best source for recruiting people into the information systems department? Why?
5. What will the information systems department look like in the year 2000?
6. Take one side or the other: There will be more/fewer people in information systems by the end of this century.
7. If an employee of the company is committed to defrauding the company, could any security procedures detect or prevent it? Are security procedures not directed mainly against external threats?
8. Research the events at Equity Funding Corporation, leading to the conviction of its top corporate officers and report your findings to the class. Could it have been detected and prevented?
9. How does one set up an effective training program for both systems and user personnel?
10. How important is an MBA in rising to top corporate positions?

10

MICROS AND MAINFRAMES

ISSUES

- How can businesses use personal computers? What are the risks and problems?

- Should management control microcomputers the same way they control mainframes?

- If ownership of data in a corporation rests with the users, why restrict their access and use of this data via a microprocessor?

- Will the applications development backlog be reduced through end user applications on microprocessors?

- What should be the role of an information center?

- Should there be a corporate policy on microcomputers? What should it include?

ACE RECORDING COMPANY

Ace Recording was a record company specializing in producing specialty albums sold through television mail order and selected retail outlets. Its revenue in 1983 exceeded $200 million with most of it coming from the North American market. Ace also had operations in the U.K., France, Italy, Germany, Japan, Australia, and Canada. Some of their more popular albums consisted of artists from the 1950s and 1960s, as well as popular versions of classical music. Production of these albums meant getting permission from the recording company to include one of their recordings or tracks in a new album, and paying royalties to the company and the artist. These royalties were based on the number of records sold, and paid once annually. During the year, strict accounting had to be kept on sales and royalties due artists. Of course, until the royalties were paid, they provided the company with a good cash flow.

Ruth Birnbaum was a financial controller at Ace Recording and was responsible for cash management, budgeting, and management reporting. The company practiced centralized cash management with all cash generated daily placed into a "cash pool" managed from company headquarters. The cash pool was an accounting entry only since in practice, each country kept its cash and used it for daily operations. Surplus cash would be remitted to headquarters when needed for royalty payments. On the other hand, headquarters often had to provide cash for production projects in each country. Ruth needed to forecast cash needs and project income quite carefully so that she could minimize bank borrowings. Cash forecasts and income projections were intitially set in the annual financial plans, prepared in conjunction with the annual budget exercise. Each country presented its operating plan for the year indicating recording projects, new releases, special promotion campaigns, and based on this operating plan, projected its revenues as well as its expenses. The shortfall, on a monthly basis, became its projected cash need. If there was a cash surplus, it was carried forward on a monthly basis to offset any future cash shortfall. If no shortfall was foreseen, surplus cash was repatriated to the United States, unless the dollar was so strong against that country's currency, that cash could be invested in local short-term, high-yield investments. Quite often, the local controller would play the foreign exchange market with surplus cash.

Local controllers had learned how to budget and estimate cash requirements so that there was never any projected cash surplus. Without a surplus in the initial financial plan, head office could not ask for repatriation of funds. As the year progressed and cash surpluses were generated, Ruth's boss usually got furious at the financial planning and budgeting process and asked for immediate updates of the original plan and budget. He reviewed the new estimates and arbitrarily set new goals and cash projections for each country. Then followed lengthy discussions and arguments over the new targets, with a compromise reached between the local controller and home office. This procedure generated a tremendous amount of paperwork as budgets and projects were set, changed, revised, changed, and thrown out just to start over again. Of course, Ruth had to make all the changes and consolidate all the countries for head office management reporting.

Up to 1980, all of these procedures were done manually. In the late 1970s, the vice-president of finance had asked data processing to develop a financial information system on the company's IBM mainframe which would include cash management, budgeting, and financial reporting. The first version, done with little input from Ruth and no inputs from any of the local controllers took two years to complete, and the users refused to use it after it was released by data processing. They would have had to add people to their staff just to prepare the manual inputs for submission to home office. Their view was that if home office needed the data to prepare reports for themselves, let them pull the data out of the reams of reports they had already submitted to the head office. Moreover, during these discussions, the foreign subsidiaries would often resort to the trick of not understanding what was being said, or claiming that the transatlantic or transpacific connection was bad and break off the conversation. The financial vice-president was unhappy with the reports because they did not reflect his latest thinking on the information needed to control cash and to project financial requirements. Data processing went back to the drawing boards, this time involving the users of the financial informations to "retrofit" the systerm. To Ruth, "retrofit" was a face-saving way of saying scrap the system and start all over. The second attempt had been ongoing for 18 months and data processing predicted that the project would be completed within the year. Ruth had not had contact with data-processing personnel for over nine months, so she was convinced that the new version would probably wind up on the scrap heap just like the old one.

As Ruth struggled to put the 1983 budget together and cope with the changes from both higher up and from the local controllers, she decided that she would try doing this on the IBM PC and VisiCalc. She found that once the data were entered, changes were easy to make, and the spreadsheet could be formatted so that reports were prepared at the press of a button. She started to enjoy her work now that the tedious tasks of posting figures and updating reports were automated. She found that the year-end reports and issuing of the new financial plan could also be done using spreadsheet and word-processing software. Ruth approached the vice-president of finance to see if all the overseas entities could install IBM PCs and link them into a network of terminals for financial management. At this point, data processing told them that they were in the final stages of debugging their financial information system and that the system would be available for use "shortly." How long "shortly" was could not be determined other than "within the next three months or so." Since equipping all the subsidiaries with IBM PCs and communication would cost over $100,000, not including the software, the vice-president of finance decided to wait for data processing to finish their system.

Meanwhile, Ruth noticed that some of the inputs she was getting from the overseas office were computer generated, and looked suspiciously like outputs from a spreadsheet program. She started to investigate quietly, and discovered that almost every subsidiary had a personal computer of some sort that they were using to prepare the budget, do forecasting, and all other financial updates. In addition, some had their general ledger stored on the diskettes and could rebudget or reproject financial data with ease. Unfortunately, Ruth also found that every country used a different type of computer. Germany had a Nixdorf, France used a Machine Bull computer, Spain had an Apple, England had an ICL system. Any attempt to exchange data by sending diskettes back and forth was impossible. Trying to link them into a communication network was out of the question.

The new financial information system was finally ready and, to data-processing's credit, was a significant improvement over the old one. Data gathering was to be done by installing terminals in each controller's office and linking them to regional computers in Europe and Asia, then sending the information to the U.S. for processing. Procedures for collecting, encoding, and sending this information were well documented for the users. Training data as well as a model to test the accuracy of the procedures were also included in the package. The plan was for a team of data-processing people and financial people to visit each overseas office and help them develop plans for acquiring the terminal and installing the system. An IBM 4341 mainframe would be installed in London and Singapore as regional concentrators for the collection and dissemination of data from countries in their region.

As the orientation tour progressed, it was apparent that London and Singapore were excited about the proposed project. They welcomed a mainframe system to process area paperwork and transmit information to the U.S. The other countries were noncommittal at first, then hostile to the idea. The system called for "dumb" terminals to be installed in the other countries for use as on-line input devices to the regional computer. Data-processing people made a tactical error of trying to sell the concept of using the terminal also as a time-sharing terminal so that such things as modeling programs and corporate information could be accessed from the local terminal. The countries did not want a "dumb" terminal, they wanted to access the computer via their microprocessors. Since there were as many makes and models of personal computers in use as there were countries, this became an impossible situation. At this point, it seemed that every foreign controller lost his complete literacy in English. They claimed not to understand what the data-processing people wanted to do, that procedures needed to be translated into their languages before they could be evaluated, that local government regulation would not permit the cross-border transfer of data (this happened to be true in France), and so on. These roadblocks and tactics were aimed at delaying their commitment to using the new system, and they worked. The installation team was so dejected that they returned to the U.S. with a recommendation that the system be installed but that the inputs be submitted manually from the overseas location. This would mean considerable savings since all the hardware planned for the overseas offices would not have to be bought. Ruth and her boss fought with management not to accept the proposal since an on-line system was desperately needed to cope with a growing cash flow problem. Cash management was the key to the survival of businesses in the music-recording field. However, management could not resist the savings in expenditures and accepted data-processing's recommendation.

For the next year, microcomputers proliferated in the company. With no central direction and guidance, each country, each office bought whatever they wanted. The London office alone had seven different makes of computers, all duplicating each other's spreadsheet packages and word-processing packages. Some more adventurous offices even used graphic packages to help develop advertising and other promotional displays. This improved the productivity and efficiency of operations in each of the offices, and for each of the managers with access to a personal computer. It did not help the cash management or financial planning efforts to any large degree. Information generated by spreadsheet programs was sent to the home office and entered into Ruth's personal computer manually. After processing the data on her PC, Ruth printed a report which was then keypunched for entry into the financial information system. The turnaround time was slow and the data was not too accurate since the overseas controllers were still playing games with their cash forecasts to minimize the potential of having to remit cash to the U.S. As one controller said, "You never know when something unexpected might come up and we would have a cash requirement which we could not satisfy if we sent all of our excess cash to the U.S." The atmosphere between the financial analysts and the data-processing department had chilled to the point that neither side really cared about the accuracy or timeliness of the reports being generated. The vice-president of finance relied on his own records, Ruth used the information from her personal computer, and the financial information system produced reports that were distributed around the world and trashed in local wastebaskets.

In late 1984, the company filed for protection under Chapter 11 of the Bankruptcy Act when their major bank refused to "roll over" a large loan that had become due.

Personal computers are becoming as commonplace as telephones in large companies. By 1990, over half of the white-collar work force (about 35 million people) will use microcomputers in their daily work (see Figure 10-1). In this chapter, we will explore the growing use of personal computers in business: what is a personal computer, why it is in high demand for business use, and the problems in controlling its proliferation and use.

FIGURE 10-1   **PROJECTED PC PENETRATION OF WHITE-COLLAR WORK FORCE**

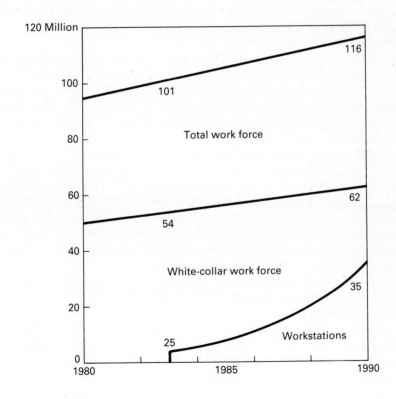

Source: "Personal Computing: The Challenge to Management," A Forbes Advertising Supplement, *Forbes,* May 21, 1984.

THE ROLE OF PERSONAL COMPUTING

Personal computing is the use of computers by individuals to help in their daily work. This support may be one of three categories: decision support (spreadsheets, database), communications (word processing, electronic mail), and convenience (personal diaries, "tickler files", daily schedules). In using the personal computer for support, there is direct interaction between the individual and the computer. It provides the individual with the ability to have real time capability at the workplace, that is, the ability to get an immediate response to a question put to the computers. Senior management of most corporations has come to appreciate the benefits of personal computing and is looking at microprocessors as tools to service their customers more effectively as well as making their internal operations more efficient. However, introducing personal computing into the workplace involves risks and poses significant problems. How each company handles this introduction will be the challenge for management. Since each company is unique, it follows that each will have a unique personal computing solution. The organizations that plan and manage the transition stand a far better chance for success than those who let personal computing grow without direction or management. Smart management will set goals for the use of personal computing to improve productivity and then rely on its information systems personnel to work closely with end users to achieve those goals.

The days when information systems personnel viewed personal computers as a threat to their jobs are rapidly fading. Today, the systems department is besieged by end users asking for computer resources and services which the systems department cannot provide. As users turn to personal computing to solve their problems, new problems are created for the systems department. As users work at home or at their desks, they want access to corporate information stored in the central data bases; how will the systems department control access to this information and preserve the integrity of the data in the files? Issues of data accessibility, consistency and compatibility, and security must be addressed prior to allowing widespread use of personal computers linked to mainframes in the organization. As users gain in experience using their personal computer, they will want to do more, learn more sophisticated techniques. Those who have used software packages may want to develop some custom-coded routines to do special analysis on their personal computer. They will come to the information systems department for training and assistance, perhaps exacerbating an already overworked staff.

Many of the problems for the information systems department will be new. As new information management products arrive, organizations will need to address how they can be effectively connected to each other and to products already in use, how they can be technically supported, and how independent, redundant development efforts within the organizations can be eliminated. Management's greatest challenge may be in bringing personal computing to its work force, in organizing it to improve productivity rather than wasting valuable time in trial-and-error efforts to make it work effectively, and in linking it to existing mainframes so that corporate information can be used, on a controlled basis, throughout the organization.

While management will have a great deal to say about how personal computers will be used in each organization, it will be the end user who will shape the nature of personal computing. By definition, personal computing provides end users with an unprecedented level of control and involvement in establishing and maintaining information resources. Few end users are equipped to identify or address the responsibilities they will face. They have had little reason to be sensitized to most information systems policies and in many respects, the personal computer was a revolt against the mainframe and policies of the data-processing departments. If management tries to control microprocessors the way they control mainframes, many of the potential benefits offered by personal computing will be sacrificed. The proper way to establish control and manage the growth of personal computing is to assess why and how people use personal computers, then develop procedures to facilitate their use and ensure the integrity of data used on the computers.

THE USE OF MICROCOMPUTERS

What, exactly, are microcomputers accomplishing today? What might they accomplish tomorrow, and how will organizations get from here to there? What role will information systems managers play as their companies make fundamental changes in the way they handle information? These are the questions facing all businesses today as their employees embrace personal computing with a passion. However, it seems that the growth of these little machines raises more questions than it answers.

People initially buy personal computers because they want to do better quality work. Productivity and cost justifications are secondary. At the outset, they are concerned with four main application areas: spreadsheets, word processing, data base, and simple business graphics. These are the areas where software vendors have concentrated their efforts. They can get by without accessing mainframes, minis, or other micros. But once users become familiar with these initial applications, they begin to see good reasons to make contact with the outside world where the data they use for input reside. It does not take long for users to realize that the data they use for their spreadsheets, their data bases, or their graphic presentations come from computer generated reports. Why should they be forced to reenter all this information? Why can they not retrieve this information directly from the mainframe files? Users who want to access the data available on the corporate mainframe do not want mainframe terminals sitting beside the personal computers on their desks, so they install some mainframe terminal emulation hardware and software, and log on to a mainframe from their personal computers just as if they were using a dumb terminal.

What can users do with the ability to make their personal computers act like terminals directly connected to the mainframe? There are essentially three applications. First is the ability to access mainframe time-sharing. Many large companies and most universities already have personal computing facilities in place on their mainframes. They are the financial planning packages, such as EPS and IFPS, and end user oriented file management systems such as NOMAD, FOCUS, and RAMIS. APL modeling is another kind of end user computing. These packages run on the mainframes and are accessible by terminals. Now, users with personal computers can also access these facilities through their micros, and after running some financial projections using IFPS, they can save the model on disk, switch from using the personal computer as a terminal to using it as a microprocessor, and use the information saved on disk in a report prepared by word-processing software, using charts prepared by the spreadsheet software and/or graphics prepared by the graphic software package.

The second use of the microprocessor as a terminal is to access external proprietary data bases such as the Dow Jones, Financial News Network, InfoGlobe (Canadian), and other networks. With their wealth of current information, these can be excellent research tools and can be useful for nonbusiness purposes, tracking specific stocks and the market, for example. Communication in this case is normally implemented using asynchronous terminals, so the microcomputer is connected to the mainframe using modems, dial-up lines, and asynchronous protocols.

Finally, the microcomputer can act as a terminal for a mainframe's on-line transaction-processing systems. Many companies have their "bread and butter" transaction systems—payables, receivables, general ledger, and payroll/personnel—on the mainframe as on-line transaction driven systems. These applications contain much information of interest to the users and because micros can be made to look like mainframe terminals, they should be able to access these mainframe applications. However, unlike access to mainframe personal computing facilities, for which the user interface is typically line oriented, these transaction-processing systems are dependent on the processing of complete screens of information at a time. Thus, terminal communications are normally based on the IBM 3270 type bisychronous protocols rather than the asynchronous protocols common among time-sharing applications. For now, most personal computers' access to transaction-processing applications involves some sort of protocol conversion. This may be done in software, or in some intermediate hardware box. The personal computer uses an asynchronous protocol, which is then converted to a bisynchronous protocol before accessing the mainframe application. As the use of micros increases even more rapidly, plug-in bisynchronous boards with associated software will be available to make the connection even easier (see Figure 10-2).

One other kind of microcommunication should be mentioned although it does not involve a mainframe. This is a form of electronic mail. Word-processing packages are widely used and the penetration has just begun. It is often held that these packages will not be used by managerial and professional staff; however recent surveys indicate that many professionals and managers are finding it worthwhile to reach a level of keyboard fluency adequate to use these programs because the time saved by delegating typing to a secretary is lost in proofreading and waiting for turnaround. Documents are now commonly being entered by the secretaries and directly corrected by the user, or the users are entering the documents themselves.

Some of these documents are destined for remote locations, others for people in the same buiding. Sending the text in the mail involves printing it out and giving directions to secretaries. On the other hand, electronically transmitting the document by dial-up lines requires relatively little effort, and obviously the delivery time is far shorter. One company found that it took an inter-office memo four days to go from the 6th floor to the 17th floor. Sending the same document from one micro to another via some store-and-forward facility could reduce mailing time significantly.

FIGURE 10-2   **HARDWARE EVOLUTION**

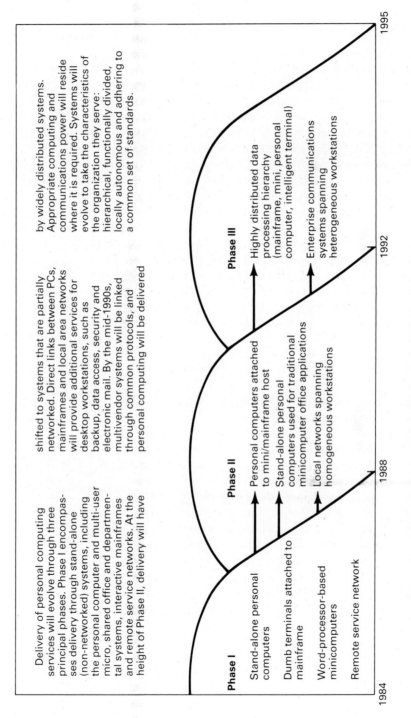

Delivery of personal computing services will evolve through three principal phases. Phase I encompasses delivery through stand-alone (non-networked) systems, including the personal computer and multi-user micro, shared office and departmental systems, interactive mainframes and remote service networks. At the height of Phase II, delivery will have shifted to systems that are partially networked. Direct links between PCs, mainframes and local area networks will provide additional services for desktop workstations, such as backup, data access, security and electronic mail. By the mid-1990s, multivendor systems will be linked through common protocols, and personal computing will be delivered by widely distributed systems. Appropriate computing and communications power will reside where it is required. Systems will evolve to take the characteristics of the organization they serve: hierarchical, functionally divided, locally autonomous and adhering to a common set of standards.

Phase I

Stand-alone personal computers

Dumb terminals attached to mainframe

Word-processor-based minicomputers

Remote service network

Phase II

Personal computers attached to mini/mainframe host

Stand-alone personal computers used for traditional minicomputer office applications

Local networks spanning homogeneous workstations

Phase III

Highly distributed data-processing hierarchy (mainframe, mini, personal computer, intelligent terminal)

Enterprise communications systems spanning heterogeneous workstations

1984   1988   1992   1995

Source: "Personal Computing: The Challenge to Management," A Forbes Advertising Supplement, *Forbes*, May 21, 1984.

MICRO-MAINFRAME CONNECTIONS

The micro-mainframe connection opens the door to more imaginative uses of the personal computer in business. First of all, micros will become very active front-end and back-end processors for existing large-scale mainframe applications. Today, branch offices, warehouses, remote locations all typically save data generated during the day, batch them for data entry to the mainframe computer at night or at periodic intervals during the day. The data entry takes only an hour or two and is done on remote dumb terminals. Once the data are validated, the mainframe processes them, updates files, produces reports and sends information back to the user in report form. This usage is perfectly standard and does not involve the use of micros. However, personnel at these offices can make very good use of a micro. The branch manager can use a spreadsheet, for example, to plan and revise budgets, and to plan and schedule the work force requirements. Other analytical tools can be used to help in daily decision making. Clerical staff can use a simple list-processing system to keep track of inventory, prices, and other job related information. Word processing can help in mass mailings, communication with customers and employees. Branch managers can cost justify microcomputers and use them to do data entry at no additional cost. Once they have micros, they can use them for back-end processing. Today reports are never in the format that the user wants. The data is extracted, retyped, cut and pasted, and redistributed. If reports are distributed to users electronically, they can make their changes using a word-processing package. They can add footnotes to explain variances in the data, change the format, supply detailed narratives, and change headings. While this may or may not improve productivity, it certainly has a great effect on the appearance and quality of the materials that are passed on and greatly speeds up distribution time. Once the changes have been made, the user can simply have the report typed on a local terminal. It is a lot faster than going through the traditional iterative cycle of alteration, typing, and proofreading.

Another type of micro-mainframe connection is the data download (see Figure 10-3). This involves cases where the main application is developed for the personal computer but needs data from the corporate data base. These applications tend to be small, specialized systems that could not be justified on the mainframe computer, but are viable on a micro using high-level software development tools, or it might be a spreadsheet application on a micro which requires data from the corporate data base. An example might be a plant manager wanting to do analysis on absenteeism of plant employees to determine the profile of productive employees. Employee information is kept at the central data base located in the mainframe. The plant manager can enter information at a personal computer, but to enter the data for several thousand employees would be tedious and time-consuming, especially when the information is captured for payroll processing on the central files. Obviously, the thing to do is to download the required data from the mainframe. This would require help from a systems programmer and the data base administrator. Fields have to be extracted from the data base and presented to the user with what looks like a flat file. These fields may have to be extracted from several records, some not related. The user can select the fields he needs using Boolean logic and the particular record downloaded to the personal computer. The destination of the downloaded data could be directly

FIGURE 10-3   **MICRO-MAINFRAME DATA DOWNLOADING**

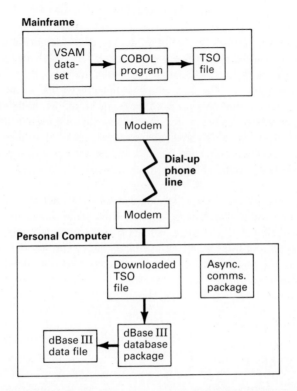

In this example, VSAM data must be downloaded to the dBase III application generator on a PC. Using today's tools, some effort is necessary to implement a suitable interface. The kind of arrangement required follows:

1. An applications programmer writes a COBOL program to transfer VSAM data into a TSO file, TSOFILE.DATA.

2. An applications programmer familiar with dBase III defines a personal computer file called DOWNLOAD, whose structure corresponds to that of TSOFILE.DATA. He does this using dBase III's CREATE command.

3. The personal computer user emulates a tty-type terminal using a modem and a standard asynchronous communications package, and logs into TSO. Using the file transfer utility that comes with the async package, he downloads the TSO file. To satisfy dBase III conventions, the downloaded file must have TXT as suffix, so it is renamed TSOFILE.TXT.

4. The user then disconnects from the mainframe.

5. The user then gives two dBase III commands to read the downloaded file into a dBase III file.

  USE DOWNLOAD (i.e., open the DOWNLOAD file)

  APPEND FROM TSOFILE SDF (reads in the file, appropriate converting the formats).

into a spreadsheet, or more likely, into a micro data base where they can be further processed and distributed when necessary into other micro packages such as a word processor, spreadsheet, or graphics processor.

Downloading of data from the mainframe to the micro might pose a technical problem, but uploading of data from a micro to a mainframe poses significant data integrity problems. Consider for example, the use of financial data downloaded from a financial model on the mainframe (see Figure 10-4). After manipulating this data on a personal computer, the financial analyst wants to change the results of the model stored on the mainframe. The data could be uploaded from the micro to the mainframe, but what about the other users of the financial model on the mainframe. They would have no way of knowing that the results now represented by the model are not the results of the model's calculations but the results of further manipulation by an analyst on a personal computer. Should this be allowed to happen? We will look at this problem later in this chapter when we discuss management control of microprocessors.

There are many other uses that one can think of once the micro is connected to the mainframe and all the data and power of the mainframe is available to the user with a personal computer. The implementation of these micro-mainframe connections will require skills, but these skills are available today. Further, the task will be made easier as more building block tools are released by vendors. What is most exciting about this development is not the technical issues but the business opportunities they bring to the information systems department.

USER ASSISTANCE

Users today may feel confident in mastering the use of spreadsheet and word-processing packages on their personal computers. The fact is, few of them understand systems development and they do not realize that as the portfolio of applications grows, so do the problems of integrating the applications with the underlying data base and keeping various versions of the programs synchronized. Nor do they understand that it pays to invest time during the design stage to define all requirements and interfaces, and to make sure that all the applications are well documented. Users find that the information systems department will quote several hundred thousand dollars and a year to implement an application. They can do the same thing in less time and more cheaply on a micro. What they are not aware of is that a few years hence, when they have a number of applications running on their micros, they will face the same kind of maintenance and system integration problems that slow down the information systems department. Rightly or wrongly, users do feel that the personal computer is the panacea to their problems, and as they implement applications that information systems personnel said would take forever to do, professional analysts and programmers are losing credibility with the user community. The pending demand for micro-mainframe connections may well be an opportunity to change that as users are forced to come to the information systems department for assistance. Data communication is too technical a world for end users. As soon as they are faced with asynchronous or bisynchronous transmission, ASCII code conversion, and communication protocols, it will become obvious that they need assistance. Vendors and consultants will not be able to help because only the information systems department is familiar with the corporate communication network, the communication hardware

---

FIGURE 10-4   **MICRO-MAINFRAME FINANCIAL MODELING**

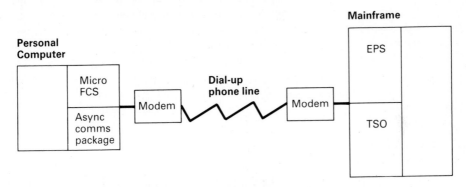

A branch office manager of a multidivisional company uses a personal computer running Micro-FCS, the micro version of the mainframe EPS financial planning package. Micro-FCS is used to enter and correct financial data, without incurring line and mainframe connect charges. At the end of each week, the new data file is uploaded to the mainframe for consolidation into the central corporate model, a large affair that cannot be supported by today's micros. Typical user procedures are straightforward. For example:

1. Branch managers use the Micro-FCS editor to capture financial data and store it in binary format on diskette. It is stored in a row and column format specified by the EPS support group.

2. At the end of each week, the branch manager uses Micro-FCS' REPORT command to convert the data file from its binary format into ASCII format. He then sends this to a TSO file on the mainframe, using a modem and an asynchronous communications package.

3. A staff financial planner using EPS on the mainframe uses its REPORT command to translate the ASCII file, and others like it, back into binary format.

4. The financial planner then gives standard EPS commands to consolidate the fresh financial data with others like it that have just been received and converted back into binary format.

5. Multilevel consolidated reports are then automatically generated by EPS.

6. Copies of consolidated reports can then be passed on to management, and appropriate subsets can be downloaded back to branch managers for immediate display.

and software installed, and the protocols necessary to link equipment to the mainframe. The same holds true for data base problems. Only the information systems department can advise on what data is available, where it is stored and how to get to it. Finally, if microprocessors are to be used for front-end or back-end processing, only information systems can make the necessary hardware and software link-ups to the mainframe.

If information systems personnel make the effort to determine what the major future requirements will be in micro-mainframe processing, they will be able to offer new services to the end users. These new opportunities include:

- Training. Information systems can offer classes to end users on how to link their micros to the company's mainframe, how to download data into the software packages used by the micros, when to use the modeling packages on the mainframe versus the spreadsheet package on the micros, and other technical considerations in using the micro as a terminal to the mainframe.

- Installation assistance. Once micro users decide what they want to do with the mainframe, they must have help in configuring communication hardware and software and writing programs to perform code conversion and data format changes.

- Post-installation support. After the micro-mainframe connection is completed, users will still need help on communications issues such as a new release of an operating system causing terminal support problems, or how to exchange documents between different text processors. As new software is installed on the mainframe, users will need to be upgraded and informed as to the new information and processing tools available.

Finally, all of this assistance may even be profitable. Currently, users think that they can get all the support they need on their micro for free through the local retailer, software vendors, and local consultants. As their appetite for mainframe access sharpens, they will soon develop a better understanding of the limitations of existing support and return to the information systems department for help. If the department has a chargeback scheme installed, users will understand and accept a reasonable level of chargeback for consulting, training, and installation support.

REDUCING THE APPLICATIONS BACKLOG

If one of the reasons that users are migrating to the personal computer is disenchantment with information systems ability to service their request for application development, will the personal computer reduce the backlog of user requests awaiting development? The figure most quoted for the backlog of applications awaiting development is about three years with some as high as seven to ten years. The three-year figure is the formal backlog, or the backlog resulting from formal requests made to the information systems department. There is another backlog called the "hidden" backlog which includes those applications where a request has not been submitted to the information systems department because the application is not essential or serves only a few people. Requests for developing these applications have not been submitted because the user knows that they will have the lowest priority, so it is not worth the effort to go through the justification process required in submitting a formal proposal. The formal backlog includes three types of projects:

- Requests for changes and enhancements to existing applications. These are really maintenance requests and account for over 60 percent of the department's workload in a typical installation.
- Requests from new systems and applications that must interface to existing systems and data bases.
- Requests for new systems and applications that stand alone and do not interface with the existing applications.

The hidden backlog consists of small applications that are only required by one person or a small group of people. Department requests usually have enough support to land on the formal backlog, but if the project is only important to a few people, it is usually not submitted and remains as a hidden backlog. Both backlogs, hidden and formal, exist because there are not enough people in information systems to service all the requests for applications from users. It is not the result of a lack of hardware or processing capacity. This means that if personal computing is to reduce the backlog of applications awaiting development, it can do so by increasing the productivity of people who are designing and installing systems, or by increasing the number of such people.

The backlog is not just programming work. It includes all the tasks from requirements definition through conversion and maintenance. There would be a backlog even if no programming were required. For example, replacing existing systems with application packages can require very little or no programming. Yet installing the new package would most likely take six months to a year. The time is required to change the way things are being done now to conform to the procedures required by the new application package. The alternative is to modify the package, something that most installations do only as a last resort. Changing and documenting existing procedures, training the users, converting and testing the new system, all take a considerable amount of time and manpower.

Today, the backlog problem itself causes friction between users and systems personnel. Even though the systems department does not set priorities for development unilaterally, users whose projects do not command high priority feel that the systems department, with its huge budget, takes an inordinately large share of the company's resources without showing many results or being able to deliver on its promises. This translates into a feeling of ''they never do anything for us.'' To the systems department, the backlog is an indication that they are understaffed, overcommitted, and subject to the insatiable demands of the users. Unfortunately, up to now, the systems department had the sole responsibility of reducing the backlog. They were the only ones with the technical competence to solve the problem and the end user could not become part of the solution.

Advantages and Disadvantages of the Micro

The question of whether the micro can help reduce this backlog can be addressed by looking at what the micro can do, and what it can not do. The advantages of a micro are its low costs, its user-friendly software, its processing speed, and its freedom from the establishment.

The basic personal computer costs a little more than a terminal on a mainframe system. More and more businesses are using their micros as terminals to mainframes. They offer an abundance of computing power which is cheap to increase. On a heavily loaded mainframe, adding five additional terminals may require equipment upgrade with significant incremental costs. To give users five additional micros would cost less than $25,000 with a letter quality printer thrown in for each user. Another cost advantage for the micro is its low fixed cost. The more computer time used on a mainframe, the more it costs. However, once the micro has been purchased, a job can take all week to process and it would only cost the electricity to run it. Therefore, mistakes cost less on a micro, taking the tension out of using a computer. Just as important, when mistakes are made, only one user is affected. If a user starts a runaway job on a shared mainframe, all users suffer.

The micro gives a more consistent response and often a faster response than a large computer that is used concurrently by many users. Three shifts of operators are required to make the mainframe available to users. Time has to be scheduled for preventive maintenance and file backups. Large batch jobs and file sorting limits access to the system and degrades response time. The micro is available wherever there is an electric outlet. You do not have to ask anyone's permission to use a micro. If you do not use it for several months, you do not have to get your password reinstated and explain why you kept files in the active system when you had no plans to use them. People do not look at your printouts and ask why you are doing personal work on the computer or playing games. A large part of the appeal of the micro is the opportunity to bypass the information systems department and truly have your own computer to do whatever you want to do. What is even more appealing is the ease of use. There is nothing approaching the difficulty of using job control language (JCL) in a mainframe. The micro operation systems, MS/DOS, CP/M, and P-System are all easier to use than TSO or MVS on a large mainframe. Spreadsheet analysis, word-processing systems, small data base systems, mail merge systems, and the interactive languages like Pascal on the micro are all superior to those found on large computers.

Even with all of the advantages, there are things that micros cannot do. Micros were designed for interactive computing; large mainframes were designed for batch processing. High speed I/O selector channels, fast tapes and disks, and all the buffering built in the operating systems of large mainframes were designed for quickly moving a large volume of data in and out of the CPU. In interactive processing, all of the buffering and high speed channels go to waste. On the other hand, the micro excels in interactive processing but is poor at moving a large volume of data. In terms of processing power, a typical micro supplies more than is needed for most applications. It should not be forgotten that a micro has more power (storage capacity and processing speed) than a 1401 or 360/30, systems that sold for several hundred thousand dollars. While micros are great for doing a million calculations, if you have to sort ten thousand records, it dies. Consequently, the micro is poor for the transaction driven systems which form the backbone of most business applications.

Another disadvantage of the micro is the things that the user has to do (Figure 10-5). The user is the operator; and it is the user who has to make backup copies of vital files, monitor the printer, feed it paper and change its ribbon, and watch it for paper jams. The user has to listen to its incessant clatter. When the user wants data stored on the mainframe, he or she has to download the data. This could take patience since uploading or downloading a file of any size using a 1200 baud modem would require half a day for a diskette full of data. This assumes that the process goes without any hitches.

Finally, micros cause security problems. While the data when residing on the mainframe are protected by several layers of access security, once data are downloaded to a micro, all that protection is lost. It is up to the user to lock up the data in a safe. In a sense, the micro is potentially more secure than the mainframe since diskettes locked in a safe are more secure than any software protection on the main-

---

FIGURE 10-5   END USER PERSONAL COMPUTING CONTROL RESPONSIBILITIES

N = None L = Low M = Medium M-H = Medium-High H = High	End User Personal Computing Control Responsibilities				
	Tradi-tional	Micro-computer	Depart'l office	Inter-active Mainframe	Service Bureau
Hardware Operation	N	H	M	N	N
Systems Programming	N	L	L	N	N
Application Development	L	M-H	M	M	L
Application Maintenance	N	M-H	M	M-H	L
Problem and Change Management	M	M-H	M	M-H	M
Capacity Management	N	H	M	L	L
Vital Records Program	L	H	M	M	M
Data Security	L	H	M	L	L
Hardware Security	N	H	M	L	L

Source: "Personal Computing: The Challenge to Management," A Forbes Advertising Supplement, *Forbes,* May 21, 1984.

frame. But there is no way to ensure that all users will lock sensitive data in safes. Furthermore, the worst security with a micro is that the entire system could be stolen.

Impact of Micros on the Applications Backlog

Most microcomputers in use today are in the hands of the end users. Whether they will have an impact in reducing the backlog will depend on what the end user can do with these computers. Users have proved that they can do computing with packages such as Visicalc, Lotus 1-2-3, IFPS, dBase III. The question is whether they can do computing without becoming programmers. Users bring knowledge of the application to computing. They know what they want to do, and if they can use software routines to do it, they will be successful. Programmers know programming, but are usually not familiar with the application and its requirements. Therefore, if the application requires that special programs be written in procedural languages to achieve a solution, it can best be done by the staff of the information systems department. If the users try to write the programs, they will become programmers, something most end users do not want to do. Experience has shown that any application with the following characteristics would not be a good candidate for handling on a personal computer:

- A large application handling large volume of input and output data
- A complex application requiring data reformatting and extensive use of Boolean logic
- An application to be used often and by many users thereby dictating that it operate as efficiently as possible.
- An application that requires extensive interfaces to other mainframe systems.

Besides the applications that are susceptible to microcomputers, there are differences in the way end users approach implementing an application and the way systems personnel approach the same problem. First, end users always use a higher-level programming language. In applications that lend themselves to high-level tools, such as word-processing and spreadsheet analysis, end users are far more productive than the COBOL programmer. They can often achieve in a short time what would take a COBOL programmer months to do. Since users also know their application better, they can program an application in less time than it takes to explain to a programmer. This also means that end users do best when the application is one in their own department and does not cross departmental lines. But end users do not write applications that are generalized or ones for company-wide use. End users worry about their own problems. Systems personnel worry about problems of others and have learned through experience that solutions should be as general as possible so that every one can use them with minor modifications. Applications written by end users for their own work may need to be completely rewritten if others are to use them.

The approach to system development is different. Systems personnel are taught to use structured methodologies in defining requirements, performing system analysis, structuring systems, and coding programs. End users tend to let systems grow through trial and error. They believe in the prototype approach; put something together fast, then modify and refine it through repetitive use. Prototypes replace the present analysis function. End users are far more forgiving with their own systems than with professionally designed systems. A system requiring the maintenance of 10 diskettes would not be acceptable if developed by the systems department but is acceptable if done by oneself. It also is not true that systems developed by end users are more user-friendly than those developed by the systems department. Quite often the opposite is true. End user systems are poorly documented and use abbreviations and notations known only to their author. Since these systems are used by the author, few applications are documented to the point where they may easily be used by others.

Perhaps the differences can be summarized by the statement that end users are consumers of data, whereas the information systems department is a supplier of data. End users program for themselves while the systems department does it for others. With this in mind, we can examine the application backlog and determine if end user computing can reduce the backlog significantly.

Requests for changes to existing applications and systems. These maintenance items are not suitable for micros because they require the modification of existing programs coded in COBOL or FORTRAN and running on the mainframe. If the request for change is for generating new reports, the user can use his micro to generate the report by downloading the necessary data from the mainframe data base. Since over half the backlog is represented by this category, and of that half, 20 percent is for generating new reports from existing systems, the micro could be of some use in reducing the backlog.

Requests for new systems that interface with existing systems. The value of the micro here would depend on the scope of the proposed system and its size. If the new system is a small one that only affects one department, perhaps the users can develop the system and interface it with the mainframe systems, assuming that it does not require interfacing with many mainframe systems. On the other hand, a small system, affecting one department and interfacing with only one existing system would probably not be on the formal backlog but on the hidden backlog. So using the micro to solve these problems would not affect the formal backlog significantly.

Requests for new stand-alone systems. This appears to be the one area where the micro can help reduce the formal backlog. Our consulting experience indicates that the typical mainframe application system involves over 50 programs, 20,000 plus-lines of source code, 2 to 4 master files, 2 transaction files, a data base of over 15 megabytes, and at least 20 to 30 predefined reports. Systems of this size would not be suitable for development on microcomputers. Therefore the micro could help reduce the backlog only for small applications, which most likely are not in the formal backlog.

The conclusion that can be drawn is that the formal backlog would not be reduced significantly through user personal computing. A better area to concentrate one's effort in reducing the backlog is through user developed systems on the mainframe using prototyping techniques and interactive programming. The micro could be used to reduce the hidden backlog since most of these are small applications affecting a few people. The micro is a natural for these systems. However, in attacking the hidden backlog, the users will require support from the systems department in downloading data, and in teaching them how to interface with mainframe programs. These tasks will be of high priority and will take resources away from handling the formal backlog. This points out the necessity for the organization to have a policy for personal computing and to plan for an orderly implementation of micro-mainframe connections so that interruptions to mainframe priority developments are minimized.

MANAGING THE GROWTH OF MICROCOMPUTERS

There is no way of avoiding it, microcomputers will grow in every business and in many levels of the organization. Today this growth is unmanaged and if continued, will result in a nightmare for the information systems department as dozens of non-compatible personal computers seek data from the corporate mainframes. When the director of information systems is called into the "corner office" today, the question most likely to be asked is: "Which personal computer should I buy?" Unless there is a policy established for the company, what could the director answer? Furthermore, if there is to be a policy, it will have to be drafted by the information systems director and sold to top management. After all, if CEOs need advice on what personal computers to buy, they certainly have no idea of the policy needed to manage the growth of microcomputers in their organizations.

In developing a policy, the purpose should be to provide guidelines for how microcomputers are to be used in the organization, provide standards for acquiring both hardware and software, identify responsibilities of the users and the information systems department, and present plans for integrating microcomputers with the company's mainframes. It is important that the policy not be viewed by users as a layer of control to inhibit them from purchasing and using personal computers. Instead, the policy should encourage the use of microcomputers and offer procedures for users to get the necessary training and technical assistance in their use. Management should also realize that any policy on microcomputers will be greeted with cynicism by a large portion of the company. There will be many users who have purchased micros because the information systems department has not responded to their needs. They have successfully used software packages and may be attempting to write more complex programs without understanding why systems definition, design, and documentation are necessary. Most of these programs will not work properly, and those that do work will require data from the mainframe. Sooner or later, the information systems department will be called in to pick up the pieces. Unfortunately, this is happening at a time when systems personnel are already busy with a growing backlog of applications and demands for new systems, a time when they can least afford to be diverted from their main task. To prevent this situation from happening, a clearly defined statement of the company's position on microcomputers is needed. The policy statement should say to everyone: "This is the way microcomputers will be acquired and used in this company." Employees can still take the attitude that they can purchase whatever personal computer they want to and use it in any way they wish, but only if they purchase the micro with their own funds. If they are to access the company's mainframe for data, or link to other microcomputers in the organization, or use the micro in a word-processing network, it must be compatible with the firm's computer and communication hardware and software. If they are to request support and assistance from the information systems department, the micro must be one approved by the company since the information systems department does not have the time or manpower to learn about and support every microcomputer sold in the market. Not only should the company's policy statement establish responsibilities for microcomputers, it should offer potential users incentives for supporting its policy.

A Policy for Microcomputers

In developing a policy for microcomputers, a company might include the following:

The company's posture in the use of microcomputers. This could be from encouraging users to be self-sufficient in the use of personal computers for improving operational efficiency to applying microcomputer technology to opportunities that provide high payback and quick return. This policy should emphasize the company's desire to encourage the use of micros among end users and foster cooperation between them and the information systems department by using the most appropriate tool (micro or mainframe) on an application-by-application basis.

The role of the information systems department with respect to microcomputers. This role should be one of coordination rather than control. The coordination role would include developing a list of approved hardware and software packages. The reason for this approval is not to limit the vendors that end users can choose from but to make sure that the hardware is compatible with the company's mainframe and can be linked to it. The approved software would be those that can take data from the mainframe through downloading, and those with communication linkages to the standard protocols used in the department's communication network. By approving both hardware and software, the department can prevent the uncontrolled explosion of different pieces of equipment and programs and still provide users with a choice of vendors.

Other responsibilities of the information systems group would be to provide assistance to user departments as they learn how to use their personal computers to best advantage. This assistance might take the form of establishing a personal computing center to answer user questions and provide technical training. A business application library could be part of the center so that users would have access to programs developed by others in the company or at least learn what was under development by other departments in the business. Another objective of the personal computing center would be to help users analyze which processing alternative best suited their needs: microcomputing or using the company's mainframe. If microcomputing were the appropriate solution, then information systems personnel could help the user select the appropriate software packages and languages and help them develop an appropriate design and implementation program.

The role of users with respect to microcomputers. Users have final control over which computers to purchase and how they are to be used. This responsibility should work under the hardware and software guidelines set forth by the information systems department. Users should justify the purchase of hardware through some type of cost/benefit analysis, obtain approval of all acquisitions from their own management, and fund all hardware and software purchases from their own budgets. If purchase were approved for hardware that was not on the recommended list, an evaluation could be done by the systems department to see if the proposed hardware could be linked to the mainframe and communication networks. If not, and the user department still wished to procure the hardware/software, they could do so recognizing that it would not be supported by the personal computing center people and by the information systems department. In other words, they would be on their own. Top management may want to discourage or prohibit the acquisition of nonapproved equipment and software. Finally, it would be the users' responsibility to ensure that all legal and audit requirements were met and that adequate security over hardware, software and data was maintained. No user could update a mainframe data base or a data base stored on a remote machine. If such a capability were required and approved, it would have to be provided through the information systems department.

Justification for the purchase of microcomputers. The policy should state the justifications for acquiring personal computers. Should any employees who think microcomputers could help them be more productive and efficient be permitted to acquire them? There should be some criteria to be met prior to approval for purchase so that they do not become toys that are rarely used. Asking users to submit plans for using the computer, the tasks to be automated, the number of hours to be used a day, the outputs to be generated (how often and what volume), the source and availability of input data, would not only help in evaluating the need for a micro, but would also help in determining whether the need could best be met with a micro or with a mainframe. Users should not object to justifying a micro if they realized that all they were being asked to do was to address the specific business problems that they expected the micro to help them solve, and to show management that there was a clear business value in purchasing the equipment. Typical benefits that are often cited as justification for microcomputers include:

- Reduction in outside time-sharing charges

- Improved turnaround and accuracy in analysis and reports
- Time saving and not having to recruit additional staff
- Improved information from better in-depth analysis
- Better decisions through improved analysis of computer data
- More timely and improved client service.

It is important that this policy statement stress the fact that justification is the user's responsibility. The user must obtain the funds and information systems cannot veto a proposal. The assumption is that if employees are given responsibility to do specific jobs, they should not be denied the use of tools that they feel are essential to performing well on those jobs. If management agrees that the tool is needed, information systems cannot veto the acquisition of that tool.

Some people have suggested that rather than confront the whole issue of business justification for personal computers, an alternative that is worth considering is to assume that employees above a certain level or in particular job functions will have microcomputers for use as workstations just as they have telephones. The cost of a micro today is about the same in relation to salary as a phone was in the 1950s, and the cost is continuing to drop. Nobody has to justify phones, so why justify micros? Companies can establish the policy, select the standard equipment, and leave it at that.

The long-term goal of personal computing in the business. This last point in a policy statement might state that the long-term goal was to make personal computing an integrated part of the overall computer resources of the corporation, not something separate and different. The personal computer could eventually be a multipurpose workstation accessing the corporate data base and combining integrated office support functions with on-line mainframe services and products. Reaching this goal would involve end user computing, end user development, and a vast increase in the demand for information as a corporate resource.

Growth of Microcomputer Use

The need for an integrated policy on the use of microcomputers becomes apparent when the growth of these systems is analysed. Figure 10-6 shows the applications' evolution starting with the introduction of the personal computer in 1980. As the cost of computing power continues to decline and performance improves, the number and sophistication of personal computing applications will advance accordingly. Spreadsheet programs sparked the initial use of personal computers by business professionals. This was followed in Phase II by the use of several stand-alone applications such as text-editing/word-processing programs, simple database/filing systems, and business graphics/presentation products. These programs broadened the range of personal productivity tools available to business. In Phase III, applications included electronic mail, access to the corporate data base, improved communication linkage creating networks of microcomputers, and the integration of word processing with data processing. Moving into the 1990s, applications will become more closely tailored to a multitude of specific professional and business functions. By the mid 1990s, information systems will provide thorough indices to the information they contain, as well as to information stored on remote and public data bases. Training and tutorial courses should be available covering almost every aspect of general business and corporation-specific procedures. Expert learning systems will enable professionals to eliminate routine decisions and focus on specific areas requiring professional judgment. Information will be as critical an asset for business management as capital, equipment and labor are today. Competitive companies will depend on personal computing systems and employees with the skills to use them.

FIGURE 10-6   **APPLICATIONS EVOLUTION ON MICROCOMPUTERS**

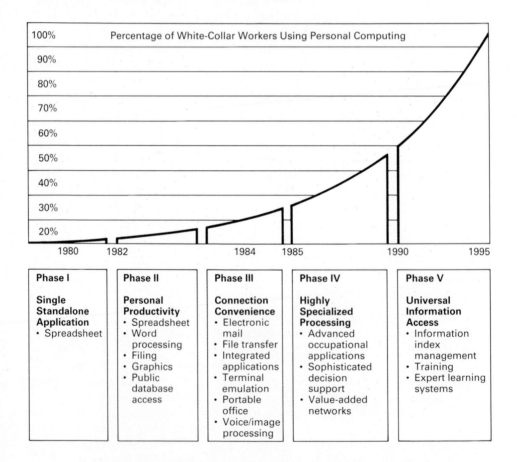

Phase I	Phase II	Phase III	Phase IV	Phase V
Single Standalone Application • Spreadsheet	**Personal Productivity** • Spreadsheet • Word processing • Filing • Graphics • Public database access	**Connection Convenience** • Electronic mail • File transfer • Integrated applications • Terminal emulation • Portable office • Voice/image processing	**Highly Specialized Processing** • Advanced occupational applications • Sophisticated decision support • Value-added networks	**Universal Information Access** • Information index management • Training • Expert learning systems

Source: "Personal Computing: The Challenge to Management," A Forbes Advertising Supplement, *Forbes,* May 21, 1984.

CHAPTER 10 DISCUSSION QUESTIONS

1. What criteria should be used in approving or disapproving requests to supply personal computer users with information stored in the corporate data base?

2. Uploading of data from a micro to a mainframe presents significant data integrity problems. What does this mean? How can the problems be minimized?

3. Do you think that managers and executives will use a personal computer or will they delegate its use to their secretaries?

4. Most users do not document their design or their end product when using a personal computer. Should they? What will happen in a few years when many applications are running on each microcomputer and changes need to be made?

5. Should the information systems department charge users for helping them use their personal computers more effectively?

6. Do you think that users can reduce the systems development backlog by implementing some of their own requests on their personal computers?

7. How can one control and protect information on personal computers?

8. What are the differences in systems development approaches as used by end users and by system department analysts/programmers? Is one better than the other?

9. Why is a corporate policy needed for microcomputers?

10. How should a company organize and staff a personal computer center? What services should be provided?

11. Should users have to justify the purchase of a personal computer? Why? Who should approve or disapprove?

11

MANAGEMENT CONTROL OF INFORMATION PROCESSING

ISSUES

- Should different management techniques be used in managing "high-tech" activities than in managing normal business activities?

- What steps can be taken to build rapport and understanding between information systems and corporate management?

- Are today's organizational structures of both the information systems department and the corporation the most effective for managing information as a corporate resource?

- If we are to encourage the use of computer resources through microcomputers and end user computing, should charging users for mainframe services be discontinued?

CREDIT REPORTING
SERVICES INC. (CRS)

Paul Gates had just settled in his seat when the 747 started to leave the Dallas/Fort Worth Airport on its way to Atlanta. Paul worked for a consulting firm specializing in purchase investigations. A client was interested in buying a credit-reporting firm and Credit Reporting Services seemed a likely target. The reports Paul had in front of him indicated that the firm was financially sound, had a good client base, and the price was reasonable when compared to its book value. Paul had traveled to Dallas to talk to CRS management and found them willing to listen. CRS was owned by two brothers who also had interests in oil, real estate, and cattle. The credit-rating firm had been started by their father and built into a sizeable company in Texas. They did credit investigations and built a data base of credit information which they sold to retail stores, banks, and any business that had need to run credit checks on their prospective customers. Several different types of information were sold to their customers, ranging from a short credit rating, to a complete credit history with financial statements, and projected earnings; similar to a Dun and Bradstreet report. The addition of CRS to Paul's client's group of companies would make them the largest credit research firm with offices covering the entire Sunbelt in the U.S. Since this was the most rapidly growing region in the country, Paul's client was anxious to add Texas to its territory. The brothers were anxious to sell so that they could devote more time to speculating in real estate development and oil drilling. Paul got the distinct impression he was on the set of *Dallas* and negotiating with J.R. and Bobby Ewing when he talked to the owners of CRS.

All of the credit data in this industry was automated. Truth-in-lending laws required that individuals have access to information and reports on their own credit ratings and companies invested heavily in systems to make this information available and to prevent unauthorized individuals from accessing any of the credit data. Paul was under instruction to look carefully at the information systems department at CRS and evaluate it as to competence and quality of service provided to customers. The evaluation would have a direct bearing on the offering price to be made for CRS since the department was key to its operations. Paul had just finished his evaluation at the Dallas computer center and was now pulling his thoughts together in a report to management.

As the plane flew eastward, Paul tried to reconstruct the meetings with data-processing people and users at CRS. The computer center was gigantic; housing an IBM 370/168 multiprocessor with over 80 disk and tape drives and 8 printers. Over 12 million records were on file. The center manager was a young man with little data-processing experience. Paul later found out that he was the brother-in-law of one of the owners. The director of data processing was an old crony of the owners and really did not seem to be up to date on what was happening in the world of data processing. He attended the seminars given by IBM and all the new product announcements. His training consisted of attending the two-week executive seminar given by IBM. The department staff had over 500 people, 50 system analysts and programmers, 21 operations center personnel, and 450 data entry clerks. The knowledgeable people appeared to be the head of systems development and the head of technical services. Both of them had been in data processing for over 12 years and were current on state-of-the-art development. As they talked to Paul, their frustrations over not being able to upgrade the system were evident.

The present system had been implemented in 1972. While there had been many changes, the basic design was an IMS data base linked with CICS communication software. Documentation had not been kept current as changes were made so the next system would most likely be a complete redesign using the latest software and techniques. When Paul asked them why the system had not been redesigned by now, the reply was" "Management is waiting for IBM to announce its Sierra line of computers." The joke was that the owners had a horse named "Sierra" and everytime they brought up the term in the context of the next generation of IBM mainframes, the conversation turned to horse racing. "I take it that the owners aren't too interested in data processing?" asked Paul. "No, they are not the slightest bit interested," was the reply. "They recognize that the business could not exist without an automated data base and on-line inquiry, but the attitude is is keep the investment at a minimum, just enough to keep it running and keep the customer happy." That was exactly what they did. The system ran well, and the customers were happy, so Paul was told.

When Paul toured the computer facility, he noticed that some of the programmers were playing games on their terminals. Discipline was lax, and the atmosphere was very informal and friendly. It was also clear that the staff enjoyed working at CRS and had a good, although to Paul, overly familiar relationship with DP management. Paul asked if they had a methodology for system development. They did not, most of their analysts and programmers were from Rice and A&M, had strong technical backgrounds and enjoyed independent work. They would not be happy if they were told how to program. "Are projects completed on schedule and on budget?" Paul asked. "Well, pretty close, but we don't keep track of schedules or budgets around here, after all we aren't paid by the hour or by the project, so unless there is another critical job waiting to be done, we don't have to rush to get it finished. The customers have never complained, so they must be happy." Paul smiled as he recalled how "laid back" and contented these Texas programmers were.

When Paul talked to the users, he found that they were mostly satisfied with the data-processing department. "Oh, there are days when the computer is down and that creates extra work, but that only happens once or twice a month. Besides, the fellows there are so nice, they let us know and try to fix it as soon as they can." "Do you work with them in developing new systems?" Paul asked. "Well, not really. They visit with us and ask us what we do and how we think the job can be improved, we do this over a beer after work, they are really nice." Paul smiled again as he recalled this conversation. "After the boys design and fix their new system, they come and show us how to use it. If we have any questions, they are real helpful." Paul decided that while there was no user involvement in the design of new applications, this user, at least, was most happy with the way things were done and had no complaints.

During his final interview with management, Paul asked them how they controlled the data-processing department, monitored progress, and made sure that they did what they were supposed to do. The reply rather surprised Paul. "Control is by trust. You gotta have trust in your people. If you pick one to run your computer, and you don't trust him, then you're bound to be in trouble. But if you trust your people, you don't have to keep hounding them or looking after them. We trust our boys in data processing, they have never let us down yet. As long as they keep the shop running smoothly, and increases in costs are in line with inflation, we'll continue to keep our faith in them and trust them."

It seemed to Paul that here was a company who did very little forward planning, had a data-processing department that the users loved, operated with systems in 1986 that were designed in 1972, was successful in developing systems without using a development methodology or instilling discipline in its staff, was loosely organized and controlled, did everything contrary to sound management practice, but was successful. How did you evaluate this kind of operation? What should he include in his report to his client?

As the plane approached the new Atlanta airport, Paul was still smiling over his recollections about an amazing group of people.

Control of the information systems' activities has always posed a problem to senior management. Much of this has to do with the lack of familiarity with the technology and the difficulty in communicating with and understanding data-processing personnel. As younger people who are computer literate and comfortable working with computer terminals and personal computers take over the management of companies, hopefully the communications gap and fear of the unknown will disappear. Managing the information resources of a company should be no different than managing any of the other resources. Yet there is a common belief that because of the rapidly changing technology and the diverse mix of skills that make up the typical information systems department, people who work with computers present a more difficult control challenge than many other organizations. If this is the case, it is a fault of management. Top management understands about sales, production, distribution, and financing because these are the necessary functions to bring a product to the market. When the marketing department develops a new advertising program for the company's major product, or when production develops a new packaging technique, or when the finance department wants to raise money through a new stock issue, top management is always actively involved in the decision-making process, and contributes to the discussions and planning efforts that precede a major business decision. When the information systems department launches the design of a major application system, or makes a capital investment in new hardware, top management rarely participates in the planning and discussions leading to decisions on hardware acquisition and software development. Yet the impact of these decisions are as important as a new stock issue or a new advertising campaign. Information systems can help in making better decisions on bringing new products to the marketplace, yet few companies make use of their information-processing resources in making major business decisions. Why? Because they do not have confidence in the information systems department, and feel that they cannot manage, understand, or control its activities.

Managing and controlling a function which is affected by changes in technology, staffed by creative, independent people, and which has significant impact on the way things are done in an organization, is not easy. But it can be done provided management understands the framework within which to develop control procedures and monitor performance. Lucas and Turner, in their article published in the Sloan Management Review[1] suggest a framework for viewing management decision areas involved in controlling information processing. This framework can provide the basis for discussing how management can regain control of the information system function.

[1]Lucas, Henry and Turner, Jon, "A Corporate Strategy for the Control of Information Processing," *Sloan Management Review*, Spring 1982.

CORPORATE MIS PLAN

Most information systems departments do some form of planning. Perhaps most common is the application development plan in which projects are identified and scheduled for implementation. These projects include system software, and installation of data base software, for example, to major applications such as the development of an on-line order entry system. Some departments will have a three-to-five-year long-range system plan that includes hardware and software acquisitions, personnel plans, and projected financial requirements for the department. Most likely, those with the long-range plans will have developed their plans independent of corporate management. While a copy of the completed plan may have been sent to management as a courtesy copy, few have had meaningful feedback from management other than general remarks such as "good effort," "very comprehensive." Very few departments will have developed their plan with the participation of top management and based their plan on the corporation's strategic plans for the same time period.

There are many reasons given by information systems managers for not having a plan tied to the corporate plan. Many companies do not have corporate plans in sufficient detail to help information systems identify corporate strategies and information needs. All too often, the information systems managers will ask corporate management for a copy of the corporate strategic plan so that they can develop an information plan to correspond to it and not be given access to one. Many companies do not have long-range corporate plans documented. One executive said: "We all know what we have to do, why spend the time writing it down; it changes often to meet our competition so documenting it would be a waste of effort." Even if the company does not have a documented strategy or plan, it is still worthwhile for the information systems department to develop one so that it can operate in a more systematic and organized fashion. In the process of developing a plan, it must have top management participation. If management does not have a plan, this would be an opportunity for the information systems executive to lead them through the thought processes of identifying the goals of the company, how they plan to meet those goals, the direction the company plans to follow in the next three to five years, and the strategies they will use to meet their objectives. As these thoughts are discussed, information systems can document them as well as the information needed to help corporate management execute its strategies. The end result in this instance would be a corporate plan and an information plan, jointly developed and supported by top management.

If the company has a set of formal plans, the information systems executive should work with management to identify the data and systems needed to supply them with the necessary information to execute their plans. This should be done in a series of planning meetings rather than asking management for a copy of the corporate plan and developing the information plan without top management participation.

Whether or not the company has documented its strategies and plans, the key is to involve management in developing the corporate information plan. This provides an opportunity for information systems executives to work closely with top management, to show them that they can communicate with them, that they understand the business problems of the company, or at least are trying to understand their problems. It should start to build the mutual confidence in each other that is essential if management is to successfully manage the information systems function.

What should the plan contain? The corporate information plan should be coordinated with corporate strategy. It should show how information systems technology will be used to meet corporate goals and objectives. It does this by showing the specific information systems tasks that must be accomplished to meet each corporate objective. These tasks would include all the activities and the associated resources needed to meet each corporate goal. Management has to set priorities for its strategies so that information systems can prioritize its development activities and allocate resources to implement its plan. The information plan would not only chart the direction for systems development, it would also provide the basis for management evaluation of its performance, a key factor in controlling the information systems department.

A top level corporate MIS plan linked to the company's strategic plan will:

- provide an opportunity for users, management, and systems personnel to work together in identifying corporate goals and the information needed to meet corporate objectives and strategies.

- set priorities for application development and establish the levels of operations support, staff, and equipment within the information systems department.

- open lines of communication between information systems management and top corporate management, and allow top management to build confidence in the ability of information systems personnel.

- provide management with a means of controlling and evaluating the work of the information systems department.

ORGANIZATION STRUCTURE

How to organize the information systems department is another area where top management can exercise some degree of control over the department. Today, whether the department is centralized, decentralized or somewhere in between is left up to the information systems department. This decision is currently made based on user demands for services or based on the type of equipment installed. Centralization implies that all systems analysis and design is performed by a central group and all equipment is located centrally. This is the traditional organization coming out of the 1960s. Decentralization is locating equipment at local sites and permitting the users to do their own analysis and design work. Some companies, very few, chose this approach with the installation of minicomputers in the 1970s. Distributed processing falls somewhere in the middle, with central and local sites tied together in a communication network to share both equipment and data resources. It would appear that distributed is the trend, especially with the rapid growth of microcomputers and the linking of micros to mainframes.

While the organizational structures of today have evolved from the centralized approach of the 1960s, corporate management should reevaluate the present structure to determine if it is the best alternative for providing information services. This reevaluation would be done taking into consideration management's plans for running the corporate organization in the future. Do they plan on keeping tight control of its activities or allowing divisions and subsidiaries autonomy in the managing of their affairs? Which organizational alternatives provide the best framework for carrying out corporate goals and strategies? Based on the structure today, how can the information department migrate to the structure best suited for managing information resources in the future, and what would be the cost of this migration in terms of people and equipment?

In evaluating organizational alternatives, management must trade off the benefits perceived by users of having and controlling their own computer resources with the need for central direction and coordination. Those companies with large central data bases and the need to access the information from all departments within the company would not select a completely decentralized organizational structure. Without centralized control, microcomputers could proliferate throughout the organization to the point where linking them into a network could be costly because of their noncompatibility. Finally, management must establish policies on the development of common systems to be used throughout the organization so that duplicate efforts are controlled or eliminated. Establishing the organizational structure for the information systems function, then, is another way to achieve management control over information processing by developing a policy that balances coordination costs and local autonomy and ensures that information services are provided in the most effective manner.

NEW APPLICATION DEVELOPMENT

Given sufficient resources, there are few applications that users want today that can be classified as being not feasible. Moreover, with the availability of low-cost microcomputers, some type of automation can be made available to anyone who wants it. It is almost a certainty that requests for new applications will increase. The information systems department already has a three-to-five year backlog of applications awaiting development; how will they cope with the inevitable request for new systems? Here is another opportunity for management to exercise control.

The corporate information plan has identified the types of information needed to support company goals and strategies and has assigned priorities for developing systems to provide the required information. Ideally, this has been done as a joint effort between end user management and information systems personnel under the direction of top management. With the information plan established, specific applications must now be considered for implementation. Some required applications will already have been implemented, but may be in need of upgrade or redesign, others will have been planned but are awaiting resources for development. The user department most affected by the application should participate in choosing the type of system, if any, that should be implemented. The alternative of "no systems" has to be considered if there is agreement that the application has too high a risk of failure for development now, or that waiting for new software developments in the future would reduce the risk of failure in implementation (waiting for relational data base software to be available prior to developing a decision support system is an example). If the decision is made to consider development, several alternative implementation methods should be evaluated by the users and information systems, and a recommendation presented to top management. The alternatives include:

- Custom development. The most costly and time-consuming choice. However, if the application is to be commonly used by many in the organization, the use is to be frequent and involve access to corporate data bases, and operating efficiency is a prime consideration, there may be no choice but to custom develop the system. Custom development should be considered as a last resort, used only if the other alternatives have been analyzed and are deemed to be not feasible.

- Application package. There are many software packages on the market today, especially for personal computers. Mainframe packages are available for most transaction systems, that is payroll/personnel, accounts receivable, accounts payable, general ledger, as well as for data manipulation and report generation. It would seem advantageous to replace aging transaction systems with an on-line package and modify it to meet local requirements rather than custom develop these applications. Most companies have found that application packages, even with extensive modifications, have been less costly to implement and operate than custom developed systems.

- User developed systems. Some applications are most suited for end user development. The main criteria is that the end user has to want to develop his own system and be willing to maintain it. These applications are of interest only to the user and consist of projects such as models, decision support systems, and special analysis programs. They can be developed with high-level software and with prototyping tools. If this alternative is selected, the information systems department should create an organization to help the user use special development tools and train them in the rudiments of design and programming. This center should enable the user to develop systems quickly and not waste time trying to reinvent the wheel. It would also help build those needed bridges of confidence between user and technical personnel.

- Moving to a micro. Instead of replacing an aging application with a newer mainframe package, consider moving it to a micro. This usually means taking an old system written in COBOL and replacing it with a mix of packages and custom code, using BASIC, Pascal, or even the COBOL that is now available for microcomputers. It also means that the information systems department achieves two important results: a needed application gets modernized, and a micro performs a real, justifiable job. Moreover, systems managers gain a new and swifter way to update old systems and the approach offers an opportunity for them to assert greater control of the ways micros are used in their organizations. This alternative is not for the large transaction systems involving thousands of records, each of 3000 bytes each. However, if there are two or three files, each containing a thousand or so 500-byte records, the micro's size will not be a problem. Do not forget, the 1401 only had 12K of main memory and the 360 model 30 only 65K. Many old systems were originally written for machines that were smaller, or not much larger, than current microcomputers. While a micro is not an IBM 3090, it is a machine with enough memory and storage capacity to satisfy many applications.

■ Using outside resources for development. Not all systems have to be developed in-house. There are occasions when the use of outside resources can be an effective way of implementing a critically needed application. These applications might include state-of-the-art technology developed by an outside company, or a unique software package which can be better modified and installed by the developer than by company personnel. A consulting organization that has helped design a new system should be able to program and install the design more efficiently and effectively than training in-house personnel to do the job. The selection criteria become time, cost, and the probability of success, when evaluating whether outside assistance should be selected for implementation.

■ Alternative design considerations. In addition to selecting the development approach, for example custom, application package, user developed, or consultants, another decision is the design approach. Should the proposed application be on-line or batch? Interactive or transaction driven? Hierarchical or relational data base? This is an area where users will need technical help and guidance from systems professionals. Systems people must be able to explain the differences in approach, the advantages and disadvantages of each, and the risks involved in selecting each design consideration. All of this has to be done without resorting to data-processing jargon and technical terms. On the other hand, requiring that the user participate in making these decisions will result in more support for the development effort and the end product produced. They will understand why a certain design methodology was selected and what they have to do to make it work.

The most critical issue in management control of the information systems department is control over systems design and implementation. It accounts for over 75 percent of the work performed in the systems department and, if lucky, gets 10 percent of top management's attention. Management is always surprised when projects are completed with cost overruns of 300 to 500 percent and anywhere from six months to several years behind schedule. Did anyone react when the scheduled completion date become due and slipped past with no system being delivered? Who approved the increase in budget to complete the project? Should management not have known that the project was in trouble and slipping behind schedule long before the project leader announced that it would take another six months to complete the job? If the project was a new plant being constructed for the company instead of an information system, would management have tolerated this type of performance? What would have happened to the contractors and the project manager if a construction project for a new plant came in 200 percent over budget and one year behind schedule?

Management control of the system design and implementation function involves three critical activities: First, management and user personnel must participate in the requirements definition and in the selection of implementation alternatives. The system to be built must be one with the wholehearted support and active participation of the users most affected by the proposed system. Second, the system must be built using an approved system development methodology which calls for milestone reporting and "go/no-go" management decision points. Management must monitor the progress of the construction of the system just as it monitors the progress of the construction of a major physical facility. There may be a time when management loses confidence in the project team's abilities to complete the project and either replaces the team or calls for outside help. This is preferable to spending millions of dollars on a project that does not work. Even today, many large data-processing organizations admit to having a system development methodology but not using it because " . . . our analysts and programmers don't want to be tied to one way of doing things. They like to be innovative and creative in their work." Until management recognizes that system development is a costly production effort, not an experimental project to test new theories and ideas, or a place for creative programmers to perform their artistry, they will continue to have costly failures in building information systems. A great symphony orchestra is composed of virtuoso performers, each a talented, creative artist. Yet to make the music work, they must follow a score and play as the conductor wants them to play. It would be chaos if each decided on his or her own interpretation of the music. Even in the arts, management and control is essential to artistic success.

Finally, management has to do more than pay lip service to project management activities. If there is a management steering committee to monitor progress and control changes, then top management should participate. Far too often, the CEO shows up at the project "kick-off" meeting and tells everyone how important the project is to the company, why the company is spending significant sums to ensure its completion, and how the new system will make the business more competitive in the market. The CEO then disappears and never shows up at another meeting other than the final one with the board of directors to explain why there is the significant write-off out of this year's earnings due to a canceled computer project. It is not too much to ask the CEO to spend a few hours a month monitoring a project that costs millions and that affects every area of the company. This presence and participation shows that the CEO is interested in the project and not just paying lip service. When project personnel recognize this, there will be more incentive to complete the project as designed, on time, and on budget.

OPERATIONS

Control over computer operations provides management with an indication of the service levels provided by the computer center and the credibility they have with the users. If users have no confidence in the service they are getting from the computer center, they will have no confidence in the ability of the information systems department to develop new systems. Late and inaccurate reports, multiple reruns of jobs, excessive computer down time, are all indications to the users that things are not going well in the "computer department." Yet, evaluation of the quality and level of service provided by the operations group is rarely offered by the users. Instead, the techniques used to evaluate service levels and the evaluation itself are done by the information systems department. To find out if the product or service is any good, ask the consumer, not the producer. Had Coca Cola asked more consumers about its "New Coke," it would have found that there was a large segment of the market that just did not like its taste and preferred the "Old Coke." This would have saved the company a lot of embarrassment in its marketing campaign to switch to the new product.

To improve performance evaluation of the quality of service provided by operations, management should not only look at the reports produced by the information systems department (the percentage of output reports produced on time, the availability of the computer, the number of transactions processed), but periodically should survey users to ascertain their view of the service provided by the department. Management could adopt a technique used by General Motors. GM launched a "Commitment to Excellence" program in 1985 where purchasers of a GM product received a survey asking how satisfied they were on the service provided by the dealer before purchasing the car, taking delivery of the car, and after purchase servicing of the car. The survey was confidential with data processed at GM headquarters. It provided management with the consumer assessment of each GM dealership and supplemented data from the dealers on cars sold, and serviced. At the end of each development project, the users could be surveyed as to how they assessed the performance of the information systems department in each phase of the system life cycle and could offer suggestions for improvement on future projects. Similarly, once or twice a year, users of computer services could be surveyed to get their reaction to the level and quality of service provided by operations. This technique would provide a measurement and evaluation based on the criteria most important to the users as well as indicators from the operations group.

EQUIPMENT AND STAFFING

Management control in this area has been limited to approval of major equipment purchases and approval of annual budgets which then dictate staffing levels within the department. If top management includes the information systems department in developing the corporate strategic plan, a by-product of that planning process will be the determination of the level of information-processing resources required to support the plan. Requirements can be compared with available resources and the incremental equipment and staff resources needed to execute the plan can be easily identified. This procedure permits top management a better understanding of why additional resources are needed and a better basis for deciding on the criticality of that portion of the corporate plan which generates the additional information-processing resource requirement. If it is critical, then management approves the additional resource; if it is not critical, management can shift priorities and defer costs for implementing that part of the plan. This is certainly a better method of controlling equipment and people resources than approving a budget formulated by the systems department with no input from the corporate level and no real understanding of the need for equipment upgrade or additional staffing (see Figure 11-1).

It seems almost certain that equipment costs will decline in the future and as more microprocessors are used in the organization, the demand for systems personnel will increase. This suggests that either more systems personnel will have to be hired, or more of the system development work will have to be done by user personnel. In any case, the company must have a policy as to their approach to the growing use of personal computers, and how these computers will interface with the information systems department's other resources. The policy selected will impact both equipment and the level of staffing for the information systems department. With the increasing use of computers in all aspects of corporate life, top management can no longer avoid participating in the decision-making process and delegating all technical decisions to the director of information systems. In the end, it is the CEO who is responsible for managing the information resources of the company.

CHARGEBACK

A traditional way of controlling information systems costs is to install a chargeback scheme, sell services to the users rather than give them away. Sometimes this has resulted in the opposite of what management wanted to achieve. An organization where the data-processing department did not have the confidence of the users found that a charge-out policy resulted in the users rushing to buy personal computers in hopes of developing the systems themselves and justifying their purchases by the money saved in not using the data-processing department. Others have used the charge-out policy as an excuse not to automate.

There are a number of advantages and disadvantages in charging for information-processing services. Primarily it will influence user behavior and their use of the services provided at a price. It can work where the users are sophisticated in the use of computers and have always worked in an environment of close budget control over expenditures. Where users are relative novices in computer technology and management is trying to encourage greater automation throughout the organization, charge-out procedures will inhibit rather than encourage greater computer use. If computer workstations are to be as common as telephones in the 1990s, computer costs will probably be absorbed as administrative overhead just a telephone costs are absorbed today. A charge-out policy based on usage will penalize those departments who use the computer in high-volume transaction processing, for example payroll, customer service, accounting, and help those who use the computer occasionally such as for planning models developed for corporate planning, even though the costs of

---

FIGURE 11-1   **DATA PROCESSING COSTS**

A. Personnel Costs

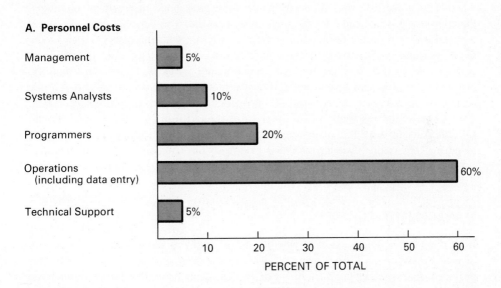

B. Costs by Category

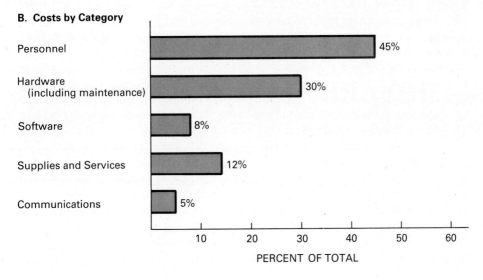

developing the planning models far exceeds the costs of purchasing an accounting package. On the other hand, charging for system design and development may discourage the use of computers for other-than-essential, high-volume transaction systems where reduction in clerical personnel can help offset the development and processing costs.

Probably the most satisfactory way to control and allocate the cost of information-processing services is to use the overhead allocation method. Total data-processing costs can be included in the business's administrative overhead. Allocation of this overhead to the departments can be based on the size of the department. Departments will be encouraged to use the computer since they are paying for the overhead whether they use it or not. As departments make greater use of personal computers, the approach of overhead allocation has greater appeal. The personal computing centers staffed by information systems personnel offering consulting services and technical assistance to users can become part of the corporate overhead. This will encourage end users to seek out this service and learn how to use their microcomputers properly. A refinement to this policy may be to charge for special projects that are of interest to only one department and have limited value to the entire corporation. The purchase and installation of a graphics processor to produce three-dimensional, full color displays for the advertising department could be a special one-time charge to advertising rather than an overhead charge to the company-wide administrative overhead. It should not be too difficult to determine which system benefits the whole company and which benefits one department only.

MANAGEMENT CONTROL

How does management evaluate whether the information services are under control or not? Today, the criteria is primarily whether the users are happy with the services provided, and whether the department delivers systems being developed on time and on budget. While these are two valid criteria, they do not measure whether the department is contributing to corporate goals and strategies. If management agrees that information is becoming a critical corporate resource, then the information services organization should be evaluated and controlled based on their ability to deliver the information needed to accomplish corporate goals and objectives. This information is defined in the strategic planning process and collected and processed in applications and systems defined in the information systems plan and agreed to by user and top management. The performance of the information systems department should be evaluated with respect to how well they execute the information system plan.

There are specific control mechanisms to assess how well the information systems department is progressing as it implements the plan on a priority basis. For design activities, management can monitor the progress of specific projects as each goes through the various stages of the system life cycle. At the completion of the project, a post-implementation audit can be conducted to see if the original goals, budget, and specifications of the project were met. At the same time, the benefits identified by the users in their cost/benefits analysis can be reviewed to see if they were achieved. The operations group can be evaluated based on their performance against plan and on how users perceive the level and quality of service provided by the group. Where possible, management should provide the information systems department with performance criteria and the department should report on how well they are meeting these criteria to top management.

What should top management do if it appears that part or all of the information systems department is out of control? If the department has participated in defining corporate objectives and goals, identified the information needed to meet those goals, and been provided with the necessary resources to develop systems to provide the needed information, then the manager of the information systems department should be replaced. If the procedure outlined above has not been followed, then management should take a careful look at how it is contributing to controlling information processing. Have they helped in developing a plan for information systems? Were they involved in the selection of applications and the determination of priorities? Do top user personnel set the objectives for new systems and participate in their design? Have they helped in setting policies to govern the direction and growth of hardware and software? Perhaps changes in personnel are necessary when the operation is out of control, but management should also determine why it got out of control and what steps must be taken to prevent the situation from happening again. The first step in exerting control is knowing what to measure and conducting the evaluation. The next step is to determine what action is needed to correct any deficiencies in controls.

QUALITY ASSURANCE

In evaluating the performance of the information systems department, it is not enough to assess whether the users are satisfied with the outputs or whether the project is completed on time and on budget. Perhaps even more important is the quality of the product produced (see Figure 11-2). The managing director of Matsushita Corp. defines quality as follows: "Quality means conforming to customer expectations, as dictated by how the product is represented through documentation and marketing." There is an emphasis on customer expectation—what the user expects from the product. Second, the definition stresses that quality issues are not limited to the product itself, but include the entire package created—documentation, marketing material, training, and support. This whole package sets the customer's expectation.

Quality of the product produced by the systems department—programs—is rarely controlled as we would control the quality of a manufactured product. For example, factory production lines have separate test and inspection and quality assurance personnel to check the quality of the product manufactured. In programming, the programmers do the testing and the inspection themselves, and pass judgment on the quality of their own work. Nevertheless, we do have the tools to ensure quality and one of the responsibilities of managing the information systems effort is ensuring that these tools are used effectively.

Testing and Debugging

The key quality control procedure in today's programming environment is testing and debugging. It can improve the quality of the systems produced if it is explicitly

FIGURE 11-2   **THE COMPONENTS OF QUALITY**

Quality ——— **Correctness**
———— Completeness
———— Consistency
———— Traceability

Efficiency
———— Conciseness
———— Execution efficiency
———— Operability

Flexibility and Maintainability
———— Complexity
———— Concision
———— Consistency
———— Expandability
———— Generality
———— Modularity
———— Self-documentation
———— Simplicity

Integrity
———— Auditability
———— Instrumentation
———— Security

Interoperability
———— Communications commonality
———— Data commonality
———— Generality
———— Modularity

Portability and Reusability
———— Generality
———— Hardware independence
———— Modularity
———— Self-documentation
———— Software system independence

Reliability
———— Accuracy
———— Consistency
———— Error tolerance
———— Modularity
———— Simplicity

Testability
———— Auditability
———— Complexity
———— Instrumentation
———— Modularity
———— Self-documentation
———— Simplicity

Usability
———— Operability
———— Training

Source: Reprinted with permission of *Datamation,*® Magazine. © Copyright by Technical Publishing Company, A Dun & Bradstreet Company, Dec. 15, 1984, page 116. All rights reserved.

planned, rigorously executed, and formally evaluated. Unfortunately, this is rarely the case.

Test data should be compiled in an organized manner and should systematically test all conditions in a program. It should consist of two parts, a unit test of the program, and an integration test where the program is tested together with other programs in the processing flow. Today, the programmer generates his own test data and usually tests his "main line" flow, not all conditions. Once the program passes the main line test, the programmer sends it into integration testing. This is usually performed under deadline pressure, toward the end of the project. Data for integration testing is provided by the programmers. Since they have little knowledge of the "real world" that the system will operate in, the assumptions and biases that are built into the code are likely to remain undetected by testing that probably contains the same assumptions and biases. The tight deadlines probably orient the programmers toward making the programs run rather than making them fail.

When errors are detected in these tests, the programs are usually patched, instead of rewritten or repaired. Any structure that existed in the original code gets corrupted. Program documentation may or may not be updated to reflect the corrections. Systems documentation is rarely updated to reflect programming changes.

After unit and integration testing, there should be a third test phase called acceptance testing. The users must generate the data for acceptance tests, for they will "accept" the system based on the results of the test. All too often, users will use one day's transactions as the acceptance test and if it can process one day or even one week's transactions, they accept the system. This certainly will not test the month-end, quarterly, or year-end routines, or the exceptions, or the high-volume days. If an acceptance test is to be effective as a quality control measure, it should be carefully planned to test all possible conditions and all features built into the system.

Finally, testing rarely addresses the noncoding aspects of the systems, the manual procedures, supporting systems, training, user documentation, system documentation, recovery and restart procedures. Moreover, the knowledge gained from testing is not made available to the rest of the department or to the users. If testing and debugging remains as the key quality control procedure, then management has to spend more attention on improving the procedures and controlling the test environment so that programs produced are quality products.

Inspections and Walkthroughs

These are reviews by senior people who are supposed to be able to spot weaknesses in the design and coding. They can be very helpful only if the people doing the review are thoroughly familiar with the requirements of the system, the design philosophy, and the structure of the programming modules. Unfortunately, the reviewers rarely spend the time to learn the background of the system and the other factors that would make a walkthrough meaningful. Today, they look at the documentation and the coding and impose their own standards and techniques on the programmers. If management is to use inspection and walkthroughs as a quality assurance tool, they must plan for their use rigorously, provide indoctrination to the reviewers, establish precise inspection criteria, and provide follow-up to ensure that suggestions for improvement are carried out.

High-Level Languages and Application Generators

These tools are probably the best means now for achieving quality, simply because they impose a defined way of performing certain functions, and less code from the programmer means fewer chances to make mistakes. However, these tools are limited for now, and design and other noncoding issues are not addressed. Testing, debugging, and walkthroughs must still be used.

System Development Standards

The most effective way to ensure quality in the design and implementation of systems is to rigidly adhere to a set of systems development standards that specify how each phase of the development life cycle is to be executed. The good standards on the market today all specify the correct ways to test, debug, and do structured walkthroughs. In addition, they cover the noncoding aspects of system development such as requirements definition, preparation of functional and technical specifications, conversion requirements, development of user procedures, and training programs. The fact that these standards are not used accounts for most of the programming and system development disasters that one hears about so frequently. They are not used because of the attitude of information systems management that system analysts and programmers are free spirits and have a strong need to do creative work in an uninhibited mode. Yet we all know that they should be as creative as a bricklayer in following a construction blueprint. It is up to top management to enforce the strict adherence to a set of development standards. Those who do not wish to conform to these standards should be replaced. Top management does not tolerate "creative accounting" from the chief financial officer, they should not tolerate creative programming from the systems department.

Customer Satisfaction

This is the most important factor in reviewing the quality of the product produced. We know very little about defining the quality of customer satisfaction and we have difficulty quantifying it. We can infer the level of customer satisfaction by measuring operating data. It is likely that customer satisfaction is inversely proportional to the number of bugs found in the system after it has gone into production. However, if we measure customer satisfaction relative to the expectation of the customers, then we can quantify expectations into measurable attributes. For example, an on-line order entry system may have customer satisfaction attributes such as: under three-seconds response time, uncluttered screen, ease of entering data on screen, minimal user keystrokes, clear messages to users, friendly error recovery, and easy-to-use menu. The quality check is to review the system produced against these attributes and assess how well the system meets the attribute. This should be done as part of the quality assurance procedures in each system developed by information systems.

As the use of computers grows, the demand for quality software will increase. Software packages developed for personal computers have given users a taste of what quality software is all about. They will demand the same quality in software developed by the systems department. It is crucial that we use the tools at hand and improve upon them. We have to search for new, more repetitive, more predictable and perhaps, more automated processes to improve quality. If top management insist on high quality products, the information systems department should be able to rise to the challenge.

CONCLUSION

Many companies today have computers processing applications designed ten to twenty years ago. The work performed on these computers does not help management meet competition nor does it help them achieve corporate goals and objectives. Computers are used as transaction-processing systems, reducing the clerical workload in accounting and order entry applications. Yet, these companies are on the Fortune list of the 500 largest corporations and many are leaders in their field. Their lead may be short-lived if competitors recognize the value of using computers to provide information that helps management make decisions to gain a competitive edge in the market. Information is a corporate resource; those who use it wisely will knock out their competition easily. Management can no longer ignore the computer. It is here and people in their organization are using it more and more every day. The secret to success in the decade of the 1990s may be how well management controls the growth and use of computers in their organization.

CHAPTER 11 DISCUSSION QUESTIONS

1. Why are data-processing departments managed and controlled differently than other departments in the company? Should this be changed? How?

2. What do you think the most common organizational structure for information systems will be in the future and why?

3. Should users have and control their own computing resources in light of the fall in equipment prices?

4. Data-processing has, in the past, rejected applications for development because they were "not technically feasible." Is this reason valid today for any application? Why?

5. What are the critical issues in management control of the information systems effort and why?

6. How does management regain control over information processing?

7. What are your feelings towards insisting that all analysts and programmers follow a system development methodology rigidly in designing and implementing systems?

8. Why do top management personnel not take a more active role in managing information resources? How can this change?

9. What criteria should be used to evaluate the performance of information services?

10. Is a charge-out scheme an effective way to control information-processing resources? What alternatives do you suggest?

11. How can quality be built into the systems development product?

12

FUTURE CHALLENGES

ISSUES

- What are the present and future challenges to corporate management in managing information resources?

- Will the paperless society occur in our lifetime?

- How will new technology affect the way corporations are managed in the future?

- Will we still have to program computers, or will manufacturers be able to develop systems with artificial intelligence?

PROFESSIONAL APPLICATION

THE UNFINISHED REVOLUTION[1]

Somewhere along the way, the computer industry has begun tripping over itself in the race toward the automation of America, falling short of its own ambitious goals. The computer revolution was supposed to liberate workers from mindless drudgery, yield soaring increases in productivity, automate the office and home alike, and uplift the lot of virtually every soul. And it has, to a point. But even the industry's most enthusiastic visionaries now admit it will take decades, perhaps a century, to truly fulfill such vaunted promise.

"The usual futurist projections are too optimistic in the short term and too pessimistic in the long term," says Robert N. Noyce, Intel Corp.'s vice-chairman and one of the two inventors of the integrated circuit that is the heart of the micro-chip. That historic breakthrough in 1959 ultimately put room-sized computer power on a sliver of silicon smaller than a contact lens. "Where we went wrong in our over-expectations," he says, was the computer industry's inward focus and its inability to "project itself out to the plumber and what he does."

"We thought it was too easy," says Daniel S. Bricklin, one of the two designers of VisiCalc, the personal computer's first software milestone. "We're really still in the very early stages. The computer doesn't even do the tasks we originally thought it would—watering your lawn, scheduling your appointments. VisiCalc's ability to recalculate lengthy rows of figures in a spreadsheet amazed managers back in 1979," he says, but these days, "people have gotten spoiled."

The technophobic need not fear. Experts say things aren't moving all that fast and haven't gone all that far. They say the widely proclaimed computer revolution is, in reality, a plodding process of evolution, advancing much more slowly than the industry hype would have everyone believe.

In fairness, computers have brought tremendous change and performed remarkable feats since the first commercial model of the vacuum tube powered UNI-

[1]This entire Professional Application is directly quoted from Dennis Kneale, "The Unfinished Revolution," from a special report on "Technology in the Workplace" appearing in the *Wall Street Journal*, September 16, 1985. Reprinted by permission.

VAC I was delivered to the U.S. Census Bureau in 1951. They have been an enormous boon to scientific research, business, medical care, bridge and building design, air safety, meteorology and countless other aspects of life. People use "transparent" computers every day in automated tellers, carburetors, calculators, clocks, videocassette recorders, dishwashers and microwave ovens.

All the while, the cost of technology has plunged. As measured by dollars and computations per second, computing costs continue to fall 30 to 40 percent a year. In 1957, a single transistor cost $10, a Cadillac limousine $7,600; if the limo had followed the semiconductor's cost curve, it would sell for three cents today instead of $40,000. That decline spurred rapid expansion. Internaional Data Corp., a market research firm, estimates that the U.S. population of mainframes, minicomputers and "multi-user" systems serving as many as 16 people, doubled in only four years, to nearly 1.3 million machines in 1984 from 605,000 in 1980.

But it was the revolution in desktop personal computers for individual workers that brought the once arcane world of computing down to millions in the rank and file. It vastly enhanced basic typing and filing. "How could you ask a secretary now to retype an entire 20-page document? It would be almost morally wrong," says Mr. Noyce.

But the wider audience also created higher expectations for computing, fueled partly by computer makers' sky-high advertising claims, and apparently stirred more frustration when the machines fouled up. Customers are pausing to "digest" the systems they've purchased in recent years and to figure out whether the machines are worth the money. Among the signs of discontent:

■ Denver psychologist Charles J. Spezzano, aggravated by the difficulties of using his new IBM PC, jokingly forms the Society for the Prevention of Cruelty to Users. Several hundred frustrated people take him seriously, joining the group and calling him from as far away as Australia. "They wanted revenge for what they felt were these horrible experiences with the products they bought," Mr. Spezzano says. The deluge was so time-consuming that he ultimately disbanded what began as a farce.

■ A New York computer consultant advises a small food-marketing concern to forget about automating its accounting operation and to stick with Esther Katz, the bookkeeper. "The invoices were out on time, the books were completely up to date, every tax form was filed on time," says the consultant, Richard De-Simone of Information Management Group, Inc. "There's no way a computer can compete with Esther—it can't. Too dumb."

■ A survey estimates that 30 percent of businesses with annual sales less than $10 million use their personal computers less than one day a week. It also finds that six of 10 people who shop for software at a computer store leave empty-handed because their needs aren't fulfilled; that 48 percent of computer users want software programs that don't yet exist; and that a fourth of the users of Lotus Development Corp.'s 1–2–3 and Ashton-Tate Co.'s dBase II want extra, better features a year or so after buying the programs.

"There's a real frustration out there. The industry pretty much razzled-dazzled everybody with the promises of these things," says Gerald Van Diver, president of the survey firm, Micro Information Publishing & Research Inc. in Minneapolis. Micro Information tracks the products of 14,000 software companies and provides referrals to thousands of people calling a toll-free number, soliciting survey data in return.

■ *"Computers and Productivity—The Emperor's Clothes,"* a recent report by Philadelphia securities firm Butcher & Singer Inc., says businesses may spend more than $100 billion on office automation in the next five years and contends customers feel *"past performance has fallen woefully short of expectations."* Elizabeth H. Menten of Gartner Group, a Stamford Conn., consulting firm, says 60 percent of her clients now want more ways to document personal computer productivity and in some cases decide *"they could live without it."* *"From here on out, a PC on every desktop isn't quite the scenario we're envisioning,"* she says.

Experts cite several reasons for these problems. The biggest: computers remain frustratingly hard to use. (A book titled "Your IBM PC Made Easy" is 438 pages long.) That stems from the industry's insular, techie orientation, critics say, and the tough technical challenges of making computers "friendlier."

There are other factors. Customers are faulted for being lazy and unwilling to take time to learn their way around the machines. Commercial constraints mean that many potentially useful programs aren't ever made because their audiences are too thin. And not every job is suited to a computer anyway.

Indeed, computers still haven't moved beyond the first wave of customers to what Apple Computer Inc.'s faltering MacIntosh campaign called "the rest of us." "Mac really isn't the computer for the rest of us, it's the computer for the next of us." says Mr. Bricklin, the VisiCalc designer. Beyond basic writing, filing and figuring, the machines aren't yet used for much else. Andrew S. Grove, Intel's president, says customers get great boosts in productivity from personal computers, but still exploit only 5 percent of the machines' full capability.

Moving past that initial group of computer users will be even more difficult. Last year, for instance, 16.4 million personal computers were in schools, homes and offices in the U.S.—a paltry penetration compared with the nation's 80 million households and 60 million white-collar employees, the most immediate market.

"The problem in the computer industry today is both sides of the house are entirely driven by computer engineers," argues Richard P, Koffler, a Santa Monica, California consultant who studies how people work with computers. *"When large computer companies talk about users, they aren't talking about you—they're talking about the computer department and the data-processing manager. And in the end, you have systems that are useless, impossible to support or work with."*

Mr. Grove of Intel counters: "Computers aren't that hard—we people are impatient . . . I've never in my life looked at a computer manual." He adds, "The average PC is used for one function today, and it could be used for five. But we are lousy students and lousy readers."

The ultimate computer will work for literally anyone, conversing affably and carrying out casually requested tasks. Mr. Noyce predicts progress on that score in the next 25 years. But going "the whole nine yards," he says, is likely to be "a continuing evolution—for the next century or so."

The challenge to corporate management today is to get involved in managing information resources and use computer technology to help in executing corporate strategies. There are still corporate management who are afraid of technology and do not want to get involved. They recognize the power of computer technology but do not know how to harness it to make it work for them. They are waiting for someone to tell them what to do. This is where the challenge for information systems management comes in. The information systems manager cannot go to top management and say, "Hey, you've just got to get involved in managing information as a corporate resource." Top management will say, "Sure, we want to be involved. What do we do?" At this point, the information systems manager must give them a detailed action plan, a methodology, and hold their hands right through the plan. If they cannot do this, if they do not have a plan that top management can get excited about, it is not going to work.

THE COMPUTERIZED CORPORATION

This book has presented an action plan for managing information resources. It starts with participating with top management in setting corporate goals and objectives, identifying strategies to meet corporate goals, and the information needed to execute the strategies. It continues with managing how to capture, process, and provide that information to top management—the system development life cycle. Challenges and opportunities created by new technologies have been discussed, and a methodology for monitoring progress and ensuring quality has been presented. In helping top management understand computer technology, the most important thing for top information systems executives is to be a businessperson: to think like a businessperson, to understand how the business works, and to understand the businessperson's vocabulary and the businessperson's needs. At the same time, top management must understand that if they are going to be competitive, they have got to be operating a highly computerized corporation. So it becomes the job of the CEO to make sure that a highly efficient computerized corporation comes into existence. General Motors has set the example by purchasing EDS Corporation to expand its resources in computer technology, and then designing and building a highly computerized corporation to produce the new Saturn automobile. Top GM executives did not come from the data-processing areas; they are production and finance people who know the automobile industry. They are learning about computers because they have to, because the only way to improve productivity and remain competitive with the Japanese is to automate the factories. The executives in GM can communicate with their counterparts in EDS. They speak in business language. There is no need to tell top management that intersection data in IMS can be handled by physical or virtual pairing with bidirectional pointers. You can phrase the whole thing in simple language which they can understand. This is part of a very basic communication process and that process is necessary if there is going to be good communication between computer specialists and top management.

FORECASTS

The challenge of today is to get management involved in building a computerized corporation. What will the challenges of tomorrow be? It is always dangerous for an author to predict the future, for once committed to print, it is just a matter of time before the accuracy of the predictions is determined. However, in the field of computer technology, no forecast can be too wild. Arthur C. Clarke, the science fiction writer, divides forecasting failures into two classes: failures of nerve, and failures of imagination. Forecasting in the computer technology area fails for lack of imagination. Look back 15 years, would you have believed 15 years ago that there would be tens of millions of personal computers in existence, that they would be used for video games as well as for business applications? Would you have believed that a computer chip the size of a fingernail would hold 256 thousand bytes of information? Or that a computer that fits on top of your desk would hold ten times more information than the IBM 360 model 30 and cost under $10,000. Nobody 15 years ago would have predicted fiber optics, today's data bases, industrial robotics, and communication advances. All manner of things have happened that were not predicted 15 years ago. If we look at the next 15 years, we are beyond the year 2000. If it were possible for us to see the year 2000 now, it would be apparent that many of the statements people are making today are failures of imagination. What is going to happen is going to be much more impressive than what most people are predicting today.

Just as an example, look at what education may be like in the year 2000. Instead of enrolling in a course, going to lectures, taking midterms and final exams, the student will select the courses he wants to take, check out the course material on a video disk, take it home and at his leisure, watch it on his video terminal. The course will be presented by outstanding scholars and teachers, and it will be interesting and entertaining because the market will have rejected all the boring and dull lecturers. Questions will be taken over tele-video hookups, and exams will be given via the student terminal. Questions will be on the screen, you select the correct answer on the keyboard, or write your essay answer on your keyboard. It is almost a given that everyone will know how to type in the year 2000. The money that universities spend today on physical plant, on residences, dining halls, classroom buildings, will be better spent structuring courses, improving curriculum, and most importantly, improving the quality of teaching. Advances in technology will make this possible. The X.25 networks which are now spreading, by the year 2000 will go into every nook and cranny. They will be everywhere. Everywhere there will be inexpensive access to a network which moves data around the world fast and very, very cheaply. All computers can be in communication at very low cost. By the year

2000, everybody will have a pocket terminal. Every school child will have one, and these terminals will access computers inexpensively over the common networks. The applications for these terminals are endless since they are connected to computer systems, software banks, data banks, and any source of data or information stored on computers. Every television set will be a terminal from which you can do banking, shopping, receive information (weather, theater programs, news) and get educated. The electronic society will not reduce everyone to spending every hour of the day in front of a terminal. One aspect of the electronic society is diversity. There will still be books, newspapers, magazines, movies, live performances in theaters and concert halls. There will be more leisure time for people to take advantage of these events. There will be as many stores in the year 2000 as there are today, perhaps more. The fact that you can shop via your home terminal does not mean that nobody will go to the stores. You can shop today via catalogs, yet people still go "shopping". The shopping will be easier because you can find out, via the terminal, where the sales are and do comparative price shopping at home before making the actual purchase at the store. The terminal will be used in the year 2000 just as the telephone is used today, certainly not a frightening thought.

If we look at the technological advances today, the growth in automated office systems, the rapid growth in communication technology, the increased use of robots in industry, and the use of microchips in cars, household appliances, toys, as well as in computer technology, the inescapable conclusion that can be drawn is that there will be changes in the way work is performed today. There is no question that people will be displaced from their jobs, but if we are socially responsible, there should be mass displacement, not mass unemployment. Displacement is not necessarily bad because the jobs which are automated tend to be the rather inhuman jobs, the assembly line, the paint shop, the welders and riveters, the routine paperwork jobs, and so on. As these jobs are automated, people displaced have to move up to jobs which are more demanding. Their skills have to be upgraded and they have to be retrained. As the economy grows, they will earn more than on their old job, and they will have more leisure time to enjoy the fruits of their labor. They will live longer and enjoy better health because of advances in medicine and medical care. The combination of all these factors means that we are a changing society and the rate of change in the next 50 years is going to be greater than the rate of change *ever* in any 50-year period in history. The change will be driven by technology: genetic engineering, hydroponics to grow more food, space technologies, marine biology, new energy sources, and electronic technology.

New technology may be the factor which most changes the way corporations are managed over the next 15 years. Information will become a competitive weapon and the successful corporation will have learned how to manage it as a corporate resource. How will this be done? Today, many companies rely on the director of information services to provide all of the technology needed to provide computer resources and services. Some ask the information systems department to assist in corporate planning and policy making. The key, however, is top management involvement, not information systems involvement. The top information executives cannot know what the CEO knows, they cannot know what the board of directors know. It takes the CEO to identify the type of information needed to run the company. Once the CEO does this, the information systems manager can translate those information needs into data models, get those models independent of technology, translate them into today's data bases and into distributed data bases, then construct a communication network to get the information to where it is needed for executing strategies. The collection process works the same way: identify the information needed, structure it into data models and get the information into data bases.

CHANGES IN ANALYSIS TECHNIQUES

Determining information needs and developing data models to meet those needs is different from traditional data processing. Traditional data processing examines processes. Conventional system analysis looks at processes and determines what files or data are required for operating the process. For example, it looks at the payroll process and determines what files and data are needed for payroll processing. Today's structured analysis examines processes and examines the workflow. The data fall out as a byproduct of doing that.

The technology of the future is the opposite of the traditional data-processing model. It starts with looking at the information needs, translates the information needs into data base structures, makes the data base structures as stable as possible, then uses high-level languages (much higher level than COBOL) for generating the processing on top of the data base with maximum productivity. That is almost exactly the opposite to the traditional way of doing processing. Developing the methodologies to do this will be the challenge for system designers in the next five years. Much of the information resources to be managed in the future will be in data structures stored through the corporation. It will be accessible via networks, distributed processing, personal computers, small decision support systems, as well as on large mainframes.

In planning the data resources for a corporation, it is important to realize that there are four different types of systems in a business, and that each of these system types has different data requirements. First are the transaction systems. They process high-volume routine work and are completely predictable. They will continue to form the core of processing work on the company's mainframes. The second type of system is the information system. This is a system that does not change the information but makes information available where it is needed at the right time in the right level of quality and with the right type of presentation. Passenger reservations and credit card authorization are two typical examples of information systems. Development work will continue in this area to download the information from central data bases to microcomputers so that managers can access the corporate information resources from their workstations. The third type of system is a decision support system. This takes some particular type of decision and uses both information and algorithms for enabling that decision to be made much better. It needs data organized in a relational data base for better decision making, and software efforts are currently underway to improve on existing decision support software. Most decision support systems will be user designed and driven, most likely operated from personal computers. The fourth type of system is a highly specialized system such as an expert system, operations research model, or a language-processing system. In planning the corporate-wide structure of information resources, it is essential to understand the different data needs of each of these different types of systems.

PRODUCTIVITY IMPROVEMENTS

With the future trend toward data bases, the need for large mainframe systems to manipulate these data bases will continue to grow, as will the need for microcomputers to access the data bases and process the data for decision support use. Large computers will be faster and cheaper than those today. This will lead to an interesting dichotomy. The number and costs of programmers who will be needed to program these computers almost make the large mainframes uneconomical. The amount of application programming, systems programming, and systems analysis that is going on with the average IBM 30XX mainframe today is totally out of balance with the cost of the machine. This disparity will worsen in the future as the cost of equipment drops and the price of labor increases. The cost of getting the large mainframes to work is too much compared to the cost of the machines. The solution has to lie in ways of improving programming productivity. Structured programming and other tools in use today increase productivity by about 10 percent. That is definitely not the answer. We need far more powerful tools with far greater orders of magnitude. Perhaps the answer is to move existing software into the hardware. A data base machine would eliminate all the efforts devoted to making IMS or IDMS work. This would require a machine that understands the data by having the data described in a dictionary that is built into the system. Query languages built specifically for a data base machine can be simple enough for an end user to use without the help of professional programmers. Query languages flow directly into report generators with graphic capabilities, and report generators can flow directly into graphic languages.

Another way of improving productivity is application development languages of which there are several hundred today. The languages work in many different ways. Some are report generators, some are query languages, some are application development facilities, but all provide the ability for high improvement in programming productivity. For example, in the generation of queries, it might take a COBOL programmer a week to create a query of a certain type for a user to employ at a screen. The user can do it himself, using a query language, in ten minutes. Some corporations have measured the productivity which they have achieved with high languages in terms of equivalent lines of COBOL, in other words, how many lines of COBOL would they have had to write if they had done it in COBOL. Some of them are quoting figures of more than 1000 lines a day of equivalent lines of COBOL. The national average for COBOL programming is 7–40 lines of code a day, varying with the skills of the programmer. The difference between those two figures is so huge that we are forced to look at it very hard and ask why that has not happened to everybody. A good part of the answer is that these languages still need improving. They are not yet good enough for everything one would like to do with them, but the software and mainframe vendors recognize this and are working hard to improve them. In the next 15 years, we will see dramatic improvements in the languages for application development without conventional programming.

DEVELOPMENT WITHOUT CONVENTIONAL PROGRAMMING

In the same vein, application development without conventional programming is what is driving IBM's data base philosophy. IBM realizes that despite the success of their personal computer, the mainstay of the company's product line is its mainframe computers. They also recognize that the trend in using a mainframe is for data base processing, and that the effort to program these data base applications is frightening enough users so that they delay implementing data base systems, hence they delay purchasing IBM mainframes. IBM would like to see the data dictionary built into the data base facilities. They want eventually to get a higher level of hardware involvement, to improve substantially the hardware for data base usage, including expanding what they have already done with the System/38 where the entire DBMS and the data dictionary are built into the hardware and the microcode. The most important part of IBM's strategy relating to data bases is to get high-level languages that will create applications in a short time with a very high level of productivity on the part of the application developer. These will be both languages for the professional and also languages for the end user. Today they have four such languages: GIS, Query by Example, ADF, and DMS. The future will most likely see substantial upgrading of all of these and possibly the introduction of new ones. Certainly one can see many improvements which are needed in today's ADF, but at the same time, one can find examples of ADF being used with an extremely high productivity of application development compared with the development that would be possible in languages like COBOL. If we look at data base systems five to ten years in the future, there will be some technicians left who will be arguing about the internal structure of the data base. What they will be arguing about is how the data base is perceived by the end user who wants to develop applications. The end user, the corporate planner, the resource manager will be the prime movers in data base design and usage, they will drive the architecture and possibly the machine design itself.

MANAGING INFORMATION RESOURCES

Managing information resources in the 1990s should be easier than today. By then, management will have recognized the importance of information as a resource and will have become involved in its management. People in the business world should be more computer literate and treat the computer as they treat the hand held calculator today. Today, computing has forced the flow of information in a business into a structure that is quite different from the natural organization of the corporation. With the linking of personal computers to mainframes and the growth of distributed processing and distributed data bases, computers and information sources will be placed in the departments where they are used. Perhaps the danger ahead lies in giving everyone complete freedom to put anything they want into the company's computer system. A corporation is still one entity, and it has one balance sheet, and one set of financial records. It is important that all the computer hardware fit together to contribute to the overall goals and mission of the corporation. That needs corporate management of the company's information resource.

CHAPTER 12 DISCUSSION QUESTION

1. Make predictions on what your area of specialization, for example, marketing, finance, production, accounting, will be like in 15 years. What role will computers play in your predictions? Are you comfortable with that environment and are you looking forward to working in it?

SELECTED BIBLIOGRAPHY

Alter, Steven. *Decision Support Systems: Current Practice and Continuing Challenges.* Addison-Wesley, 1980.

Anthony, Robert. *Planning and Control Systems: A Framework for Analysis.* Harvard University Press, 1981.

Bennett, John. *Building Decision Support Systems.* Addison-Wesley, 1983.

Biggs, Charles, and Birks, Evan. *Managing the Systems Development Process.* Prentice Hall, 1980.

Buss, Martin. "How to Rank Computer Projects," *Harvard Business Review,* Jan-Feb 1983.

Buss, Martin. "Managing International Information Systems," *Harvard Business Review,* Sep-Oct 1982.

Cash, James, and McFarlan, Warren. *Corporate Information Systems Management.* Richard D. Irwin, 1983.

Curley, Kathleen, and Pyburn, Phillip. "'Intellectual' Technologies: The Key to Improving White Collar Productivity," *Sloan Management Review,* Fall 1982.

Davis, Gordon, and Olson, Margrethe. *Management Information Systems.* McGraw-Hill, 1985.

Dickson, Gary, and Wetherbe, James. *The Management of Information Systems.* McGraw-Hill, 1985.

Dizard, Wilson, *The Coming Information Age.* Longman, 1985.

Gibson, Cyrus, and Nolan, Richard. "Managing the Four States of EDP Growth," *Harvard Business Review,* Jan-Feb 1974.

Grindlay, Andrew. "Managing the Information Systems Function," *The Business Quarterly, Winter,* 1979.

Hussain, Donna, and Hussain, K. M. *Information Resource Management.* Richard D. Irwin, 1984.

Interim Report on Study and Research on Fifth-Generation Computers. Japan Information Processing Development Center, Nichigai Associates, 1980.

Kanter, Jerome. *Management Information Systems.* Prentice Hall, 1984.

Long, Larry. *Design and Strategy for Corporate Information Services: MIS Long-Range Plan.* Prentice Hall, 1982.

Lucas, Henry, and Turner, Jon. "A Corporate Strategy for the Control of Information Processing," *Sloan Management Review,* Spring, 1982.

Lucas, Henry. *Information Systems, Concepts for Management.* McGraw-Hill, 1982.

Managing and Using Computers. Harvard Business Review No. 21340, Reprint series, 1981.

Martin, James. *Computer Networks and Distributed Processing.* Prentice Hall, 1981.

Martin, James. *Design and Strategy for Distributed Processing.* Prentice Hall, 1981.

McFarlan, Warren, and McKenney, James. *Corporate Information Systems Management—The Issues Facing Senior Executives.* Richard D. Irwin, 1983.

McFarlan, Warren, McKenney, James, and Pyburn, Phillip. "The Information Archipelago—Maps and Bridges," *Harvard Business Review,* Sept-Oct, 1982.

McFarlan, Warren, McKenney, James, and Pyburn, Phillip. "The Information Archipelago—Plotting a Course," *Harvard Business Review,* Jan-Feb, 1983.

Murray, Thomas. *Computer Based Information Systems*. Richard D. Irwin, 1985.

"Planning Your Future Information System," *EDP Analyzer,* January, 1983.

Rockart, John. "The Changing Role of the Information Systems Executive: A Critical Success Factors Perspective," *Sloan Management Review,* Fall, 1982.

Rockart, John. "Chief Executives Define Their Own Data Needs," *Harvard Business Review,* Mar-Apr, 1979.

Scott-Morton, Michael, and Keen, Peter. *Decision Support Systems: An Organizational Perspective*. Addison-Wesley, 1978.

Synnott, William, and Gruber, William. *Information Resource Management—Opportunities and Strategies for the 1980s*. John Wiley, 1981.

Thierauf, Robert. *Effective Management Information Systems*. Charles E. Merrill, 1984.

Tricker, R. I., and Boland, Richard. *Management Information and Control Systems*. John Wiley, 1982.

Zuboff, Shoshana. "New Worlds of Computer Mediated Work," *Harvard Business Review,* Sept-Oct, 1982.

APPENDIX A   IBM Family Tree

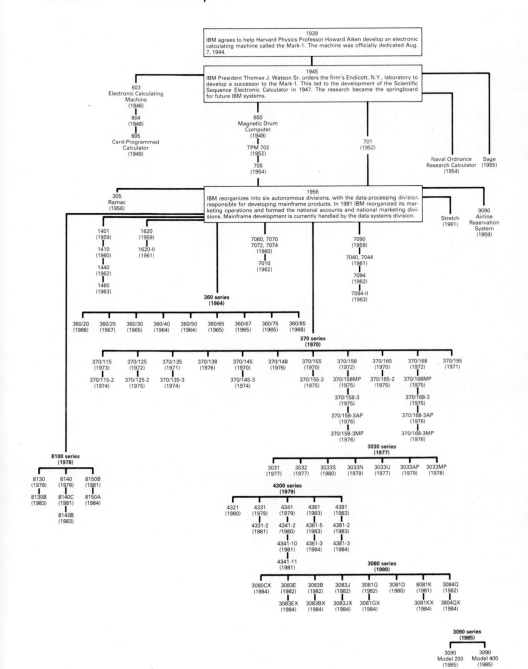

APPENDIX B   IBM Major Large System Announcements

Model	Announced	Delivered	MIPS	Price	$/MIPS	AV $/MIPS
360/50	Apr '64	Aug '65	0.2	1,200,000	7,018,000	6,150,000
360/65	Apr '65	Nov '65	0.6	3,000,000	5,282,000	—
370/155	Jun '70	Jan '71	0.6	1,600,000	2,667,000	2,386,000
370/165	Jun '70	Apr '71	1.9	4,000,000	2,105,000	—
370/158	Aug '72	Apr '73	0.9	1,400,000	1,628,000	1,689,000
370/168	Aug '72	May '73	2.4	4,200,000	1,750,000	—
370/158-3	Mar '75	Sep '76	1.0	1,600,000	1,684,000	1,745,000
370/168-3	Mar '75	Jun '76	2.5	4,514,700	1,806,000	—
3031	Oct '77	Mar '78	1.1	1,000,000	909,000	—
3032	Oct '77	Mar '78	2.5	1,900,000	760,000	782,000
3033	Mar '77	Mar '78	5.0	3,380,000	676,000	—
3033S4	Nov '80	Jan '81	2.4	1,190,000	492,000	—
3033N4	Nov '79	Jan '80	4.0	1,800,000	450,000	447,000
3081-D	Nov '80	Oct '81	10.0	4,003,000	400,000	—
3083-E	Mar '82	Apr '83	4.0	1,400,000	354,000	—
3083-B	Mar '82	Oct '82	5.7	2,100,000	367,000	—
3083-J	Nov '81	Oct '82	7.5	2,700,000	360,000	—
3081-G	Nov '81	Sep '82	10.5	3,543,000	337,000	345,000
3081-K	Nov '81	Apr '82	13.5	4,603,000	341,000	—
3084-Q	Nov '81	Oct '83	25.7	7,982,000	311,000	—
3083-CXO	Oct '84	Jun '85	3.2	871,000	277,000	—
3083-EXO	Feb '84	Jun '84	4.2	1,400,000	333,000	—
3083-BXO	Feb '84	Jun '84	6.1	2,100,000	344,000	—
3083-JXO	Feb '84	Jun '84	8.0	2,700,000	338,000	—
3081-GX1	Feb '84	Jun '84	11.4	3,543,000	312,000	315,000
3081-KX1	Feb '84	Jun '84	14.9	4,603,000	310,000	—
3084-QX3	Feb '84	Jun '84	27.8	7,982,000	288,000	—
3090-200	Feb '85	Nov '85	28.0	5,085,000	182,000	186,000
3090-400	Feb '85	Apr '87	50.0	9,468,000	189,000	—

Source: Arthur D. Little, Inc.

INDEX